The Nightly News Nightmare

The Nightly News Nightmare

NETWORK TELEVISION'S COVERAGE OF U.S. PRESIDENTIAL ELECTIONS, 1988–2000

Stephen J. Farnsworth and S. Robert Lichter

ROWMAN & LITTLEFIELD PUBLISHERS, INC.
Lanham • Boulder • New York • Oxford

ROWMAN & LITTLEFIELD PUBLISHERS, INC.

Published in the United States of America
by Rowman & Littlefield Publishers, Inc.
A Member of the Rowman & Littlefield Publishing Group
4720 Boston Way, Lanham, Maryland 20706
www.rowmanlittlefield.com

PO Box 317, Oxford, OX2 9RU, United Kingdom

British Library Cataloguing in Publication Information Available

Library of Congress Cataloging-in-Publication Data Available

0-7425-1905-8 (cloth : alk. paper)
0-7425-1906-6 (pbk. : alk. paper)

Printed in the United States of America

∞™ The paper used in this publication meets the minimum requirements of American National Standard for Information Sciences—Permanence of Paper for Printed Library Materials, ANSI/NISO Z39.48-1992.

CONTENTS

TABLES

ACKNOWLEDGMENTS

The support, encouragement, and advice of Diana Owen and Jim Lengle of Georgetown University and Jack Kramer and Lew Fickett of Mary Washington College proved invaluable in helping us develop the ideas and arguments that appear in this volume. But a project of this scope would not have been possible without the efforts of many individuals over the years. First and foremost are Richard Noyes and Mary Carroll Willi, who directed the CMPA Election News studies on which this book is based. When Rich directed the first CMPA study in 1988, no one had imagined that a "real-time" content analysis of election news was possible. By the time he directed his final study in 1996, he was a nationally recognized authority on media and campaigns whose insights are summarized in *Good Intentions Make Bad News* (Rowman & Littlefield, coauthored with Robert Lichter). Rich Noyes was ably assisted in 1992 and 1996 by Mary Carroll Willi, whose skills and dedication were once again demonstrated when she took over as director of Election Watch 2000. While making a smooth transition in a chaotic environment, Mary Carroll also somehow found the time to provide the updated data and tables used in this book.

In addition, CMPA Director of Research Dan Amundson helped develop the initial coding system and provided invaluable counsel and assistance. CMPA Vice President Linda Lichter contributed her expertise to developing the coding system at the outset and her patience and moral support thereafter. We also thank representatives of the George W. Bush, Bill Clinton, and Ross Perot campaigns and the Clinton and Bush White House staffs for providing us with access to campaign speeches and television ads.

Tanya DeKona offered not only her support but also her patient, careful reading of this manuscript. Without her continuing encouragement, this project would not have been possible. And from inception to publication, the patience and dedication of our editor Jennifer Knerr serve as a reminder of how great a contribution a good editor can make to a manuscript, a lesson the publishing business seems to be rapidly forgetting. We also thank April Leo and Renée Legatt of R&L for their help with this project.

Over the years, too many journalists for us to single out have given us the benefit of their insights into how the process works from the inside. They include the reporters and editors of the Washington Bureau of the *Los Angeles Times*, the *Kansas City* (MO) *Star* and *Times*, the *Burlington* (VT) *Free Press*, the *Rutland* (VT) *Daily Herald*, States News Service, and Fairchild News Service. But special thanks go to four who contributed lengthy formal interviews for this book, and to Luke Britt, who conducted the interviews: Michael Barone of *U.S. News and World Report*, Larry Barrett of *Time*, Peter Brown of *Scripps Howard*, and Joe Klein of *Newsweek*. Similarly, our research depended on the efforts of many other CMPA staff members, student coders, and research assistants, whom we also thank collectively.

Among the scholars upon whose personal support and expertise we relied over the years, special thanks go to Stephen Hess and Tom Mann of the Brookings Institution, Norman Ornstein of the American Enterprise Institute, Bruce Buchanan at the University of Texas at Austin, Larry Sabato at the University of Virginia, Tom Rosenstiel of the Project for Excellence in Journalism, and primus inter pares, Marvin Kalb and Tom Patterson of the Shorenstein Center on Press, Politics, and Public Policy at Harvard University. We benefitted as well from the writings of other scholars who have done pioneering work on the media's role in elections, including Michael Robinson, Doris Graber, Chris Arterton, and Kathleen Hall Jamieson.

Finally, this project was made possible by the generous support of several private foundations and universities. Funding for various phases of this research came from the American Enterprise Institute, Brookings Institution, Earhart Foundation, Harvard University, J. M. Foundation, John and Mary Markle Foundation, Mary Washington College, Pew Charitable Trusts, Robert Stuart Foundation, Smith College, Smith Richardson Foundation, and Wellesley College.

Even as we express our appreciation for the assistance of the foundations that supported this work over the years, the scholars and journalists on whose insights we relied, and the coworkers who contributed their efforts to this project, we recognize that many may disagree with some of the arguments and conclusions that we drew from our research. For all our debts to others, we take full responsibility for the opinions expressed in this book and for any errors or omissions it may contain.

CHAPTER 1

U.S. PRESIDENTIAL ELECTIONS AND TELEVISION NEWS
Studying Media Content

The news media are often viewed as the fourth branch of government, a perspective that bestows a sense of dignity, authority, and importance comparable to the Supreme Court, the presidency, and the Congress (cf. Cook 1998; Sparrow 1999). This vision of the news media as the "fourth estate" is not misplaced, since the news media influence the presentation and interpretation of campaigns as well as the performance evaluations of those who ultimately are elected. For generations, journalists have been vital sources of information regarding American government, policies, and politicians. In recent decades, a time marked by rapid change in both the political and media environments, reporters have become even more important sources of information for citizens. Smoke-filled rooms where party bosses selected presidential nominees have been replaced by nationwide televised primary debates. Candidates themselves have adapted by increasingly becoming individual political entrepreneurs selling their messages to the voters directly, often through sophisticated, media-friendly (and citizen-friendly) appeals like John McCain's "Straight Talk Express" in 2000 and Ross Perot's televised infomercials in 1992 (Owen 2002; Patterson 1994; Polsby and Wildavsky 2000; Vavreck 2001). A generation ago, reporters were folk heroes of the

Silver Screen: in the hit film *All the President's Men*, two young *Washington Post* reporters are portrayed as courageous battlers who exposed the corruption and lies of Watergate. While reporters are less likely to receive such public adulation today, journalists continue to play an important role in keeping political candidates and government officials accountable (Cook 1998).

Everyone, it seems, has an opinion about the quality of media coverage: sometimes reporters are seen as establishment tools of corporate power, sometimes as leftist attack dogs, and still other times as scandal-obsessed morality cops (cf. Goldberg 2002; McChesney 1999; Sabato et al. 2000). What we offer here is evidence, and lots of it, regarding the quantity and quality of network television news coverage of the past four presidential elections. Using objective content analysis—the careful dissection of each news story into fragments that can be coded along several different dimensions—we demonstrate that the evening news programs on network television do an increasingly poor job of covering presidential elections. One need look no further than the media missteps of the 2000 presidential election to demonstrate the networks' massive shortcomings, yet we track the downward spiral through the analysis of thousands of evening network news stories over the course of the 1988, 1992, 1996, and 2000 presidential campaigns.

Our data analysis represents one of the most comprehensive quantitative indictments ever levied against network television news, an industry that, for all its visibility, has few defenders. Even network television reporters, anchors, and executives bemoan the news media's shortcomings; in fact, in the wake of every presidential campaign, reporters at least promise to improve next time and sometimes even apologize for their past performance (cf. Downie and Kaiser 2002; Russert 1990; Sabato 2002; Shogan 2001). Despite these promises and regrets, however, the content analysis evidence presented here demonstrates that network television's coverage of each subsequent presidential election does not improve and on many measures it even declines.

Media coverage of Election Night 2000, of course, was a spectacular failure, arguably the worst performance in more than a half-century of television news. On that excruciating night, and in the early morning hours that followed, the television networks declared that Al Gore had won Florida, then that the state was too close to call, then that George

Bush had won Florida, and then that the state was too close to call once again (Jamieson and Waldman 2002). Given widespread recognition ahead of time that Florida's twenty-five electoral votes would likely be decisive in the contest, the networks' mistakes effectively declared one candidate the winner of the White House, then the other, in a contest that was not settled until more than a month later when the Supreme Court stopped the recounting of Florida ballots and handed the presidency to Bush in a contentious five-to-four decision (Bugliosi 2001; Nelson 2001; Sunstein and Epstein 2001).

These devastating media miscalls, as bad as they were, are only part of a broad pattern of network news coverage steadily declining in both quantity and quality over the past four presidential elections. Starting in 1988, television news' portrayal of the presidential contests has been marked by a host of shortcomings: the damaging trend toward the horse race coverage of who is winning and losing over coverage relating to matters of substance, the less-than-satisfactory performance with respect to the journalists' cardinal issues of accuracy and fairness, and the declining amount of attention paid to candidates (as opposed to that lavished on the correspondents covering them), as well as the declining volume of coverage of the presidential election overall.

The study of television news is a very controversial area, as people tend to have strong opinions about the media's performance. These emotional reactions can make it difficult for people to evaluate the news media objectively. For example, readers and viewers often remember particular stories that resonate for them personally, including those that make them angry or irritated or provide information that is consistent with an individual's existing opinions (Paletz 2002). These isolated remembered (and sometimes mis-remembered) stories may be the source of one's overall opinions about a news outlet, regardless of how unrepresentative the stories or the recollections may be (Graber 1988). For these reasons, it is very important to study the media as scientifically as possible. This is done here through the process of content analysis, in which each news segment related to the presidential election is carefully coded into categories that describe whether the segment was positive, negative, or neutral toward each candidate as well as who the source of that commentary was (candidates, citizens, outside experts, and reporters themselves are examples). Each story is also coded into categories that describe which topics were addressed in each news segment (campaign strategy, tax cuts, or health care are examples). Each network evening news story, and there are over 1,300 of them coded here for each of the past four presidential election cycles, is analyzed along several different dimensions that allow for studies of media content from many different perspectives. These data dissect every campaign news segment that aired on the evening news programs of ABC, NBC, and CBS during every presidential election from 1988 to 2000. These data include all evening news segments from the general election period, from the primaries, and from the "preseason" campaigns that occur the year before the primaries and the presidential election.

This four-election-cycle content analysis, conducted by the Center for Media and Public Affairs (CMPA), a nonpartisan media research institute based in Washington, D.C., represents part of one of the most extensive analyses of news coverage of presidential elections in existence. Indeed, this entire analysis permits an unusually wide-ranging and thorough examination of campaign discourse. The 5,847 network news campaign stories analyzed here for the 1987–1988, 1991–1992, 1995–1996, and 1999–2000 presidential election campaign periods are part of a total CMPA content analysis of 22,386 campaign items examined from the past four presidential elections. All are employed to make the arguments in this book (though we obviously do not discuss each of them individually).

The network television data allow for a quantitative study of how television news coverage has changed from election to election along the key dimensions discussed above: the increasing focus on the horse race rather than on matters of substance, the increasing problems of accuracy and fairness, the growing focus on reporters rather than on candidates, and the declining amount of campaign coverage overall. The evidence presented here illustrates the ways that the mediated presentation of reality on network television has worsened over time.

The collected data also permit comparisons between network news and other media outlets, as well as comparisons between network news coverage and the unmediated candidate discourse. These analyses find that network news falls short when compared to other media outlets and to what the candidates and the campaigns actually said. The 16,539 items analyzed by CMPA that are not from the networks' evening news programs are segments aired by or printed by a number of media outlets, including the Public Broadcasting Service (PBS), the Cable News Network

(CNN), the *New York Times*, the *Wall Street Journal*, the *Washington Post,* and various network and cable talk shows. They also include content analysis of various forms of campaign discourse, including speeches, interviews, advertisements, and campaign web pages. Through these additional data, we compare the content of the network evening newscasts with other media outlets and with what the campaigns and the candidates themselves actually said in their speeches, debates, advertising, and web pages. This comparison, the subject of chapter 5, allows us to demonstrate the ways that the "mediated" perspectives on the campaigns on network television differ from the "mediated" perspectives offered by public television news, by CNN, and by newspapers. Both network news and other media outlets are also compared in chapter 5 to the "unmediated" message put forward by the campaigns and the candidates themselves. (The appendix contains a more extensive discussion of the campaign news items contained in this analysis.)

The evidence in the following pages points to a devastating failure on the part of network television's evening news programs on nearly every dimension analyzed by CMPA. Television coverage was poor in 1988, 1992, and 1996, and by some measures the 2000 election marked the worst performance of the four presidential campaigns we analyzed. And network television news fares even worse when compared to other media outlets and to what the candidates and the campaigns actually said.

"Mediated" versus "Unmediated" Campaign Information

Many political scientists have found fault with television news coverage in the past, but rarely have media scholars made these criticisms with the support of as extensive a content analysis as is employed here. Our comparative data allow us to say that other news outlets—including other television news outlets and several of the nation's leading newspapers—do a better, often a far better, job of providing citizens with the information needed to understand and evaluate the campaign, the candidates, and the issues. Our evidence allows us to go even further than a comparison just of network television versus PBS, CNN, and leading daily newspapers. We also compare what candidates and campaigns actually said versus what the reporters *said* the campaigns and the candidates said. The differences between the campaigns' messages and the media messages are immense. We demonstrate here that candidates and campaigns do a far better job of responding to citizen desires for substance, fairness, and comprehensiveness than the television networks do. In other words, the mediated coverage of network news has become so negative and so inaccurate that the unmediated speeches, advertisements, and Internet web pages of the highly self-interested campaigns actually qualify as the more substantive, more useful, and more accurate forms of campaign discourse. In fact, this is not even a close call: the unmediated campaigns do a far better job of responding to these important citizen desires for campaign information than do the television networks.

Examining network news coverage of the most recent presidential elections is central to our understanding of how these contests operate. Candidates and their teams design campaigns to maximize positive television exposure because television news remains a major source of public learning about candidates and political issues (Hollihan 2001; Paletz 2002). Since the vast majority of information about presidential elections received by ordinary citizens is mediated information, the television networks play a vitally important linkage role in our electoral process—arguably more important than even the political parties themselves (cf. Patterson 1994; Wayne 2001, 2003).

For good or for ill, television networks have become and remain central players in the operation of elections as well as in the process of governing in this country (Cook 1998; Graber 2002; Patterson 1994; Sparrow 1999). Reporters tell us much of what we learn about the issues, the candidates, and how they are faring on the campaign trail. More than three-quarters of those surveyed in 1996 said the news media represent their primary source of information about the campaign, while fewer than one in ten offered the second most common response, conversations with others (Dautrich and Hartley 1999:22).

For most of us, then, the mediated reality portrayed by the television networks is the reality we perceive (Iyengar and Kinder 1987; Patterson 1994). The declining quality of television's performance in covering presidential campaigns, therefore, is an important warning sign regarding the health of our electoral process. TV networks that reduce the quality and quantity of election coverage shortchange not only the candidates but also the voters who choose each successive president.

What Voters Want from Campaign News

Above all, what the voters say they want from journalists is better coverage, reporting that is more informative, more issue-based, and less biased. Arguably the most powerful evidence that the media are not giving citizens the desired campaign news content is found in the evaluations citizens give journalists at the end of the campaign season. Numerous polls in recent years have demonstrated the low regard with which the American public views the news media in general and election news in particular. The most useful long-term consideration of this public frustration with the press is found in surveys conducted by the Pew Research Center for the People and the Press, which every four years asks respondents to assign letter grades to the performance of various participants in the election process. Over the four presidential election cycles considered here, the public has consistently given the media poorer grades than the parties, candidates, pollsters, and even the much-criticized campaign consultants (Pew Research Center for the People and the Press [hereafter Pew] 2000c). After the 1988 election, a campaign that stimulated many election news reform promises and efforts, the media's "grade point average" was 1.9. It peaked at 2.0 (a "straight C") in 1992 before dropping to 1.8 in 1996 and 1.7 (a "C minus") in 2000. In 1988 the media received twice as many "F's" as "A's" by a margin of 16 percent to 8 percent. By 2000 the gap had grown to over three "F's" for every "A," a margin of 20 percent to 6 percent (Media Monitor 2000).

Given these scores, it should come as no surprise that the public would not mind if the journalists were less influential in presidential elections. A November 2000 postelection survey by the Pew Center (2000d) found that 53 percent of those surveyed felt that the news media had too much of an influence on the political process, up from 47 percent in 1996 and 46 percent in 1992.

The increased media coverage of the horse race in recent elections is not simply a response to what viewers want from media coverage of campaigns and elections. There is considerable evidence from several elections that suggests that we the people want more substantive coverage than we get from the television networks. A study of the 1984 presidential election, for example, found a substantial difference between the media's agenda and the public's agenda (Robinson 1985). An examination of the questions asked by citizens calling in to *Larry King Live* on CNN during the 1992 campaign also found a gap between what the media focused on—campaign strategy—and the issues that mattered to those ordinary citizens—trade with Mexico, aid to Russia, how to make the economy work better—who queried then President Bush that year (Patterson 1994:55–56). Reporters clearly have a different perspective about what citizens need to know than citizens themselves do.

> The voters possess a different schematic outlook [than do reporters]. They view politics primarily as a means of choosing leaders and solving their problems. As the voters see it, policy problems, leadership traits, policy debates and the like are the key dimensions of presidential politics. (Patterson 1994:59)

A November 1996 telephone survey of 3,004 Americans by Louis Harris and Associates found deep citizen concerns about media bias. A total of 63 percent of those surveyed said that they believe the news media tend to favor one side when presenting news on social and political issues, and 77 percent said that they believe there was a "great deal" or a "fair amount" of political bias in the news coverage they see (Smith et al. 1997:119). Conservatives are particularly troubled by what they perceive as media bias: 45 percent of Republicans said they viewed journalists as more biased than most people, as compared to 27 percent of the Independents and 28 percent of the Democrats (Smith et al. 1997:101).

In a December 2000 Gallup poll, 65 percent of those surveyed said they believed reporters' news stories were "often inaccurate," up from 45 percent in a July 1998 survey, 44 percent in an August 1989 survey, 48 percent in a January 1988 survey, and 34 percent in a June 1985 poll (Wayne 2003:131).

The Pew postelection survey of November 2000 also showed some citizen concern over bias, particularly among Republican voters. Overall, 18 percent of those surveyed thought both major party candidates for president were treated unfairly, as compared to 12 percent who said the media were fair to Gore only and 5 percent who thought the media were fair to Bush only (Pew 2000d). Among Republicans, traditionally far more negatively disposed regarding the news media, 25 percent said both candidates were treated unfairly, 23 percent said only Gore was treated fairly, and just 2 percent said that only Bush was treated fairly (Pew 2000d). Overall, 60 percent said both major party candidates were treated fairly, a statement made by 47 percent of the Republicans, 61 percent of the Independents, and 68 percent of the Democrats. A preelection survey on media bias by the Pew Center (2000b) during October 2000 found very similar results: a majority of people felt that reporters were fair to both candidates, and far more Republicans than Democrats perceived bias in the media coverage of their party's nominee.

In a study of perceptions of bias regarding various media outlets, C-SPAN programming, the *NewsHour* on PBS, the Sunday morning news magazines (like *Meet the Press*), and CNN were seen to be particularly evenhanded, while local call-in talk radio and Rush Limbaugh's talk radio programs were seen as the most biased (Dautrich and Hartley 1999:100). Network news finished in the middle of the pack, just below local newscasts and just above the *New York Times*.

Negativity is also a major concern among those participating in the 1996 survey, with 61 percent saying the media place too much attention on negative news (Smith et al. 1997). Citizens want reporters to do a better job of sticking to the facts and leaving the more analytical observations to others. "A strong majority of the general public believes that the news media should just report the facts and then let people make up their own minds on issues rather than weigh the facts and offer suggestions about how to solve problems" (Smith et al. 1997:83).

In the November 2000 Pew Center postelection survey, citizens expressed great frustration with media inaccuracy generally, and with that year's election night miscalls in particular (Pew 2000d). Anger and/or disappointment over the media's performance was expressed by 69 percent of the voters surveyed, and 87 percent said they wished the networks would not announce a winner in future presidential elections until nearly all the votes had been counted (Pew 2000d).

But public opinion regarding journalists is not entirely negative, particularly when reporters are compared to politicians. Three-quarters of those surveyed by Louis Harris and Associates in 1996 expressed support for the news media's role as a watchdog on government and 63 percent on balance think that reporters help democracy more than hurt it through their reporting (Smith et al. 1997). Three-quarters of those surveyed said that reporters should hold public officials accountable for what they do, and two-thirds of those surveyed said it was "very important" for the media to protect the public from abuses of power (Smith et al. 1997:50). In fact, more than 40 percent of those surveyed called for a more aggressive media, saying reporters could do more to scrutinize public officials and to guard against government abuses of power.

Ellen Hume, at that time the executive director of the Democracy Project on PBS, said at a December 13, 1996, news conference releasing the Harris survey's results that it is important for reporters to make more of an effort to tailor their reporting to such public concerns, rather than just focusing on negativity and crime:

> Journalists dug up the Indonesian contributions to the Democratic National Committee in this last election [1996]. That was a watchdog function that worked, or if they don't write about that during the election, there is a big difference there. One of the things I found in trying to look at all this is we should try to design news programming that actually helps citizens figure out what their role is in this great landscape in America. So often the news is encrypted in Washington. It is about what the insiders are saying around the dinner table. That might be interesting to some people, but I do think that citizens deserve better. (Hume, quoted in Smith et al. 1997:5)

Another major piece of evidence that points to the overall failings of network television is found in the steady erosion of network television's audience and the rise of other alternative media, including cable television and to a lesser extent the Internet (Pew 2000d). Respondents to the Pew Center survey gravitate to online information sources both for convenience and for specialized information that is more readily accessible on the web. Although the Internet was a leading source of information for only about one in ten citizens looking for news about the 2000 presidential election, it is likely to become a far more significant source of campaign news in future years as the technology advances and becomes even more widespread (Farnsworth and Owen 2001; Pew 2000d). Even before the Internet became a readily available source of campaign information, viewers expressed a great deal of interest in the less mediated campaign formats, including the citizen-questioners debates and the call-in shows that were a prominent part of news coverage of Campaign 1992 (Just et al. 1996:139).

What Voters Get from Campaign News: Past Content Analysis Research

HORSE RACE VERSUS SUBSTANCE

More than two decades ago, political scientist Thomas Patterson (1980) observed that television focused greatly on the question of which candidate was ahead and who was behind, a far cry from the much more issue-oriented coverage of the 1940s. Although Patterson focused on the 1976 presidential election, the same trends were found in subsequent contests. As the 1970s gave way to the 1980s and 1990s, we as news media consumers increasingly were told more about who was ahead in the polls and who was behind, rather than where candidates stood on the issues (Lichter and Noyes 1995; Patterson 1980, 1994).

In their comprehensive study of campaign coverage by CBS News and by the United Press International wire service during the 1980 presidential contest, Michael Robinson and Margaret Sheehan (1983) found that 59 percent of CBS election news stories failed to contain a single issue sentence, even though the scholars identified more than 90 issues on the 1980 campaign agenda. For UPI, 55 percent of the stories failed to reference a single issue.

> "Horse race" permeates almost everything the press does in covering elections and candidates. We found that in our wire copy and videotape about five of every six campaign stories made some meaningful reference to the competition, but, by comparison, well over half of the same stories made no mention of issues. (Robinson and Sheehan 1983:148)

In recent presidential campaigns, new polls are sometimes conducted every day to give us constant updates regarding the fortunes of each candidate. In the New Hampshire primary, for example, daily tracking polls measured the horse race every 24 hours during the month before the 1992, 1996, and 2000 Granite State primary contests (Farnsworth and Lichter 1999, 2001, 2002). Reporters may have little understanding of the uncertainties of polling, including such things as margins of error, but that does not stop them from talking about polls frequently during the half-hour nightly news programs (Larson 2001; Owen 2002).

But voters do more than learn regularly of each candidate's standing;

they actually began to support in greater numbers the candidate who reporters said was winning. Patterson (1980) called this a "bandwagon" effect. Bandwagon effects make it harder for a candidate who is believed by reporters to be behind—or who really is lagging in the media-reported polls—to catch up with the front-runner. If news consumers effectively are told over and over again by media outlets that the poll numbers are the most important thing in the campaign, it should come as no surprise that the voters also consider poll standings when comparing candidates.

> The press game schema is more pervasive now than it was even a few decades ago. The change coincides with the shift to an electoral process that depends upon the press as its chief intermediary. In the same period that the press has taken on the mediating role once performed by the political party, a number of trends within journalism have combined to make election news a less suitable basis for voter choice. (Patterson 1994:60)

Our data in the chapters that follow show that conditions have deteriorated even further in the presidential elections in the years since Patterson wrote those words. Questions of the heavy horse race emphasis of network television news is taken up in chapter 2.

SCANDAL COVERAGE

Past researchers have also found that the campaign agenda, as defined by network news content, also tilts heavily toward scandal coverage, which like horse race coverage can also crowd out coverage of policy matters. (While issues of character may be somewhat more significant to candidate evaluations than horse race standings, that does not necessarily make character issues more important than policy matters.) Larry Sabato (2000) found a growing emphasis on scandal among the reporters making their living in the wake of Vietnam and Watergate, when public lies by government officials had become commonplace. The rise in recent years of "new media," including cyber-journalism and a revived talk radio, has increased the opportunity for scandals to become leading controversies rapidly (cf. Davis and Owen 1998; Seib 2001; Drudge 2000; Hall 2001).

Of course, even when some individual reporters and editors may want to restrain themselves from scandal coverage, they will find it hard to do so, given this increasingly competitive new media environment. Being left behind is not an appealing prospect for any reporter or editor, given the intense public and media interest in personal scandals like (to name a few) the Clinton/Lewinsky matter (Sabato et al. 2000), the antics of first brother Billy Carter in 1980 (Patterson 1994), reports in mid-1988 concerning how Dan Quayle—at the time the Republican vice presidential nominee—avoided service in Vietnam (Hershey 2001), stories involving Bill Clinton's own efforts to avoid service in Vietnam and allegations surrounding his relationship with Gennifer Flowers (Baker 1993), and, most recently the 2000 reports concerning George W. Bush's quarter-century-old drunk driving arrest (Burger 2001).

In fact, just being a responsible journalist may mean being left behind in scandal coverage. During the 1992 presidential primaries, all three networks at first refused to run a story on Gennifer Flowers' statement that she and Bill Clinton had had an extramarital affair when Clinton was governor of Arkansas because they were not sure what to make of the allegations. One NBC news executive, though, was shocked to find the story leading the 11 P.M. local news on his network's New York affiliate that same night (Rosenstiel 1994:63).

The same thing happened to *Newsweek* several years later. The weekly magazine lost out on its "scoop" of the Clinton/Lewinsky matter to Internet journalist Matt Drudge in January 1998, largely because *Newsweek* executives wanted more time to evaluate the reporting on what they knew would be one of the most explosive presidential scandals of the decade (Drudge 2000; Sabato et al. 2000; Seib 2001).

Our analysis of the news media's focus on scandals is found in chapter 3.

FAIRNESS, ACCURACY, AND ALLEGATIONS OF MEDIA BIAS

The news media's power to set the agenda is particularly troubling if reporters fail to meet standards of objectivity and fairness. Conservatives are more likely to charge that reporters are biased toward the Democrats, though in the 2000 election many liberals alleged the reporters were being too easy on Texas Governor George W. Bush and were unfairly keeping Green Party candidate Ralph Nader off the air. In the 1992 campaign, when allegations of media bias were particularly high, many Republicans put a bumper sticker on their cars that read "Annoy the Media: Re-elect Bush."

Scholars have a range of opinions on the question of whether reporters are biased. Some say that reporters are biased only to the extent caused by the norms of the news business: things such as deadline pressures and the need to make stories interesting enough for them to be published or aired and also to be attended to by the public (Robinson 1976). Others say that reporters try to be fair, but when inadvertent bias finds its way into news stories it is more likely to reflect the liberal perspectives held by most journalists (Lichter et al. 1990). Still other media researchers, generally found on the ideological left, focus on the corporate structures of the news business and argue that the generally conservative orientations of publishers, owners, and other corporate executives are the true sources of bias (Herman and Chomsky 1988; Ginsberg 1986; Gitlin 1980). As the diversity of opinion suggests, media researchers have not yet reached a consensus on the nature of an alleged media bias. In this project, we use the CMPA content analysis to search for evidence of bias on the network news and to see whether any such network bias is reflected in other media coverage and in the candidates' campaign discourse. Our analysis regarding questions of bias in the content of the evening news programs is found in chapter 4.

While scholars and politicians may argue over the existence of ideological bias, there is much stronger evidence that the television networks' coverage has become increasingly negative in tone over the past several elections (Lichter and Noyes 1995, 1998). This negativity, directed against nearly all viable candidates, can have powerful impacts upon public orientations regarding government. Citizens exposed to the cynicism found in media portrayals of political candidates and of government are thought to become increasingly negatively disposed toward government (Cappella and Jamieson 1997; Hetherington 2001). Voter turnout has been falling during the years of increased media negativity, and many scholars think the media's performance is one of the reasons why half of the nation's eligible adults have chosen not to vote in recent presidential elections (Putnam 2000). An examination of media negativity and its consequences can be found in chapter 4.

Future debate over the media's ability to get the facts right will doubtless begin with the television networks' miscues on Election Night 2000, our flawed and most recent presidential election (Owen 2002; Sabato 2002). But the debate shouldn't end there. As in every presidential election at least since the 1960s, the news media—especially television—

established the information environment within which the general election was contested. Public debate over media coverage began long before the double miscalls that left the network anchors with not just egg but an entire omelet on their faces, in Tom Brokaw's wry image. At various points in the campaign, commentators complained that news reports were distorting the images and trivializing the messages of both major party candidates (Cook 2000; Kurtz 2000a). During the party conventions, other critics charged that the broadcast networks, traditionally the industry leaders in covering presidential elections, were ignoring their public service responsibilities by basing their diminished coverage on ratings rather than the intrinsic importance of events (AuCoin 2000; Kloer 2000). And throughout the fall campaign, media critics and journalists alike debated the scope, focus, and tenor of campaign coverage (Buckley 2000; Hess 2000a, 2000b; Papai and Robinson 2000; Taylor 2000). The events of Election Night 2000 were not the first examples of network news errors, and this study devotes considerable attention in chapter 4 not only to the events of Election Night 2000 but to earlier news media errors in the coverage of American political campaigns.

THE SHRINKING SOUND BITE AND JOURNALISTIC SELF-OBSESSION

Of all the declines in the quality of network television news in recent decades, perhaps none has been as dramatic as the reduction in a presidential candidate's ability to address the issues in his or her own voice on network television news during the presidential campaign. A study by Kiku Adatto (1990) found that the average length of time a presidential candidate spoke in his own words on network television news during the 1968 campaign was 42 seconds. The average sound bite length in 1988 fell to 10 seconds, a decline of more than three-quarters over that twenty-year period (Adatto 1990). The results triggered a good deal of soul-searching among reporters when they were first released, and the networks promised longer candidate sound bites in 1992 (Patterson 1994:160). Nevertheless, the CMPA data, presented here in chapter 3, demonstrate that these snippets of candidate discourse have shrunk even further in the presidential campaigns that followed Adatto's original analysis.

If the candidates aren't doing the talking, who is? The reporters, mostly, according to the CMPA data analysis. Thomas Patterson (1994) described media coverage of a presidential election as a struggle among reporters and candidates to be heard and to set the tone. The reporters of course have a great advantage in this struggle as they have access to the news programs in a way that candidates do not. As a result, we hear a lot more in campaign coverage from the reporters than from the candidates, even though the candidates, not the reporters, will end up being elected and having to govern. In the 1960s, candidates and other partisan sources were much more able to set the tone of an article, and to be heard at greater length, than has been the case in more recent decades (Patterson 1994). Matthew Kerbel (1998) found in a later study of campaign coverage on ABC and CNN in 1992 that the trend has become overwhelmingly biased toward the reporters and away from the presidential candidates. We apply the CMPA data to this issue in chapter 3.

The question of content cannot be considered effectively without considering the question of how much impact the news media have over voter perceptions of the candidates, of the campaigns, and of the most important issues. Although our focus is on the content of media messages rather than their effects, a brief consideration of past research regarding media effects can help place the content analysis research in perspective.

Content's Consequences: Three Models of Possible Media Effects

THE HYPODERMIC EFFECTS PERSPECTIVE: HEAVY MEDIA INFLUENCE

In addition to the study of the content of news, political scientists have also focused their attention on the impact of media content on public opinion. This area of research properly begins with the Martians on the radio. When Orson Welles broadcast a fictionalized radio account of an alien invasion of New Jersey as a Halloween prank in 1938, millions of Americans were fooled (Cantril et al. 1940). The effects of this "War of the Worlds" broadcast suggested that citizens may be highly susceptible to media images (Cantril et al. 1940). Seeing (or hearing, mostly, at that time) was believing, as the saying goes. Scholars dubbed this perspective on media influences the "hypodermic effects" model, as the effect of mass media content was seen as immediate, direct, and powerful—much like getting an immunization at the doctor's office.

The rise of Adolf Hitler in Germany and Benito Mussolini in Italy shortly before World War II are thought to be additional examples that support this theory of very powerful media effects on public opinion. Both came to power in part through their news appearances in the relatively new media of radio and filmed newsreels, both of which allowed for rapid and easy transmission of messages to large numbers of people. *The Triumph of the Will,* a virulently pro-Hitler pseudodocumentary made during this era by Leni Riefenstahl, was seen as one of the most effective exercises of propaganda ever: the film starts with Hitler descending through the clouds as if he were an Aryan god (he is returning to earth by airplane) and shows Hitler receiving the fervent adoration of cheering multitudes throughout (Mast 1971). Scholars who looked at the Nazis' effective use of the media became convinced that ordinary citizens were very susceptible to media messages, particularly messages that have been put before our eyes and ears over and over again. To this day, totalitarian societies try to create cults of worship of the national leader through this sort of propaganda. A China once filled with portraits of Mao and an Iraq filled with portraits of Saddam Hussein are recent examples.

Radio and film were not the first media formats, of course. But they were the first *national* media sources, particularly in the United States. They were the first to provide identical messages from coast to coast through broadcast networks and through national distribution in motion picture theaters. Newspapers, even when part of a national company, tended to be much more localized in their coverage and did not provide a pervasive national message comparable to that offered by radio networks, by the newsreels, and by the television networks that came subsequently (Postman 1985; Schudson 1978; Smith 1977).

Although the hypodermic effects model may seem appealing at first glance, it didn't seem to work all that well, at least in the United States, once social scientists developed techniques sophisticated enough to allow for data-based studies of media effects upon public opinion. The researchers looked for opinion change among voters after they were exposed to media content about candidates for office, but they did not find much evidence that would support the hypodermic effects approach (Lazarsfeld et al. 1948). The hypodermic effects theory may have explained media influence on citizens in the 1920s and early 1930s when radio and film were novelties—but the model was not supported by quantitative evidence that examined media use and candidate preferences of U.S. voters in the 1940s (Lazarsfeld et al. 1948).

Why didn't this first theory work better in practice? There are several possible explanations. Perhaps U.S. citizens became more sophisticated with respect to media messages as we became more accustomed to these new media sources, more wary of propaganda as a result of World War II, and less susceptible due to steadily increasing education levels in this country. Perhaps this model of heavy media influence does a better job of explaining cultural trends than partisan political behavior. Or perhaps the model never was all that effective. We just don't have enough public opinion research from before World War II to know for sure whether the model ever worked well. Some researchers believe that, upon further reflection, the early studies that laid the foundation of this perspective were not that solidly constructed to begin with (McQuail 2000).

THE MINIMAL EFFECTS PERSPECTIVE

If the news media could not change minds, as scholars started to observe in the late 1940s and 1950s, perhaps mass media sources were not so influential after all. Scholars then reversed course and settled on the idea of "minimal effects" to explain the relationship between the media and the people. They proposed a "two-step flow," in which media messages were particularly influential upon political elites—opinion leaders like executives, union officials, and heads of families (Klapper 1960). These elites then used what they learned to organize their own discussion of issues, thereby transferring the substance of the media message to those who might have missed it or were not paying attention.

But this theory of modest media effects also became unpopular as scholars began to look for evidence to support this perspective regarding media influence. Unfortunately for the theory's supporters, the evidence against this approach seemed consistent and powerful, almost from the time the theory was first offered. Civil rights became a front-burner issue in the 1960s, and it did so once television started broadcasting pictures of African American children being attacked by police dogs and adults being clubbed by southern sheriffs (Graber 2002). Public support for U.S. involvement in Vietnam declined drastically once the television networks began suggesting the war was a stalemate in the wake of the Tet Offensive

(Braestrup 1983; Mueller 1973). More recently, a variety of issues—homelessness, health care, nuclear weapons proliferation—became highly important when television focused upon them, only to lose their importance to citizens once the networks moved on to other topics (Adams et al. 1994; Iyengar and Kinder 1987; Paletz 2002).

THE MEDIA EFFECTS PERSPECTIVE: SETTING THE PUBLIC AGENDA

For the past quarter-century, many media researchers have favored a third theory, known as "media effects" or "more-than-minimal effects." This perspective, pioneered by Michael Robinson (1976) and Maxwell McCombs and Donald Shaw (1977), is located between the high-impact and low-impact extremes contained in the earlier hypodermic and minimal effects theories. They argued that the media's most powerful influence on American society relates to agenda-setting—not telling us what to think so much as telling us what to think about. There is a lot of survey research to support the media effects position. People seem to evaluate candidates and government officials, for example, along the lines of the issues that are the focus of televised news reports. Studies show that citizens are "primed" to focus on what reporters have told the country were the most important matters, such as whether Vice President Hubert Humphrey should be blamed for the war in Vietnam during the 1968 presidential campaign, whether President George H. W. Bush should be fired for alleged economic bungling in 1992, and whether Bill Clinton should be impeached and then removed from office over the Clinton/Lewinsky matter and the subsequent cover-up (Iyengar and Kinder 1987; McGinniss 1969; Owen 2000; Robinson 1976).

The media effects theory does not presume the overwhelming media impact suggested by the hypodermic effects model, but the agenda-setting function is still seen as an important source of media influence (Iyengar and Kinder 1987; Iyengar 1991). Scandal coverage demonstrates how media messages do not translate into public opinion that agrees with the content of these media messages. President Clinton was treated extremely negatively on television for his handling of the Clinton/Lewinsky matter, yet public opinion consistently opposed his removal from office (Sabato et al. 2000). At most, this highly negative media treatment of Clinton over the Clinton/Lewinsky matter and the subsequent cover-up triggered modest declines in public ratings of his personal character, though public evaluations in that area were not that high before the scandal became public (Sabato et al. 2000). Media treatment of Clinton scandals involving Gennifer Flowers and allegations of draft-dodging during the Vietnam years were likewise heavy and quite negative in tone before the 1992 New Hampshire primary, and many media pundits thought the Clinton campaign had been fatally wounded by the scandals (Kurtz 1992a). But then Governor Clinton weathered the storm and finished second in the contest (Farnsworth and Lichter 1999). The second-place finish in this pivotal primary allowed Clinton to declare himself "the comeback kid" and put the Arkansas governor back on track to win the Democratic nomination and then the presidency in the months that followed (Ceaser and Busch 1993; Palmer 1997).

Another reason why one should not perceive media effects research as a return to the more powerful hypodermic effects model is because of growing evidence that citizens remember only some of the news they hear, see, and read. A news item is most likely to register and be remembered if it is consistent with one's core values about people and politics (Graber 1988).

The agenda-setting idea suggests that the topics that television reporters choose to emphasize in their broadcasts will also play an important role in citizen evaluations of the candidates. The changing role of economic evaluations in presidential elections provides a useful example of how this agenda-setting process works. Economic conditions are usually one of the most important measures by which incumbent presidents (and subsequent nominees of the president's party) can be rewarded or punished, according to many researchers (Campbell 1992; Fair 1978; Lewis-Beck and Rice 1992). In a year—like 1992—when negative economic news abounds, there is little an incumbent president can do to reverse the tide flowing away from his candidacy, as President George H. W. Bush found to his regret in 1992 (Fitzwater 1995; Gold 1994).

In fact, media agenda-setting effects sometimes are strong enough to outweigh personal experiences. One study of the effects of economic news coverage, for example, found that people who were exposed to a large amount of macroeconomic news tended to emphasize societal economic conditions and de-emphasize their own personal economic situations, even though they would know more about the latter (Mutz 1992).

Conversely, if the media focus is not on the economy, the public focus is also likely to be directed elsewhere. In 2000, when reporters said little about the condition of the national economy—which had been growing at a healthy pace for the eight years of the Clinton presidency—one would not expect the national economy to be that significant a factor for citizens. Indeed, exit polls in 2000 showed that only 18 percent of those casting a ballot in the Gore-Bush contest considered the economy to be the most important issue that year, as compared to 43 percent who thought so eight years earlier, when Clinton defeated President Bush and Texas billionaire Ross Perot (Frankovic and McDermott 2001). With examples like this to draw upon, it is no wonder that the media effects perspective became popular among media and elections scholars relatively quickly.

Network news, with its national reach, offers the opportunity for a shared national "schema," or shared orientation toward a particular subject (Graber 1988)—or at least network news did offer that opportunity for a shared perspective before parts of its audience moved away in the direction of the much wider range of information and perspectives provided by such media as talk radio, cable news channels, and the Internet (Davis and Owen 1998; Owen 1996). The fact that the networks have faced more competition in recent years is an important issue to consider as we examine media coverage of recent presidential elections.

At the same time, the media effects perspective is far removed from the minimal effects model. Citizens are consuming much of the network news themselves, rather than having others digest it and translate it for them. Indeed, the fact that an increasing number of citizens is seeking out sources beyond the television networks—talk radio, the Internet, and so on—is hardly an approach consistent with the "two-step" flow of information at the center of the minimal effects model. The media effects approach, which seemed to make sense to many media scholars before the Internet, appears even more relevant in a time when individual news consumers are being drawn increasingly to search for their own news content.

The Changing News Media Environment

The last four presidential elections, the period of this study, have taken place during a time of rapid transformation of the news media environment. When Michael Dukakis and George Bush did battle over the opportunity to succeed Ronald Reagan as president, there was no Internet, there was hardly any talk radio worth mentioning, and the Cable News Network was a barely watched upstart news operation that posed no competition to the dominant television networks (Davis and Owen 1998; Graber 2002; Kovach and Rosenstiel 1999). At the start of this period, network television stood astride the media world as an 800-pound gorilla. The networks dominated the campaign strategies of candidates, they were far more influential with citizens than print, and to compare ABC, CBS, and NBC with CNN (derided by some critics in its early days as the "Chicken Noodle Network") would have provoked gales of laughter (Goldberg and Goldberg 1995:261). Every night, at 5:30 P.M. or 6 P.M. or 6:30 P.M. (depending on the time zone and media market in which you found yourself) America stopped to listen when America's network anchors described the most important events of the twenty-four hours since they had last visited our living rooms. The share of the network news audience had fallen some, from 75 percent of the audience in the 1970–1971 season to just under 70 percent in the 1980s, but when Dan Rather, Peter Jennings, and Tom Brokaw spoke, America listened (Kurtz 2002b).

What a difference four presidential elections can make. CNN, with its 24-hour-a-day news coverage, came into its own with the 1991 Persian Gulf War, becoming the place to turn for up-to-the-minute news during times of international crisis (Goldberg and Goldberg 1995). The CNN talk show *Larry King Live* became the place in 1992 to see Ross Perot tell America he was planning on running for president. Indeed Perot ran for president in 1992 largely through CNN appearances and through his own self-financed and highly rated infomercials on network television (Baker 1993; McWilliams 1993). Rush Limbaugh became a talk radio icon at about the same time. Limbaugh, an in-your-face conservative who drew considerable public attention during the 1990s, peppered President Clinton with a never-ending series of attacks and helped promote the rise of a more combative Republican Party that achieved majority status in the U.S. House and Senate following the 1994 elections (Owen 1996, 1997). The Internet likewise became an obsession for millions of Americans and the source of constantly available news and information—sometimes of dubious quality, depending on the source—about virtually any topic (Davis and Owen 1998; Drudge 2000; Hall 2001; Seib 2001).

And the once-dominant Big Three television networks? Their audience share has plummeted to 43 percent of the audience, a drop so dramatic that media experts are wondering if the half-hour nightly news programs—the jewels in the crowns of three of America's most influential media companies—are long for this world (Kurtz 2002b).

"When Brokaw, Jennings and Rather retire, it is a perfect time for these corporations to decide that their newscasts are no long worth it," said Ken Bode, a former NBC correspondent who teaches at Northwestern University's Medill School of Journalism. "Unless something dramatic happens, inevitably, the network newscasts are gone" (quoted in Kurtz 2002b:A1).

Howard Kurtz, who covers the news business for the *Washington Post*, blames demographic and technological changes for the decline of the network evening newscasts:

> The audience is shrinking—and graying—because of changing lifestyles and more media choices. Older folks who came of age in the pre-cable era are accustomed to tuning in for news at 6:30. Most younger people never acquired the habit, are still working at that hour or are just plain less interested in news, surveys show. A growing number get their information online, essentially becoming their own editors. (Kurtz 2002b:A20)

Attention paid to network news coverage of presidential elections has shown the same dramatic decline in viewers, and in influence, as has network news overall. Table 1.1 contains the results of a series of election-year surveys that show what news sources citizens say they are using as they collect information about that year's presidential contest.

News consumers are voting with their eyeballs with respect to the network news coverage, and as more alternative sources have become available they have been looking elsewhere. Citizens are choosing sources that our content analysis demonstrates in chapter 5 are more thorough, less negative, and more informative than network news. The expansion of cable news in particular has cut greatly into network television's share of the news audience. In 2000, for the first time, more people turned to cable news than to the networks for information about a presidential election. In 1992, 55 percent of the people surveyed said that the network news programs were one of their top two media sources for information about presidential elections. By 2000, only 22 percent made the

TABLE 1.1 Media Use Trends, 1992–2000 (results in percentages)

Question: "How did you get most of your news about the presidential election campaign—from television, from newspapers, from radio, from magazines, or from the Internet?" [Accept two answers. If only one response is given, probe for one additional response.]

[If the respondent answered television, ask:] "Did you get most of your news about the presidential campaign from network TV news, from local TV news, or from cable news networks such as CNN or MSNBC?" [Accept up to two answers.]

	2000	1996	1992
Television (overall)	70	72	82
Network	22	36	55
Local	21	23	29
Cable	36	21	29
Other [volunteered]	1	4	2
Don't know [volunteered]	1	2	1
Newspapers	39	60	57
Radio	15	19	12
Magazines	4	11	9
Internet	11	3	n/a
Other [volunteered]	1	4	6
Don't know	[a]	1	1

Source: Pew Research Center for the People and the Press 2000b.
Note: Because two answers were accepted, columns do not add up to 100 percent.
[a]Less than 0.5 percent.

same claim. Other media sources have also seen declines, though they tend to be less dramatic. The audience share of local news fell from 29 percent to 21 percent over the eight-year period. Newspapers became the leading source of campaign news in the Pew survey of media use during Campaign 2000 (Pew 2000b). This print advantage was largely achieved by default: the 39 percent of respondents who listed papers as a major source had fallen considerably from the 57 percent of those surveyed eight years earlier who said that they relied on newspapers. Network television's fall was simply much more rapid.

Despite these declines, network television news continues to attract huge audiences, and many of the cable alternatives are in fact network-owned offshoots that sometimes use the same reporters and even the same stories. A case could be made, to paraphrase Mark Twain, that reports of the death of the network evening news programs have been greatly exaggerated. During an average week in March 2002, for example, the three evening newscasts drew a nightly average of 23 million viewers—and over the 2001–2002 season were seen by an average of 43 percent of the audience watching television during their time slots (Kurtz 2002b). Although these audience figures are smaller than they were, the audiences are vastly larger than those who tune in to leading cable news outlets or public television (Kurtz 2002b; de Moraes 2002). In contrast, *Wall Street Week*, the only public television show to rank first in its category, was drawing 2.7 million weekly viewers before longtime host Louis Rukeyser was dumped in March 2002 over concerns that the weekly business show did not draw enough younger viewers (de Moraes 2002). Bill O'Reilly, who hosts one of the leading cable news programs on the Fox News Channel, in early 2002 was bringing in about 2 million viewers a night, a fraction of the number any broadcast news show needs in order to survive. Other prominent cable news shows do not even do that well. On CNN, Aaron Brown's news show averaged about 825,000 viewers a night in early 2002, and *The News with Brian Williams* on MSNBC was drawing an average audience of about 375,000 viewers a night (de Moraes 2002).

News coverage of the past three presidential elections has been marked by a particularly steep decline in public attention to the Big Three evenings news programs, as viewers appear to have moved in the direction of higher-quality news. In 1992, network news was roughly as commonly used a source of election information as newspapers. But a steady decline since then in network news performance—a decline amply demonstrated through our content analysis—has led to a dramatically increased gap between these two influential formats. A 2- percentage-point gap favoring print in 1992 opened up into a 17-percentage-point gap favoring newspapers over network television news eight years later. Network television news had a 26-percentage-point advantage over cable news in 1992; by 2000 this had become a 14-point deficit.

These survey results suggest the great decline and the great challenges faced by today's evening television news programs. Citizens have grown more negative about the news media's performance, criticizing it as too negative, not focused enough on the issues, and too biased. As table 1.1 shows, citizens have turned away from network news with a vengeance not seen previously in the more than half a century of television. And media researchers—ourselves included—find that television has become even more worthy of criticism in its coverage of recent presidential elections. It is to an outline of this content analysis methodology that this chapter now turns.

An Overview of the CMPA Content Analysis Evidence

For the last four presidential elections—the campaigns of 1988, 1992, 1996, and 2000—CMPA's content analysis was applied to the Big Three (ABC, CBS, and NBC) broadcast network evening news shows. With the rise of cable news, talk radio, and the Internet in recent years, these programs are not as dominant in establishing the contours of political discourse as they used to be (Davis and Owen 1998). Nonetheless, for all their recent decline in viewers, these flagship broadcasts continue to draw by far the largest audiences of any news organizations (apart from wire services). They also control many of the alternative news outlets on cable, where material from the evening newscasts can be recycled for cable news programming (this is particularly common for NBC and MSNBC). In addition, this core network news sample provides a basis for a comparison with television news coverage of earlier presidential contests. The 2000 content analysis applied most of the same coding categories that were used in the center's studies of the 1996, 1992, and 1988 general elections, which allows for direct comparisons over time. The comparisons are further enhanced by a content analysis of the *NewsHour* on PBS during Campaign 2000, as well as an expanded version of the study for 1996, which included additional variables and a larger and more diverse sample, including print as well as broadcast outlets. The 1996 study also measured candidate discourse in several different formats, including campaign trail speeches and paid television ads. Nonnetwork news outlets are also analyzed for the 1988 and 1992 elections, allowing for content comparisons overall for all four presidential elections considered here.

The networks' evening news coverage was examined during all four election news cycles to determine its thoroughness, substantive focus, valence (i.e., positive or negative tone with respect to the candidates), and level of mediation (i.e., the degree to which the story of the campaign was communicated through the candidates' own utterances, as opposed to the comments of journalists and other on-camera sources). The amount of coverage, the topics and issues that were addressed, the context in which public policy issues were framed, the speaking time given to the candidates (both cumulatively and in terms of average duration, as measured by individual sound bite length), and the evaluative tone of comments about the candidates were among the dimensions measured for each news story.

Coders worked from videotaped newscasts. For all variables reported here, intercoder reliability—the extent to which one coder agreed with a second coder looking at the same taped news segment—exceeded 90 percent. Reliability tests were conducted on stories taken from previous applications of the system and spot checks were conducted on current stories during the 2000 campaign to provide additional confidence in the content coding. The overall news story was treated as the unit of analysis only for measures of topical focus. Other variables were measured by coding individual statements (message units) within stories. This procedure permits far more precise differentiation of campaign discourse than story-level coding affords. In all four elections, the general election study period began on Labor Day, the traditional kickoff date for the general election campaign, and concluded with the broadcasts aired the night before Election Day. The primary election news period began on January 1 and lasted until a nominee was selected, usually by mid-March. The election "preseason" covers the year before the presidential contest. Although few voters may be paying much attention a year before a presidential election, jockeying to win a party's presidential nomination starts even earlier than that, particularly in Iowa, home to the first caucus, and in New Hampshire, home to the first primary (Broder 2001).

What Comes Next?

This first chapter has introduced the research project and outlined the previous academic research on content analysis research. The first chapter also has discussed how the dominant theory of media influence (the media effects paradigm) relates to media coverage of presidential elections, and how citizens feel about the news coverage they receive. We now conclude with a brief discussion of what will be covered in subsequent chapters of this work.

Chapter 2 begins by comparing the content of network television newscasts from the past four presidential elections. Here we will demonstrate how the amount of coverage overall has declined over the past four elections and how the coverage that remains has grown increasingly focused on the horse race rather than more substantive matters, like discussion of policies and character—areas that would be very useful for voters trying to decide which candidate to support.

Chapter 3 deals with another damaging change in the way reporters have covered presidential campaigns over this period: the steadily increasing amount of time that reporters and anchors devote to themselves. Not only has the amount of coverage overall declined but so too has the amount of coverage in which candidates speak for themselves. The content analysis reveals candidates have small shares of correspondent reports devoted to their own comments and that the fragments of candidate remarks (called "sound bites") broadcast on the Big Three networks have become smaller and smaller. In this chapter, we demonstrate how this degradation of coverage forces candidates to reduce their ideas to the simplest and most "media-friendly" descriptions if they expect to receive media attention. The trend even encourages candidates to pepper each other with "sound barks," rather than reason with each other, on the campaign trail. Finally we also consider the ways network television reports "frame" candidates, reducing some of them to little more than stereotypes on the campaign trail.

Chapter 4 turns directly to questions of negativity, accuracy, and bias in a consideration of network coverage of Election 2000 as compared to previous elections. The astonishing series of media blunders that marked the Bush-Gore contest comprises only the latest errors of judgment in a process that has been marked by less accurate and more negative coverage over time. The decision by the television networks to pool their resources to create the Voter News Service has led to similar errors in the past, including when the networks erroneously reported in 1996 that Sen. Bob Smith (R-N.H.) had lost his bid for re-election. The race to be first, which has intensified as media technologies have improved and as use of the Internet has become more widespread—has led to increasing recklessness in the calling of elections, and not just in Florida (Nelson 2001; Owen 2002; Sabato 2002).

Errors are only part of the problem relating to accuracy and bias, though. The past four elections have been marked by a steady decline in the civility of the coverage, with reporters increasingly focusing on the negative aspects of each candidate. The media cynicism created more than a quarter-century ago by the lies of Vietnam and Watergate continues to deepen, as a decreasing fraction of what is said about a candidate qualifies as positive. This negativity may make it particularly appealing for potential voters to "tune out" the candidates and not even go to the polls on election day.

In chapter 5, we argue that the evidence against the television networks is particularly compelling when they are compared to other media sources, including public television and leading daily newspapers that help set the national media agenda—papers such as the *Washington Post,* the *Wall Street Journal,* and the *New York Times*. The *NewsHour* on PBS offers the most important contrast. Despite having a slightly smaller amount of airtime, PBS devoted far more air time to Election 2000 news than the Big Three evening news shows combined, was far more focused on substantive issues than on the horse race, and was less prone to bias. The average candidate sound bite on PBS in 2000, for example, was nearly seven times the length of the average sound bite on ABC, CBS, and NBC.

Chapter 5 also discusses the large gap between the way presidential campaigns are presented by the news media and the way that these campaigns actually unfold. There is a great deal of difference, the CMPA content analysis demonstrates, between what the candidates said and what the networks said they said. This discrepancy is found across the types of campaign discourse, including candidate speeches, campaign web pages, and even the much-maligned campaign advertisements.

Chapter 6, the final chapter, presents potential reforms to improve the performance of network television or in the alternative to make the networks less significant in citizen assessments of presidential candidates. While network television does not appear likely to follow the lead of the *NewsHour*, which has far lower ratings than any of the three network evening news broadcasts, there are possible ways to improve the broadcast networks' performance in covering presidential elections. Potential reforms debated here include hour-long network newscasts, free broadcast airtime for candidates to present unmediated messages, and the growing opportunities for interested citizens to go beyond the nightly news through consultation of Internet sources.

CHAPTER 2

A NEED-TO-KNOW BASIS?
Covering Issues of Substance and the Horse Race

Every fourth November, roughly 100 million Americans cast a vote for a presidential candidate. The campaigns for president, and before that the preliminary battles for the Democratic and Republican presidential nominations, are extended seminars on the state of the nation: how well (or how poorly) the incumbent president has handled the always pivotal issues of war and peace and of the economy. Candidates debate other issues that could affect presidential performance as well, which—depending on the year—could include energy, the environment, health care, tax cuts, and even the country's moral climate. But more than just a look back, presidential campaigns are also about looking forward. Candidates discuss where the country should go in the years ahead and how the nation can deal with some of its most vexing problems: crime, poverty, the massive federal debt, the tens of millions of Americans who lack health insurance, and the potential insolvency of Social Security and Medicare in the coming decades. Even for a country as wealthy as the United States, there are many challenging and highly contested policy areas considered at length by people who campaign to be president.

On network television's evening news programs, though, a different picture emerges. The debate is not primarily over whether Social Security needs fixing and, if so, how to fix it. The televised discussion is not over whether the American economy needs a boost and, if so, how to provide a little macroeconomic help. Rather, network television reporters talk mostly about who is ahead and who is behind in the presidential polls. The discussion of public policy matters that does occur on network television is often framed in the context of this very same horse race. Campaign programs proposed to fix Social Security or cut taxes or revamp welfare are seen as ways to woo the farmers, the so-called soccer moms, senior citizens, or some other special interest group. As data presented in this chapter show, reporters often spend more time on air judging the political wisdom of the appeal than presenting the policy proposal and evaluating its substantive merits. While a consideration of how well a policy proposal would address a problem can be an important part of assessing a candidate, reporters focus on how politically savvy the appeal seems to be in the opinion of those same reporters and their sources. This trend has been identified by past scholars, and despite the criticism, this media approach has become more pronounced in more recent presidential elections. The networks' growing focus on horse race matters, as measured by the Center for Media and Public Affairs (CMPA) content analysis, is even more dire than past scholars have indicated.

The horse race–dominated election as presented by network television news is the one that most of us see, since television has long been the dominant venue for American political discourse (Patterson 1994). Few Americans attend presidential campaign rallies in person, and a decreasing number of us use the daily newspapers as our major source of campaign news. If we attended campaign rallies and if we read about presidential campaigns in some of the country's better newspapers, we might see or read about a somewhat different election—one where there is more discussion of policy options, more discussion of matters of substance—than the "mediated" election of network television news. But even print sources, as we demonstrate in chapter 5, suffer from many of the same problems that afflict network news.

This chapter presents the broad outline of network television news coverage of presidential elections from 1988 to 2000. Using a massive content analysis by CMPA of every presidential campaign news story aired on every evening newscast on ABC, CBS, and NBC over the past four presidential election cycles, this chapter measures how much the total amount of presidential election coverage has declined over the past four elections. The content analysis used here also demonstrates how the television coverage that has remained has grown increasingly focused on the horse race aspects of the presidential campaign rather than more substantive matters, like issues and candidate character. The areas that many television reporters neglect, particularly candidates' policy proposals, could be very useful for citizens trying to decide which candidate to support.

Agenda Setting: The Power of News Content

In the first chapter, we discussed three leading theories of the news media's influence: the "hypodermic effects" model of very powerful media effects (where news content was thought to be more or less "injected" into citizens), the "minimal effects" model (where citizens were not seen to be affected very much by news content), and the "media effects" model ("more than minimal" effects), where the news media don't tell citizens what to think so much as what to think about. Few media scholars imagine citizens are "brainwashed" by what they see on television (the first perspective), and few believe citizens are only barely influenced by what is presented in the news media. Most academics who study the news media find themselves among those who consider the third, "media effects," model the strongest—that reporters and editors help set the agenda and frame the debate by the issues and perspectives they choose to emphasize (or to ignore).

Most Americans alive today grew up in homes with television, and former senator Bob Dole (R-Kans.), the Republican Party's 1996 nominee for president, was probably the last presidential candidate to grow up in the pre-television age. Given how common television has been in American life for the past half-century, it is easy to overlook how much television news has changed the political environment. Television, which became widespread in America during the 1950s, had the potential to be far more influential in politics than newspapers for a variety of reasons: (1) it offered an expanded range of information—both moving pictures and words; (2) it offered the potential for being more credible (seeing is believing, as the saying goes); and (3) it rapidly became the dominant source of information and entertainment in American households (cf. Grossman

1995; Ranney 1983; White 1961). The key events of American politics in the 1960s—the Civil Rights movement, the Vietnam War, the space race, the Cuban Missile Crisis, and the assassinations of John F. Kennedy, Robert F. Kennedy, and Martin Luther King, Jr., and their aftermaths—all lent themselves to powerful (and emotion-invoking) visual images (cf. Gitlin 1980; Grossman 1995; Halberstam 1979; Lesher 1982; McGinniss 1969; Meyrowitz 1985; White 1978). So too did the 1960 presidential election, the first to include nationally televised debates—confrontations that pitted the sunny features of a media-savvy Jack Kennedy against the pale-complexioned and otherwise unappealing visage of Richard M. Nixon (White 1961; Perret 2001). It is no wonder that citizens during these years turned to television in increasing numbers and for an increasing share of the news they consumed.

Candidates would very much like to set the agenda. Presidents in good economic times may want to make the economy the issue, as Bill Clinton wished to do in 1996 (Ceaser and Busch 1997). Presidents in bad economic times may want to make something—anything—else the issue, as George H. W. Bush did four years earlier (Gold 1994). Challengers also have their own preferred agenda, in 2000 George W. Bush wanted to run on character issues and Al Gore wasn't sure what he wanted to run on, though he more or less decided on professional competence (Abramson et al. 2002; Ceaser and Busch 2001).

But candidates do not get the opportunity to set the campaign agenda, at least not unilaterally. The real power to set the agenda is in the hands of the news media, which control access to the columns of the nation's newspapers and the segments on the evening news programs (Ranney 1983). The process can be symbiotic, as candidates try to present information in media-friendly formats to increase the chances of obtaining coverage on topics those candidates wish to see on the agenda (Cook 1998). Reporters sometimes use those "made for TV" efforts in their programming, as the media experts on the campaigns try to tailor what they offer reporters to correspond with what the reporters themselves desire to use in their stories (Cook 1998; Ranney 1983). If the campaigns succeed in offering reporters what they will use in their stories, the campaigns may get coverage in areas they want, but make no mistake about it—coverage decisions are decisions made by journalists, not by candidates.

What the reporters choose to talk about is an important matter. The research evidence demonstrates that when we as news consumers learn what reporters and editors think are the important issues, we tend to consider these issues important ourselves (Iyengar and Kinder 1987). This process, known as agenda-setting, can work in a number of different ways. When citizens are exposed primarily to horse race news coverage, they do a better job of recalling that information than more substantive matters (Capella and Jamieson 1997). If reporters talk and write about economic matters a great deal, as was the case in 1992, we as news consumers and citizens are likely to consider economic matters an important part of evaluating a president or a presidential candidate (Lewis-Beck and Rice 1992; Mutz 1992).

The reverse is also true. In the same way that reporters can put something on the agenda, reporters can keep something off the agenda, or at least minimize its impact. If the media do not say a great deal about economic matters, as was the case in 2000, economic matters are not seen by citizens as an important issue to consider when selecting one's favorite presidential candidate (Campbell 2001; Lewis-Beck and Tien 2001; Wlezien 2001).

Political scientists Shanto Iyengar and Donald R. Kinder (1987) offered one of the most extensive tests of the agenda-setting power of television news through a laboratory experiment in which subjects were assigned to watch newscasts with different content and emphases. The results were clear: the more extensively a topic was covered on television news, the more important it became to the viewer.

> Americans' views of their society and nation are powerfully shaped by the stories that appear on the evening news. We found that people who were shown network broadcasts edited to draw attention to a particular problem assigned greater importance to that problem—greater importance than they themselves did before the experiment began, and greater importance than did people assigned to control conditions that emphasized different problems. (Iyengar and Kinder 1987:113)

As noted above, reporters do not have complete control over the contents of the campaign agenda. Journalists cover candidates who are constantly trying to shape the campaign agenda in ways that advantage their own particular campaign. There are also external events, including disasters and wars, that can alter the campaign agenda regardless of the issues that had been the focus of media attention (McLeod et al. 1994).

Likewise, not all citizens accept the media assessments of the most important issues. Not every citizen is persuadable, in other words. Some voters are very strong supporters of one political party or the other, regardless of candidate, issues, or media content. Such partisan, and decisive, citizens vote Democratic even in an election like that of 1972, when George McGovern was able to win only Massachusetts and the District of Columbia, or they vote Republican even in a year like 1964, when Barry Goldwater won only the states of South Carolina, Louisiana, Georgia, Mississippi, Alabama, and Arizona (Nie et al. 1979; Perlstein 2001).

Another issue that can be seen to undermine television's influence is that not everyone may be paying sufficient attention to understand political developments. Many citizens, even those who vote regularly, are not all that interested in political news. "For most Americans politics is still far from the most interesting and important thing in life," wrote Austin Ranney (1983:11). "To them politics is usually confusing, boring, repetitious, and, above all, irrelevant to the things that really matter in life." Political scientist Doris Graber (2002) has argued that the disconnected facts received from television news make it hard for citizens to create meaningful wholes of the evidence they do receive, and this can discourage citizens from even trying to make sense of the political world. In contrast, a study of citizen discourse in 1992 found that citizens are far more capable of engaging in useful democratic discourse than many critics believe (Just et al. 1996).

Of course, not every voter has to be influenced by television news for that news coverage to be significant, perhaps even decisive, in an election. Since neither major party commands the support of a majority of voters, less-partisan voters—political independents and ideological moderates mostly—end up selecting the winner in general elections. For the voters who do not more or less automatically support a candidate for partisan reasons, news coverage of the campaign can be an important part of deciding which presidential candidate to support.

The News Agenda: It's Mostly the Horse Race That Matters

Given the dramatic visual and political events of the 1960s, it is no wonder that the agenda-setting model (part of the media effects school) has been an important area of media research over the past several decades. A pioneer in this area, Michael Robinson (1976), found that network news coverage played an important role in shaping public assessments of government. Negative portrayal of the government on television can create a sense of "videomalaise," a public frustration intensified by the more expansive medium of television (Robinson 1976).

Applying the agenda-setting perspective to the study of presidential elections means turning to the horse race, which has long been a key area of media research (Bartels 1988; Patterson 1980, 1994; Ranney 1983). Thomas Patterson (1980, 1994) was an early critic of television's emphasis on horse race coverage, saying that reporters talk too much about the electoral "game" rather than about "governing." Citizens receive information about politics as sports, but not nearly enough about issues to enable voters to choose effectively between or among the candidates. Why are reporters so obsessed with horse race matters, and as a result, with public opinion polls? Patterson laments the media's focus on polls, but he believes this pattern of modern reporting has more to do with news routines than with a deliberate choice on the part of reporters to be irresponsible.

> The news is not a mirror held up to society. It is a selective rendition of events told in story form. For this reason, the conventions of news reporting include an emphasis on the more dramatic and controversial aspects of politics. Above all else, reporters are taught to search for what is new and different in events of the past twenty-four hours. (Patterson 1994:60)

The crucial issues raised by early critics of the news media's horse race focus (cf. Patterson and McClure 1976) appear to have triggered efforts on the parts of at least one of the networks to do better in the 1980 campaign. CBS anchor Walter Cronkite provided viewers with a number of very issue-based interviews just before the 1980 election, even if it sometimes appeared during those interviews that CBS did not have an accurate sense of what the most important issues were (Robinson and Sheehan 1983:146–47).

In subsequent years, nearly every content analysis that examined network television programming has objected to the heavy emphasis on the horse race aspects of presidential campaign coverage (cf. Bartels 1988; Kerbel 1998; Lichter et al. 1988; Lichter et al. 1989; Lichter and Noyes 1995, 1998; Patterson 1994; Robinson and Sheehan 1983). "In covering a presidential campaign, the media tell us more about who is winning and who is losing than they do about who is fit to be president," complained Larry Bartels (1988:32), raising an objection widely shared by media researchers. Despite the many media critics of the practice of describing politics as sports, the media's focus on the horse race continues. In fact, as this chapter shows, the trend toward horse race coverage has become more powerful in recent elections.

From the point of view of a well-functioning democratic polity, the horse race focus seen during the nomination campaigns seems particularly troubling. Nomination campaigns are intramural competitions where citizens no longer have partisan cues to guide them and often involve several candidates who often are not all that well known, and if fiercely contested, these nomination campaigns can cripple a partisan nominee in a fall election (Lengle 1981, 1987; Lengle et al. 1995).

The concerns here, therefore, go beyond the fact that network news is paying more attention to the trivial matters of the horse race. Network television's focus on politics as sports is making this trivial matter influential—if not decisive—in the selection of presidential nominees, and that selection process itself may be an important factor in voter assessments in the November general election. A key way that horse race matters affect outcomes occurs through the process by which this coverage builds momentum for a candidate (Bartels 1988). In 1972, for example, Edmund Muskie won the New Hampshire primary by nine points, but the media's story was instead that he did worse than expected as the reporters focused on the "surprisingly strong showing by [George] McGovern" (Ranney 1983:96). McGovern eventually won the 1972 Democratic nomination, but was trounced by Richard Nixon that November (Wade 2002). Bill Clinton proclaimed himself "the comeback kid" after finishing second in New Hampshire twenty years later, and likewise the media's focus was on Clinton's stronger than expected showing and not about the candidate who actually won the primary (and won it by eight percentage points), former senator Paul Tsongas of Massachusetts (Baker 1993). "Doing best in the early primaries is not simply a matter of getting more votes than the other candidates; it is getting substantially more votes 'than expected,'" wrote Austin Ranney (1983:95). "Query: expected by whom? Answer: by the analysts of the press and the networks."

In fact, the best thing that can happen to a presidential primary candidate may very well be that the reporters are completely wrong about a candidate's political fortunes. On the other hand, this can also be the worst thing. If you are underestimated and do quite well, like Bill Clinton in 1992 and John McCain in 2000, you may bask in some of the most favorable coverage available; if you are overestimated and do not do as well as expected—even if you win—you may suffer from harsh media coverage, like President Bush in 1992. Robert Shogan of the *Los Angeles Times*, one of the nation's most experienced political reporters, laments this focus on the expectations game in New Hampshire, arguing that it has "a profound and capricious impact" (2001:31) on presidential nominations and elections.

Fortunately for the candidates who "beat the spread"—including Clinton, McGovern, and Jimmy Carter—reporters continue to play the expectations game (Maisel 2002). Being badly mistaken in their predictions, as they were in 1992, doesn't even slow the reporters down.

> Four weeks ago, just before the New Hampshire primary, the television wise men of "Inside Washington" were asked to assess the prospects for Bill Clinton's scandal-ridden candidacy. "I think he is a goner," said Carl Rowan. "I think Clinton is dead," said Charles Krauthammer. The governor of Arkansas, long since resurrected from the political graveyard, appeared well on his way to the Democratic nomination yesterday after convincing victories in Illinois and Michigan. And the press? Those folks who anointed Clinton the frontrunner long before the voters tuned in, then decided he had been de-Flowered in New Hampshire, then started chronicling his comeback? Well, it's a good thing they don't make their living playing the stock market. (Kurtz 1992a)

As political scientist Larry Bartels observes, "Analysts, observers, and pundits courageous enough to predict the outcomes of recent nominating campaigns have been routinely embarrassed" (1988:6). But the predictions keep on coming.

The erroneous predictions of Clinton's fortunes by reporters during the 1992 New Hampshire primary, and again during the early days of the Clinton/Lewinsky scandal in the late 1990s, demonstrate the limits of media effects on the viewing and reading audience. In the days following the first public disclosure of that scandal, the president was said to be finished by leading pundits, including Sam Donaldson, the longtime White House correspondent and host of ABC's *This Week*. On that show's January 25, 1998, broadcast, Donaldson opined:

> If he's not telling the truth, I think his presidency is numbered in days. This isn't going to drag out. We're not going to be here three months from now talking about this. Mr. Clinton, if he's not telling the truth and the evidence shows that, will resign, perhaps this week. (Donaldson, quoted in Jones 2001:199)

In fact, America was talking about this scandal a year later. Such dire assessments regarding Clinton's ability to survive politically would not have been wrong under the hypodermic effects model. A model based on powerful media effects would predict that if reporters said Clinton was finished politically—as many journalists said during the 1992 campaign and again during the 1998 scandal involving the president and Monica Lewinsky—the voters would have rejected Clinton (Kurtz 1992a; Owen 2000; Sabato et al. 2000).

Nevertheless, the horse race–based media expectations game can have real consequences. People can be elected president, as Bill Clinton was in 1992, at least in part because he won the expectations game during the primary season and faced an incumbent president, George H. W. Bush, weakened politically by poor economic conditions (Patterson 1994). Jimmy Carter's 1976 victory was also helped considerably by the combination of these two factors: beating media expectations and facing a weak incumbent president, Gerald Ford, who was paying a high price in public opinion for having pardoned Richard Nixon's Watergate crimes (Bartels 1988; Ranney 1983).

What do journalists do when they are wrong? They write a new story—and when necessary add a 180-degree turn to their coverage. Reporters seeking to find explanations for their previous underestimations of a candidate can be quite generous, at least temporarily. Reporters describe candidates enjoying an unexpected rise in the polls as "suddenly more decisive, committed, inspiring and in general a better candidate and person" (Patterson 1994:118–19). Candidates falling in the polls receive more negative coverage, described by that particularly undesirable quality "a likely loser" (Patterson 1994:120). Other researchers have reached similar conclusions, even though they looked at different elections. Examining the 1984 battle between Gary Hart and Walter Mondale for the Democratic nomination, for example, Larry Bartels (1988) concludes that momentum—a desire to "go with a winner"—is a very important part of the nomination process.

Agenda-setting is the process of telling voters what to think about and what to ignore, and it is also the process of telling them whom to think about and whom to ignore. When presidential candidates, like Ralph Nader and Pat Buchanan in 2000, get very little media coverage, voters are less likely to consider those candidates and their issues when deciding which candidate to support. In his report on his 2000 Green Party presidential campaign, Nader faulted the networks for not taking his campaign seriously, even though the third-party candidate generated large crowds and raised issues other candidates chose to ignore.

> There is a major problem for anyone who runs for president, especially a third party candidate. No matter how long or extensively you campaign in every state of the union, no matter how large your audiences become, you cannot reach in direct personal communication even one percent of the eligible voters. In essence you don't run for president directly; you ask the media to run you for president or, if you have the money, you can pay the media for exposure. Reaching the voters relies almost entirely on how the media chooses to perceive you and your campaign. In short this "virtually reality" *is* the reality. (Nader 2002:155; emphasis in original)

Of course media coverage is not decisive in the minds of all voters in this situation either. Despite his near-absence on network television during Campaign 2000, Nader nevertheless received the votes of more than 2.8 million citizens, roughly 3 percent of those ballots that were cast and counted (Pomper 2001).

The focus on horse race campaign news by network television news and by most other media outlets is damaging for the polity, according to some researchers. If the newspapers and television news programs focus largely on polling, we can expect at least some otherwise uncommitted citizens to pay a great deal of attention to which candidate is ahead and which candidate is behind when they decide which candidate to support (Patterson 1980). Shanto Iyengar (1991) says that the news media's unwillingness to take issues seriously undermines the ability of politicians to send issue-based appeals and of voters to receive issue-based appeals.

> Instead of forcing the candidates to address the issues of clear social or economic significance, television news coverage of the 1988 campaign focused on the Pledge of Allegiance, patriotism, prison-furlough programs,

> flag desecration, membership in the American Civil Liberties Union and other issues more symbolic than substantive. (Iyengar 1991:142)

To Iyengar and others (cf. Just et al. 1996), this trend is particularly problematic for a democratic society because it does not give citizens the information necessary to connect the dots, so to speak. How does a president (Ronald Reagan) who frequently called for a balanced budget amendment to the Constitution escape blame for creating the largest eight-year U.S. budget deficit in history? A candidate for president in 1988 (George Bush) can proclaim himself "the education president" at the same time he says "read my lips, no new taxes," and the voters do not seem to notice the inconsistencies. The fault for the public's inability to appreciate such contradictions lies largely with the media, Iyengar concludes:

> Because of its reliance on episodic reporting, television news provides a distorted depiction of public affairs. The portrayal of recurring issues as unrelated events prevents the public from cumulating the evidence toward any logical consequence. By diverting attention from societal and governmental responsibility, episodic framing glosses over national problems and allows public officials to ignore problems whose remedies entail burdens to their constituents. Television news may well prove to be the opiate of American society. (Iyengar 1991:143)

Even basic knowledge appears to be impaired as a result of media coverage patterns. Presidential scholar Stephen J. Wayne says that the horse race focus may be the reason that citizens know so little basic information about the candidates running for president:

> A national survey taken in January 2000 at the onset of the presidential campaign found that one-third of the people did not know which of the presidential candidates was currently governor of Texas, only 30 percent knew that Bill Bradley was a former senator from New Jersey, and only 17 percent correctly identified John McCain as a cosponsor of a campaign finance bill in Congress (73 percent did not know or refused to give an answer). Similarly, in December 1995, when Senate Majority Leader Robert Dole was the leading candidate for the 1996 Republican presidential nomination, only 34 percent could correctly identify the person who served as majority leader of the Senate. Vice President Al Gore did better in the same survey; 60 percent knew who he was. (Wayne 2003:136–37)

Amount of Network News Coverage

GENERAL ELECTIONS

Even before the 2000 general election was under way, the networks attracted criticism for cutting back on coverage, in this case their live coverage of the party conventions. Critics saw this reduction in coverage as the most recent instance in which the network news departments paid less attention to "hard" political news and more to "soft" news of lifestyle trends and human interest stories (Media Monitor 1997; Patterson 2000). Television executives themselves claimed that both the Democratic and Republican conventions had grown too dull and too stage-managed to justify covering extensively on network television and pointed to the fact that viewers interested in more extensive coverage could find it on cable television.

The networks' minimalist approaches toward covering the 2000 party national conventions were not isolated incidents. Indeed, CMPA studies found that coverage of both the 1999 campaign preseason and the primary battles dropped sharply from the previous presidential election. Airtime was down by 44 percent in comparison to the 1995 preseason and 23 percent for the contested period of the primaries prior to "Super Tuesday" in 1996, according to the content analysis conducted by CMPA. (The competitive period of the primaries lasted from January 1 to March 7 in 2000 and January 1 to March 12 in 1996.) This decline was all the more striking because both parties waged heated battles for their nominations in 2000, whereas only the Republicans did so in 1996. All other things being equal, there should have been twice as much coverage during the 1999 preseason and the 2000 primary season, as there were twice as many nomination contests to cover. Instead coverage in the most recent election cycle fell significantly in both periods.

During fall 2000, the tightest presidential race since the advent of television attracted just enough attention to halt this downturn, as shown in table 2.1. During the nine weeks from Labor Day through Election Day, the network evening news shows carried 462 campaign stories with total air time of 13 hours 25 minutes, an average of 12.6 minutes per night. This latest figure corresponds to an average of just over four minutes per half-hour network evening newscast. This represented slightly fewer stories but slightly more airtime than four years earlier (483 stories in 13 hours 8 minutes, or an average of 12.3 minutes per night). In fact, Campaign 2000

TABLE 2.1 General Election News, 1988–2000

Amount of Coverage	2000	1996	1992	1988
Number of stories	462	483	728	589
Minutes per day	12.6	12.3	24.6	17.0
Total time (minutes)	805	788	1,402	1,116

coverage of the general election trailed that of Campaign 1996 throughout the fall, until heavy coverage of the closely contested final days before November 7, 2000, outpaced that of the last week four years earlier. The photo-finish ending, then, led to a very slight increase in amount of television news coverage of the contest during fall 2000. Put another way, this very slight increase amounted to about four extra seconds of election coverage a night on each network evening newscast. (By way of perspective, four seconds is about how long it takes to dial a ten-digit phone number you have memorized—like your own home number.)

The three networks differed somewhat in the amount of coverage offered during the 2000 general election period. NBC had the only increase in coverage, up 11 percent from 1996 to a total of 145 stories with a total airtime of 4 hours 46 minutes. The amount of time spent on Campaign 2000 fell slightly at ABC, down 2 percent from 1996 to a total of 180 stories lasting 4 hours 38 minutes. Of the Big Three networks, the election coverage on CBS fell by the largest amount, down 10 percent from the network's 1996 coverage, to a total of 137 stories adding up to four hours of airtime.

The amount of network coverage for both the 1996 and 2000 general elections, however, pale before the massive coverage CMPA recorded for Campaign 1992—23 hours 22 minutes—and Campaign 1988—18 hours 36 minutes. The light coverage of the 1996 general election, representing barely half the 1992 level, was initially attributed to a dull and uncompetitive contest between two well-known candidates. With the media coverage of the 2000 election now precisely quantified, the decline in coverage recorded in 1996 now appears to be part of a longer-term trend of reduced network television coverage of presidential elections. After all, the 2000 total barely exceeded that of 1996, despite featuring a breakneck race with sharp policy debates and a newcomer to national politics as the GOP challenger. Presidential elections don't get much more interesting

TABLE 2.2 Primary Election News, 1988–2000

Amount of Coverage[a]	2000	1996	1992	1988
Number of stories	550	699	370	597
Minutes per day	13.4	16.9	10.7	13.3
Total time (minutes)	882	1,202	738	1,126

[a]Coverage through the Super Tuesday primaries held March 7, 2000; March 12, 1996; and March 10, 1992. The 1988 data are through the Illinois primary on March 15, 1988.

than they were in 2000, but the amount of coverage in that election was far, far less than the general election phase of the 1988 and 1992 presidential elections.

When the 2000 general election figures are combined with the decline in preseason and primary coverage from four years earlier (more information on those periods are found below), the networks' overall campaign attention deficit is all the more striking—a 22 percent decline, or roughly ten hours less airtime (from 46 hours 22 minutes to 35 hours 56 minutes) than the relatively uneventful 1996 race. While there are more alternative sources of election news today than in the recent past, tens of millions of Americans rely on the television networks as a major source of information about campaigns and elections. We are finding less and less information about presidential elections on the nightly network television newscasts with each successive election.

NOMINATION CONTESTS

From January 1, 2000, through the evening news the night before the Super Tuesday primaries of March 7, 2000, the three major networks broadcast 550 stories on the presidential nomination process, for a total of 14 hours 42 minutes of coverage. This total, found in table 2.2, represents a decline of 23 percent from the 1996 primaries through roughly the same date, even though both the Democrats and the Republicans had contested primaries in 2000. There were more stories and more time devoted to campaign coverage during the 2000 primaries as compared to 1992, but both years fell far short of the standards set in 1996 and 1988.

As was the case with the general election coverage in 2000, CBS showed the sharpest decline in coverage. The 4 hours 18 minutes of primary coverage provided by CBS represented 39 percent less coverage than that aired in 1996. ABC aired 4 hours 37 minutes of presidential campaign news during the 2000 primaries, down 29 percent from four years earlier. NBC, which offered 4 hours 50 minutes of coverage during the period, reduced its coverage by 14 percent when compared to 1996.

Within the primary season, a key period of media coverage to consider is the month or so before the New Hampshire primary, traditionally the first presidential primary. The New Hampshire primary enjoys a wildly disproportionate influence in American presidential nomination politics, as the voters of this small and unrepresentative state have long been able to narrow considerably the field of candidates for the primaries and caucuses that follow (Adams 1987; Baker 1993; Duncan 1991; Mayer 1987, 1996, 1997, 2001; Palmer 1997; Rosenstiel 1994; Stanley 1997, 2001). From the unofficial January 1 start of the 2000 primary season through the eve of the New Hampshire primary, January 31, 2000, the network evening news shows were about as likely to feature the challengers, former senator Bill Bradley (D-N.J., 67 stories) and Sen. John McCain (R-Ariz., 58 stories) as they were to feature Democratic front-runner Vice President Al Gore (67 stories) and Republican favorite then Texas Governor George W. Bush (66 stories). The networks apparently concluded that all four candidates had a reasonable chance of prevailing in the Granite State contest and gave each one a roughly equal amount of coverage. That apparent network judgment appears to be a sound one given the final poll numbers and the primary results in New Hampshire (Farnsworth and Lichter 2001).

The results of that February 1, 2000, primary changed dramatically the orientations of subsequent network news programs. After Gore secured a 50 percent to 46 percent victory over Bradley in New Hampshire and McCain crushed Bush by an unexpectedly large 49 percent to 30 percent margin, the Democratic contest became increasingly overshadowed by the more aggressively contested GOP nomination (Lichter 2001; Nelson 2001). After New Hampshire, the GOP race generated almost five times as much network news coverage as the Democratic contest. The Republicans faced several primary battles during the period between the February 1 New Hampshire primary and the Super Tuesday primaries of March 7—including Delaware on February 8, South Carolina on February 19, Arizona and Michigan on February 22, and Virginia and Wash-

TABLE 2.3 Preseason Election News, 1987–1999

Amount of Coverage[a]	1999	1995	1991	1987
Number of stories	294	485	211	379
Minutes per day	1.2	2.3	1.1	2.1
Total time (minutes)	420	842	383	683

[a]January 1 through December 31, except February 1 through December 31 in 1987.

ington state on February 29. (Bush won all the contests during this period, except Michigan and Arizona, the latter being McCain's home state.) For the Democrats, Gore secured easy victories in Democratic primaries in Delaware and Washington state during this five-week period and went on to win the Democratic nomination without losing a single primary or caucus to Bradley (Stanley 2001). The fact that network news basically stopped covering the Democratic contest after New Hampshire made it particularly difficult for Bradley to convince potential donors and voters that he was still a viable candidate. In America's heavily mediated presidential primaries, if a challenger stops appearing on television, the challenger effectively becomes invisible. Unless they have a personal fortune, they also soon stop being challengers.

Table 2.3 demonstrates that the coverage during the 1999 preseason also fell sharply from four years earlier. The combined network airtime for the candidates in both party contests during 1999 stood at seven hours, as compared to 14 hours 2 minutes during 1995, when only the Republicans faced a contested primary season. NBC led the pack in the preseason with 2 hours 33 minutes, while both ABC and CBS featured 2 hours 4 minutes of news on the campaigns during this period. The network's 1999 figures were higher than those of 1991, but both preseasons fell far short of the media coverage during the same periods of 1995 and 1987.

The difference between media coverage in 1999 and in 1995 was less pronounced when measured by the total number of stories, 294 stories during the 1999 period versus 485 four years earlier. But other issues received as much or more attention than did the presidential contests on the evening newscasts. In comparison, the Littleton, Colorado, school shootings generated 298 stories, and the presidential impeachment proceedings—which concluded quite early in the year when the U.S. Senate acquitted President

Clinton on February 12, 1999—nevertheless generated 405 stories during that year. First Lady Hillary Clinton, who decided in 1999 to run for the Senate seat being vacated by Sen. Daniel Patrick Moynihan (D-N.Y.)—and who subsequently won the seat convincingly in 2000—was the subject of 107 stories during the twelve-month period, more network news coverage during that preseason period than any single candidate seeking a major-party nomination for president. The television networks are all headquartered in New York, so the television networks sometimes take a special interest in U.S. senators from New York and the neighboring states of Connecticut and New Jersey. But it takes an extreme case of parochialism for the three networks to pay more attention to a candidate for the U.S. Senate from New York—even a First Lady—than any candidate for president; the latter is an office far more significant than that of the junior senator from the Empire State.

Among the Republican presidential contenders for the 2000 presidential nomination, Bush was featured in eighty-six stories during the 1999 preseason, former Transportation Secretary Elizabeth Dole was featured in twenty-two, McCain was the subject of seventeen stories, and publisher Steve Forbes was the subject of twelve. Further back were Gary Bauer, the head of the conservative Family Research Council, who was the focus of three network news stories; Sen. Orrin Hatch (R-Utah), who was the subject of two stories; and Alan Keyes, a former deputy secretary of state, who was not the focus of a single network news story during the period. Dole, the wife of the 1996 GOP nominee for president, had the second largest amount of attention among the Republicans even though she dropped out of the race on October 20, 1999. Undeclared candidate Donald Trump was the subject of eight stories, but in the end the famous New York developer did not mount a campaign for the presidency in 2000. Despite his ultimate noncandidacy, Trump was the subject of more network television news stories than declared candidates Bauer, Hatch, and Keyes combined. Pat Buchanan, who won the 1996 New Hampshire Republican primary but was running for president in 2000 as a member of the Reform Party, was the focus of eighteen network news stories during the period, more than Forbes, Bauer, Hatch, and Keyes combined. On the Democratic side, Gore was the subject of seventy-three stories during the preseason, while Bradley was the subject of forty stories.

Given the declines in the amount of coverage throughout recent presidential campaigns, it is no wonder that the networks' share of viewer attention has been falling steadily in recent years. If the current pattern of viewer migration away from the three networks and toward cable stations and the Internet continues in 2004, wired political junkies will be able to find all the information they desire on the cable news networks and the web sites that are maintained by all major news organizations. (In fact, these network web sites contain far more information on the election, the candidates, and their issue positions than do the nightly evening newscasts evaluated here.) Nearly a decade into the email age, though, some people continue to find it harder than others to go online. Not everyone has easy access to a computer and not everyone possesses the skills needed to scan the web for relevant information. The losers in this new information environment will be the television viewers who catch up on campaign news by watching the evening news shows, but who do not or cannot seek out more information in newspapers and on web pages, including those provided by the television networks. These trends may widen the information gap between political elites and the mass public and can intensify the difficulties faced by lawmakers trying to divine and respond to public opinion on public policy matters (Hetherington 2001). Further, these information gaps may make it easier for frustrated citizens to feel negatively about government. This negativity can lead to a corrosive cynicism that can make citizens very negatively disposed toward the federal government and less likely to support government policies and programs designed to address important national problems (Cappella and Jamieson 1997; Craig 1993, 1996; Easton and Dennis 1969; Farnsworth 1999a, 1999b, 2000, 2001; Hibbing and Theiss-Morse 1995).

Horse Race Coverage

GENERAL ELECTIONS

The thoroughness of campaign news, along with its usefulness to voters, depends on the focus of the coverage as well as its sheer volume. This issue has long been raised by critics of the media's concentration on the horse race and, more broadly, the strategies and tactics adopted by the campaigns (Broh 1980; Ranney 1983; Sigelman and Bullock 1991). But it also involves the more specific topical agenda that the news features—

the major foci of discussion. This has become more central to the debate over campaign news since the 1992 election. Many journalists regarded the 1988 general election battle between Bush and Dukakis as a campaign marred by negativity, superficiality, and factual distortions. The network news divisions responded by vowing to pay greater attention to the topics that journalists considered most relevant to the public interest, regardless of the candidates' spin on issues and events. In other words, a decade ago broadcast journalism adopted a more active role in setting the campaign agenda, in order to better serve the voting public (Alter 1988, 1992; Bode 1992; Boot 1989; Russert 1990). This commitment toward a more heavily mediated approach has been a goal of network television since 1988, though as this study shows—and as others have shown—the effects of this effort on network television have been mixed at best (Kerbel 1998; Lichter and Noyes 1995, 1998; Owen 2002; Patterson 1980, 1994).

With a more active role comes increased responsibility for the tone and substance of campaign news. How did the networks respond to this challenge in the past four presidential elections? The down-to-the-wire nature of Campaign 2000 produced by far the heaviest horse race coverage CMPA has measured over the past four general elections. As table 2.4 illustrates, 71 percent of all stories during the 2000 general election contained a discussion of the candidates' standings and prospects (we defined "discussions" as lasting a minimum of thirty seconds of airtime or one-third of very brief stories). This not only eclipsed the 48 percent figure produced by Clinton's runaway victory four years earlier, but also the 58 percent of stories that dealt with the horse race in both 1992 and 1988. Indeed nearly half (44 percent) of all Campaign 2000 stories reported results from one or more opinion polls. This total reflects the profusion of daily tracking polls, several of which were commissioned by news organizations. In contrast, the candidates' records and policy stances, which we defined as substantive or issue-oriented coverage, were covered in only 40 percent of all stories during Campaign 2000.[1]

As in 1996, no policy issue dominated the fall campaign in the way the economy pervaded public debate in Campaign 1992 or crime and defense issues defined Campaign 1988. (Stories can have a horse race focus and a policy focus—or neither focus—so the percentages of horse race and policy foci do not add to 100 percent.) In Election 2000, discussions of the two candidates' strategies easily eclipsed the policy debate. Net-

TABLE 2.4 Horse Race Coverage: General Election News, 1988–2000[a] (percentage of stories)[b]

Focus of Coverage	2000	1996	1992	1988
Horse race	71	48	58	58
Policy issues	40	37	32	39

[a]Coverage from Labor Day through the day before Election Day.
[b]Stories can include a horse race and a policy focus (or neither focus); numbers therefore do not sum to 100 percent.

work news coverage of the Gore and Bush campaigns' strategies (136 stories and 127 stories, respectively) each outnumbered stories about their competing economic policies (44 stories) by about a three-to-one margin. The only other substantive topics that were featured with some frequency were health care (27 stories), social security (22), education (18), and energy policy (16). In fact, late-breaking allegations of Bush's twenty-four-year-old drunken driving arrest generated more network news stories in the last three days before the election (16 stories) than all foreign policy issues received throughout the entire campaign (10 stories).

Network television's lack of attention to foreign stories failed to allow voters to evaluate the candidates on what was to become the single most important crisis of the first year of the new presidency: the September 11, 2001, terrorist attack on the World Trade Center in New York City and the Pentagon just outside Washington, D.C., and the subsequent military response. Foreign policy, where presidents often have a much freer hand than in domestic policy (Cronin and Genovese 1998; Neustadt 1990; Nincic 1997), is always an important issue area for evaluating a president, and the events of 2001 made this policy area even more important than usual.

Reports on Bush's drunk driving arrest demonstrate the importance of the media's agenda-setting function, as some political observers believe that the last-minute disclosures of this incident may have cost Bush hundreds of thousands of votes and perhaps even the Electoral College votes of a state or two that Gore won by a very narrow margin (Burger 2002). At the time, it would have been hard to make the case that foreign policy should take a back seat to a police arrest a quarter-century earlier. It was even more difficult, of course, to make that case a year later.

Even though there are relatively few issue-oriented news reports on television, much of the "issue-oriented" portion of the coverage is actually framed in terms of horse race news (Patterson 1994). That is, the candidates' records and positions are discussed not in terms of their relevance for public policy but as indicators of their strategies and their standings in the polls. Patterson's findings were replicated by CMPA's expanded content analysis of the 1996 election, which found that nearly half (43 percent) of all policy-oriented discussions on network news focused on the insight they provided into campaign tactics or their implications for the horse race (e.g., a story on Clinton's family leave policy that focused on whether it helped him gain votes among married women, rather than the specifics of his proposed policy or its likely impact on American society). The CMPA's study of the 1996 network news coverage also found that fewer issue stories met any of three criteria that we established to gauge the depth of policy-oriented discussions: Only 35 percent specified any detail of a candidate's position (such as the dollar amount of a proposed tax reduction), 31 percent contained any background information about an issue (such as the demographics of welfare recipients in a story on welfare reform), and 37 percent considered the consequences of any proposal for the country (e.g., whether a tax cut would create new jobs or hamper deficit reduction). A mere 9 percent of all network news stories met all three criteria. Thus, measures of both the quantity and quality of issue coverage suggest that viewers are more likely to learn more about the political consequences of policies than their substantive details. This lack of information puts viewers who depend on TV news at a disadvantage when it comes to evaluating those policies. Without specifics voters are hardly in a position to consider whether a candidate's proposal on any issue is in fact good for the country, or good for oneself.

Of course the question of who is likely to win the election is a perfectly legitimate one for the voters to hear about. This question is particularly likely to be a focus of media coverage when the answer is highly uncertain, as it was leading up to—and even for several weeks after—Election Day 2000. In 1996, when Clinton was far ahead of Dole throughout the campaign, there was far less uncertainly and correspondingly less discussion of the horse race than in more closely contested elections. In other words, horse race coverage in recent elections represented a larger share of the shrinking pie of network news coverage over this four-election period.

Citizens do not seem as focused on the horse race dimension of the campaigns as are reporters, but there is substantial evidence that citizens learn more about the race than about candidate policies. Polls have repeatedly shown that voters have a very good idea which candidate is likely to win the presidency, but voters are less able to demonstrate their knowledge of issue stands, policies, and other examples of political knowledge more removed from horse race component of campaigns and elections (Hibbing and Theiss-Morse 1995; Lichter and Noyes 1998).

Voters do not seem particularly happy about the network television trend toward greater horse race news coverage. The low grades that the reporters receive in citizen evaluations of the media lately have been a matter of "how low can they go?" As television news has become more and more focused upon campaign standings and campaign strategy, citizen evaluations of the news media have fallen. As noted in chapter 1, reporters received from citizens surveyed by the Pew Research Center a "C-minus" average grade for the Election 2000 coverage, with the mean score of 1.7 (where a 4.0 is an "A" and a 2.0 is a "C"). The 2000 media GPA is lower than the 1.8 mean grade for 1996, the 2.0 average for 1992, and the 1.9 average for 1988 (Pew 2000c).

But low grades from citizens are not the only evidence that people are frustrated with network television's approach to campaign coverage. Citizens also seem to be voting, at least in the media arena, through their news consumption choices. Surveys of media use show that citizens clearly are not endorsing the horse race–dominated network television coverage described here. As discussed at greater length in chapter 1, Pew (formerly Times-Mirror) Research Center surveys found that the percentage of people who listed network television as one of their two leading sources of news regarding the presidential election has fallen by 23 percentage points between 1992 and 2000, down from 55 percent to 22 percent (Norris 2001; Pew 2000c). The decline registered by network television, once the pride of America's corporate television empires, over this eight-year period was the sharpest of the seven media sources included in the survey. While network television and newspapers were virtually tied in the 1992 media use survey (55 percent versus 57 percent, respectively), by 2000 more people listed newspapers (39 percent) and cable television (36 percent, up from 29 percent eight years earlier) than the networks as a leading source of information about the presidential contest (since people were allowed to give up to two responses, the percentages for media use exceed 100 percent).

There is still further evidence that the television networks are on the wrong track when it comes to reporting that is dominated by horse race concerns rather than by a discussion of issues. Whenever voters are given a chance to question candidates—and in recent presidential elections they often have been given opportunities to do so—the citizens' questions focus far more on issues than do the questions asked by reporters (Just et al. 1996; Patterson 1994). The town meeting–style debate between Bush and Gore several weeks before the election—the third of three presidential debates in 2000—focused on middle-class needs and the merits of Bush's proposed tax cuts, far more substantive matters than the first debate, where reporters focused on Gore's audible sighs, his somewhat more aggressive demeanor, whether the vice president had misstated the facts concerning how long a high school student was forced to stand in a crowded Florida classroom, and which official from the Federal Emergency Management Agency accompanied Gore on a fact-finding trip in the wake of a natural disaster in Texas (Hershey 2001; Owen 2002; Stanley 2001).

The discrepancy between what the voters want (more discussion of issues) and what the networks provide (coverage dominated by the horse race) frequently has been observed by scholars. Looking at the 1992 presidential election, media scholar Thomas Patterson (1994:55–56) observed a sharp contrast between the questions asked by voters who called in to query Governor Clinton on *Larry King Live* and the campaign questions asked of President Bush by the White House press corps. On that talk show, citizens asked about U.S.-Mexican trade relations, Clinton's views on African American and African issues, whether he would increase aid to Russia and free up loans to Israel, and what policies he would adopt to help promote an economic recovery. In contrast, reporters asked Bush whether he would debate Clinton and Ross Perot, whether Bush felt Perot was trying to buy the presidency, whether the polls indicated the public has rejected the Bush message, and whether Pat Buchanan's support in the primaries suggested Republican voters wanted an alternative to Bush.

This politically focused discussion of campaign matters is a long-time staple of media coverage. This appeal goes further back than the twelve-year survey period considered here, perhaps even all the way back to journalist Theodore White's insider-oriented coverage of the 1960 presidential election (Patterson 1994; White 1961). For our purposes, though, one can examine briefly two network television reports from the 1980 presidential election, a time when reporters focused more on issues and less on horse race concerns than they do today. These two stories demonstrate that, even a generation ago, the nation's top political reporters placed horse race issues front and center in their newscasts.

When Jimmy Carter started his general election campaign for a second term in 1980, Lesley Stahl of CBS News was there. She—like so many other reporters before and since—focused on a candidate's strategy for winning rather than on his campaign issues:

> President Carter chose the heart of George Wallace country for today's traditional campaign kickoff; he chose Alabama because he was concerned that the Wallace vote among Southerners and blue collar workers may be slipping to Ronald Reagan. (Stahl, quoted in Robinson and Sheehan 1983:214–25)

Bill Plante, another CBS correspondent who covered the 1980 campaign, used a very similar approach is his discussion of how Reagan, the Republican presidential nominee and the eventual victor in the 1980 contest, sought to make his appeal to middle-of-the-road voters. Once again, the reporter focused on how issue positions relate to campaign strategy:

> As he rode through New Hampshire nine months ago, Ronald Reagan still carried high the conservative banner. For 16 years he had promised a clean sweep of liberal programs and philosophies in government, leaving a trail of conservative rhetoric in his wake. That rhetoric is what Jimmy Carter has been using for ammunition. But Reagan has proved to be a moving target. As he searches for the votes of Democrats and independents, many of those conservative positions have changed. (Plante, quoted in Patterson 1994:85)

Plante then went on in this broadcast segment, which aired October 7, 1980, to contrast Reagan's statements during the nomination phase of the campaign on a number of issues, including abolishing the Department of Education and cutting the inheritance tax, with those during the fall general election campaign. Patterson (1994:85–88) noted that Reagan had a more consistent message—including his commitment to free enterprise, less government regulation, and lower taxes—than Plante's report indicated. Patterson said the discrepancies occurred because reporters often are too focused on perceiving politics as sport to provide voters with a more comprehensive perspective.

> In the game schema, a change in a candidate's position, however slight, is a calculated attempt to manipulate the electorate. In a different schema, that of governing, flexibility and compromise are a vital part of the political process. Campaigns have historically served an educative function for candidates. As they travel the country, their ideas are tested against public opinion and regional problems. They learn which of their ideas are sound and which need adjustment if they are to garner the support necessary to make their programs work if and when the voters put them in office. The campaign would be a failure if the public's reactions did not feed back into the candidate's programs. (Patterson 1994:87–88)

These reporter comments and questions offer a distinct contrast to what citizens ask candidates when they are given the chance to do so, as has been the case in recent elections and primaries. Particularly since 1992, voters have stopped being little more than passive repositories of opinions for pollsters and reporters to survey. Citizens have also become direct questioners of candidates in talk shows and in presidential debates. For each of the past three presidential contests, one of the three general election presidential debates has been reserved for questions offered by an audience of ordinary citizens. The significance of this new campaign format was apparent from the first question-and-answer general election debate, which was held in Richmond, Virginia, on October 15, 1992. At that town hall debate, President Bush struggled with a question about how the nation's economic troubles had affected him personally. Bush's uncertain, stumbling response (see below) gave the impression of being aloof and out of touch on an issue central to many voters. In sharp contrast, Bill Clinton answered the question with a far more empathetic discussion about the severe economic hardships he knew many Americans were enduring at that time and how strongly he believed this suffering had to end (Germond and Witcover 1993; Owen 1995).

> *Audience Questioner:* How has the national debt personally affected each of your lives? And if it hasn't, how can you honestly find a cure for the economic problems of the common people if you have no experience in what is ailing them? [Perot answers first; President Bush answers second]

Bush: Well, I think the national debt affects everybody.

Audience Questioner: You personally.

Bush: Obviously, it has a lot to do with interest rates—

Moderator: She's saying, you personally.

Audience Questioner: You, on a personal basis, how has it affected you?

Moderator: Has it affected you personally?

Bush: I'm sure it has. I love my grandchildren—

Audience Questioner: How?

Bush: I want to think that they're going to able to afford an education. I think that that's an important part of being a parent. If the question—maybe I get it wrong. Are you suggesting that if somebody has means that the national debt doesn't affect them?

Audience Questioner: What I'm saying is—

Bush: I'm not sure I get—Help me with the question and I'll try to answer it.

Audience Questioner: Well, I've had friends that have been laid off from jobs.

Bush: Yes.

Audience Questioner: I know people who cannot afford to pay the mortgage on their homes, their car payment. I have personal problems with the national debt. I want to know how it affected you. And if you have no experience in it, how can you help us if you don't know what we're feeling?

Moderator: I think she means more the recession—the economic problems the country faces today rather than the deficit.

Bush: Well, listen, you ought to be in the White House for a day and hear what I hear and see what I see and read the mail I read and touch the people that I touch from time to time. I was in the Lomax AME Church. It's a black church just outside of Washington, D.C. And I read in the bulletin about teenage pregnancies, about the difficulties that families are having to make ends met. I talk to parents, I mean, you've got to care. Everybody cares if people aren't doing well. But I don't think it is fair to say, "You haven't had cancer. Therefore, you don't know what it's like." I don't think it's fair to say, you know, whatever it is, that if you haven't been hit by it personally. But everybody's affected by the debt because of the tremendous interest that goes in to paying on that debt. Everything's more expensive. Everything comes out of your pocket and my pocket. So it's that. But I think in terms of the recession of course you feel it when you're president of the United States. And that's why I'm trying to do something about it by stimulating the export [*sic*], vesting [*sic*] more, better education systems.

Thank you, I'm glad you clarified it. (Gillon 2002:4389–90)

Like that debate questioner in Richmond, reporters considered the economy a top issue in 1992. A CMPA study of issues raised in that general election campaign found that economic matters were discussed more than any other issue in network news stories—in fact the economy, along with the economically related issues of taxes, unemployment, and the federal budget deficit, ranked first, second, third, and fifth, respectively, in terms of amount of issue coverage in that election. But the coverage of these issues were almost always quite brief—"only nine percent of the references to candidates' issues were reasonably extensive, detailed, and contextually meaningful presentations of their records and proposals" (Lichter and Noyes 1995:95). The extensive back-and-forth questioning in the 1992 Richmond exchange went far beyond the often brief and routine treatment of economic matters in news stories. "Most [1992] media references (television and newspaper alike) to the candidates' programs resembled bumper sticker slogans—brief, superficial and without context" (Lichter and Noyes 1995:95).

NOMINATION CONTESTS

Horse race coverage is also a mainstay of network news coverage of primary campaigns. In the 2000 primary season, nearly half (45 percent) of all election stories contained extensive discussions of the horse race, up from 37 percent in the 1996 primaries. Discussions of campaign strategies, such as McCain's decision to forgo the Iowa Caucus and concentrate on the New Hampshire primary, followed close behind the horse race in the 2000 primaries, accounting for nearly two out of every five stories (38 percent).

As shown in table 2.5, the proportion of substantive coverage during the 2000 primaries fell by half from 1996 levels. From January 1 through Super Tuesday, 44 percent of Campaign 1996 stories discussed either policy issues or the candidates' records and qualifications for public office, as compared to only 22 percent of all election stories aired during the 2000 primaries. Much of the difference can be traced to the changes following McCain's unexpectedly large victory in New Hampshire. Bush and McCain were in a statistical dead heat in the final (January 29–31) tracking poll conducted by American Research Group, Inc., of Manchester, New Hampshire, but on primary day McCain prevailed by a margin of nineteen percentage points over Bush (Bennett n.d.; Nelson 2001). Be-

TABLE 2.5 **Horse Race Coverage: Primary Election News, 1992–2000[a] (percentage of stories)[b]**

Focus of Coverage	2000	1996	1992	1988
Horse race	78	56	55	49
Policy issues	22	44	72	16

[a]Coverage through the Super Tuesday primaries held March 7, 2000; March 12, 1996; and March 10, 1992. The 1988 data are through the Illinois primary on March 15, 1988.
[b]Stories can include a horse race and a policy focus (or neither focus); numbers therefore do not sum to 100 percent.

fore the New Hampshire contest, 35 percent of all network news stories included substantive discussions; after New Hampshire, the substantive share fell to 16 percent.

The issues most frequently discussed on network television during the 2000 primaries were taxes (20 stories), abortion (16 stories), health care (11 stories), campaign finance reform (10 stories), and the significance of the Confederate flag (10 stories). Bush and his fellow Republicans promoted tax cuts, Bradley and Gore argued over whether Gore had been consistently pro-choice on abortion, McCain and Bradley called for campaign finance reform, and Bush and McCain addressed the controversy over flying the Confederate flag at the South Carolina state capitol shortly before that state's Republican primary (Ceaser and Busch 2001; Nelson 2001; Stanley 2001).

The 2000 primary election season was the most focused on the horse race of any of the four presidential election cycles examined in this analysis. The 78 percent horse race focus in 2000 was far above the 56 percent during the 1996 primary season, the 55 percent during the 1992 contests, and the 49 percent during the 1988 primary period. The policy focus during the 2000 primary season was half that of four years earlier and less than one-third that of 1992, with only the 1988 contest faring worse on this measure than 2000.

In part because of Pat Buchanan's attacks on President Bush's handling of the economy that year, the 1992 presidential primaries involved more policy discussions than in the 1988 contest or in the 1996 and 2000 primaries. Of 424 network news stories between January 1 and March 16, 1992—the eve of several Midwestern primaries that helped secure the nominations of both Clinton and Bush—160 (38 percent) had extensive discussions of the horse race. Of the 601 network news stories during the same period of 1988, 292 (49 percent) had extensive discussions of the horse race. Network coverage of the 1992 contest was unusually gossipy as well. One out of every six campaign stories on network television (70 of 424) included references to the allegations against Clinton, whose successful drive for the Democratic nomination was marred by questions involving marital infidelity and military draft avoidance. That 17 percent of all primary stories dealt with Clinton's scandals is particularly noteworthy, given the fact that both Bush and Buchanan received more coverage during the primary period than did Clinton.

In the 2000 primary period, the most dramatic decline in substantive coverage during the January 1 to March 6 primary season occurred at CBS, where substantive coverage stood at 51 percent in 1996 and 24 percent in 2000. NBC had the highest percentage of substantive coverage in 2000 at 28 percent, but that was 24 percentage points lower than the network's 1996 level. ABC had the lowest percentage of substantive coverage during both the 1996 and the 2000 primaries, 21 percent in 2000 versus 39 percent four years earlier.

Horse race coverage likewise dominated in the 1999 campaign preseason. Of the 456 evaluations of Bush on the network evening newscasts, 53 percent dealt with horse race matters. The second largest topic of those evaluations dealt with issue stances and job performance, the subject of 14 percent of evaluations on network news during that period. A similar pattern describes the coverage of Gore, where 46 percent of the 303 network news evaluations of the then vice president dealt with horse race matters. Issue stances and job performance again came in second as a topic of evaluation, with 14 percent of the evaluations found in that category during the preseason. Much of the television coverage of the campaign during this period was actually on cable: the three Republican primary debates in December were carried by the Fox News Channel, CNN, and MSNBC, not by the Big Three broadcast networks and their local broadcast affiliates. And there was little coverage of those debates on the networks on the days following those campaign events.

As has been the case in general presidential elections, citizens have had an increasing ability to be involved in the questioning of candidates during recent primary contests. This again led to very powerful contrasts between the questions the media believe need to be asked of candidates and the questions ordinary citizens think should be asked of candidates. These contrasts can be seen across the past several presidential nomination campaigns, as the venues for citizens' questions have expanded to include debates and call-in shows, and even some news programs.

On February 19, 1996, the day before the 1996 New Hampshire primary, publisher Steve Forbes and his wife, Sabina Forbes, were interviewed by Paula Zahn, then working for CBS's *This Morning.* Although the focus of this research is on the evening news shows, these interviews on the traditionally somewhat softer morning shows demonstrates just how pervasive the horse race schema has become in network television. In that February 1996 interview with the Forbeses, Zahn asked the candidate the following four questions:

> [1] Mr. Forbes, what do you think you have to—where do you think you have to finish tomorrow to continue to have a credible shot at the nomination?
>
> [2] How do you think those ideas will be accepted in New Hampshire? Where do you predict you will end up tomorrow?
>
> [3] Can you give us any assessment of what you think has happened and why your support has apparently dropped in these polls?
>
> [4] In closing this morning, in New Hampshire, what do you think is going to be the key issue that sends people to the polls? (quoted in Lichter and Noyes 1998:71)

A number of shows on CNN during the 1996 primary period offered viewers the chance to ask questions, and in so doing provided an important contrast to the usual focus of journalists on the horse race and campaign strategy. Frank Sesno's *Late Edition,* along with *Larry King Live* and *Talkback Live*, gave citizens the chance to ask the presidential candidates a total of sixty-six questions. Of those questions asked by ordinary citizens, fully 50 percent focused on matters of substance, while only 6 percent focused on the horse race, according to a content analysis of those programs conducted by CMPA. For example, a caller to *Late Edition* asked Steve Forbes directly: "How do you plan to change the standard of living for the average American?" Lamar Alexander was asked by a caller on *Larry King Live*: "What would you do for the veterans in our country?" (quoted in Lichter and Noyes 1998:73).

What is particularly striking about this radically different approach of citizen questioning is that CBS—and NBC for that matter—had used their morning shows as vehicles for ordinary citizens to ask questions of candidates in 1992. Both networks were also of course quite familiar with the citizen-oriented 1992 presidential debate in Richmond discussed above. That both networks failed in the 2000 election to repeat the performance of this successful morning show format from 1996 is baffling. If nothing else, the networks might be more concerned about the audience gains registered by cable television, which frequently has used the citizen question format on the way to becoming an important source of election news for many Americans.

Thus, wherever one looks on the network television evening news programs, be it the coverage of general elections, primaries, or the preseason, be it the coverage directed to Democrats or Republicans, and be it the coverage of CBS, NBC, or ABC, the reporters favor a pattern of coverage heavily tilted toward the horse race rather than more substantial matters like the coverage of issues. Over time, this "politics as sports" focus—a concentration that does not appear to be shared by most voters—is becoming a steadily more dominant part of the political world as seen through the distorted prism of network television.

The Horse Race: Assessing Candidate Viability

GENERAL ELECTIONS

Scholarly concerns over horse race news often focus on the way such news crowds out more substantive coverage. And major party candidates in general elections have rarely complained about any partisan tilt in journalists' assessments of the horse race, since they are frequently based on polling data. The trend toward greater horse race coverage in recent elections is a strong one and was unusually noteworthy in both tone and volume in Campaign 2000. Overall, assessments of the candidates' viability were quite balanced; 47 percent of the evaluations of Bush's chances on the network news were optimistic, as were 52 percent of assertions about Gore's prospects. However, the cumulative balance of these assessments masks a dramatic turn in the coverage midway through the campaign. Despite polls showing a close race between the presidential candidates, the national newscasts initially portrayed Gore's prospects for winning as far more promising than those of Bush. During September, on-air assessments of Gore's election prospects were positive by a six-to-one margin (86 percent to 14 percent), while Bush's were negative by a ratio of five to one (83 percent versus 17 percent).

Such assessments typically took the form of reports on preference poll results, often accompanied by variants of the notion that the leader's candidacy was surging and his opponent's was stumbling. For example, after CBS reported on September 17 that Bush continued to trail in the polls, Bill Whitaker described his campaign as being in disarray: "After a series of blows, many of them self-inflicted, [Bush] aides acknowledge their message has been muffled." During this period, most polls placed Gore's lead in the single digits. However, the unprecedented number of tracking polls being reported on a daily basis, most of them funded by news organizations, insured frequent repetition of horse race judgments. To make matters worse, scholarly studies of the way the news media covered Campaign 2000 polls found that reporters often stumbled over important details of these surveys. In particular, many reporters failed to recognize the uncertainty represented in polls by the margin of error (Larson 2001). NBC News, which used Republican operative Frank Luntz to gauge public opinion, was censured by the National Council on Public Polls "for portraying Luntz as someone who is objectively reporting on public opinion when in fact he has strong partisan leanings, especially as no Democratic counterpart was given air time" (Owen 2002:128).

In addition to these serious misjudgments, the very closeness of the race led journalists to treat changes of a few percentage points as more newsworthy than they might have seemed to academics trained as public opinion specialists. In another demonstration of the mercurial media assessments that characterized the 2000 campaign, however, evaluations of Gore's prospects dimmed and those of Bush's brightened in October and November (41 percent positive versus 59 percent negative assessments of Gore, compared to 65 percent positive and only 35 percent negative for Bush). For example, Terry Moran of ABC observed on October 12, "Gore has suffered another stumble in what has become a campaign struggling to regain its stride." This shift occurred about the same time Bush pulled ahead into a lead in most polls, but one that was as slight and tenuous as Gore's had been. In order to make their reports fit the numbers, even numbers as fluid and dubious as those found in many Campaign 2000 surveys, reporters often concluded that a candidate with bad poll numbers cannot be doing much right and a candidate with good poll numbers cannot be doing much wrong. Slight changes in the most respectable polls led to far greater changes in the way reporters' stories framed the election.

Moreover, this mid-campaign shift in positive and negative horse race assessments represented an unprecedented divergence from the patterns that CMPA's studies had previously measured. Not only was the magnitude of the shift in assessments of electoral viability greater than for those of desirability, but no such turnaround had ever occurred during the three previous general elections of 1996, 1992, and 1988. Each time, the front-runner garnered highly positive predictions of success, while his opponent(s) fared poorly, throughout the entire fall campaign. This is hardly surprising, since all three races featured a front-runner who led in the preference polls wire to wire, whereas the 2000 race was much tighter. It is not the change in directionality of horse race judgments that is notable so much as the magnitude of the shift.

Daily reports on tracking polls reminded voters of the candidates' standings more frequently than in previous elections. The continual reiteration of these judgments may account for the fact that large majorities of the public picked Gore as the likely winner in surveys taken in September and Bush as the winner in October and November, regardless of their own preferences for either candidate (Gallup News Service 2000). Whatever audiences may have learned about the candidates' policies, substantial learning seems to have occurred about the candidates' prospects, as they were presented in poll-driven election news. Consistent with the media effects model, network television's focus on polls may have encouraged citizens to focus on the horse race as they sought to orient themselves within Campaign 2000.

Coverage of the horse race may have also influenced voter perceptions in another fashion. Because large shifts in desirability (which will be covered in chapter 4) and viability assessments both took place at the same time, and in the same direction, each candidate enjoyed a period of coverage that was at least relatively favorable on both fronts. It is more typical for the various dimensions of a candidate's media image to cancel each other out. Thus dark horses may get good press, but little of it, because reporters do not see them as viable, while the attention given to front-runners may bring unwelcome scrutiny along with it. This tendency to balance favorable coverage on one dimension with unfavorable coverage on another is sometimes referred to as "compensatory coverage" (Robinson and Sheehan 1983).

NOMINATION CONTESTS

The horse race discussion that dominated the 2000 primary election, like the premature obituaries written by reporters covering the 1992 Clinton campaign to win the Democratic nomination, suggests that *Washington Post* media critic Howard Kurtz (1992a) is right to observe that reporters are fortunate they do not make their living in the commodities futures markets. Their performance in the political futures market represented by horse race coverage, after all, often leaves a lot to be desired. Bush, who lost the 2000 New Hampshire primary in a McCain landslide but did eventually win the GOP nomination and ultimately the White House, received 91 percent positive horse race press during the primary preseason coverage (January 1 to November 30, 1999). McCain, the only challenger who received sufficient media attention during the preseason time period to allow for meaningful content analysis, received 65 percent positive horse race coverage during the period. The preliminary horse race commentary was correct in that the two major challengers for the Republican nomination were identified early on, but clearly both horse race assessments were far more positive than would be consistent with the lengthy and competitive Republican contest that followed in early 2000.

Viability predictions were perhaps even more off the mark for the Democrats. Gore, who won every single Democratic primary and caucus on his way to his party's 2000 presidential nomination, received only 35 percent positive horse race coverage in the primary preseason. Bradley, who did lead briefly in a few early New Hampshire polls but lost that primary and every other contest, received horse race coverage that was 86 percent positive about his chances during the preseason period.

Before leaving the topic of candidate viability as assessed by network television news during this preseason period, we should note that some horse race assessments aired on network television during this period were even further off the mark than those about the Democratic and Republican nomination contests. Reform Party nominee Pat Buchanan received 35 percent positive horse race evaluations during this period, but he received only 0.4 percent of the popular vote in November 2000. Even that tiny percentage of the vote is artificially high. Some of the votes recorded for Buchanan were the result of a badly designed punch-card ballot in Palm Beach County, Florida, where 3,400 voters in that heavily Jewish and African American county almost certainly voted by accident for Buchanan, who had previously expressed doubts about aid to Israel and about U.S. civil rights policies (Pomper 2001). Likewise, Hillary Clinton, who was elected to the U.S. Senate from New York relatively easily in November 2000, received 58 percent negative horse race assessments on network television during this period.

Although the network news coverage of horse race standings tends to be compensated for by an inverse pattern of substantive evaluations (that is, good horse race coverage accompanies bad substantive evaluations and vice versa), candidates sometimes get good news on both fronts simultaneously. In such instances, a burst of media momentum may occur during primary season when one candidate is presented as both a wise choice and a winning one. These conditions were fulfilled following McCain's 2000 victory in New Hampshire and the attention-getting "better-than-expected" showings by Gary Hart in the 1984 Iowa caucuses and by Jesse Jackson in the virtually all-white New Hampshire primary of 1988. Ross Perot's surge in the polls during the late spring of 1992, when he discussed running for president on Larry King's talk show, also fits this pattern. These candidates all prospered in the polls during a brief period when the media made their candidacies seem at once highly visible, viable, and valuable. But the media wave eventually crested for each of them as their newfound success attracted more probing coverage (Dye et al. 1992; Lichter and Noyes 1995).

CONSEQUENCES OF A HORSE RACE FOCUS

Many scholars of media effects in presidential elections have pointed to the role that the media have in shaping the agenda and in framing the debate. The media's greatest influence, according to most media researchers, is in the ability to tell voters what to think about. The heavy concentration of horse race matters on the flagship nightly television newscasts makes the candidates' campaign standings an important part of many citizens' evaluations of the election (Patterson 1980, 1994). This "bandwagon effect" makes it easier for candidates who hold a lead to keep that lead, as more and more undecided voters conclude that a majority of their fellow citizens are probably right. Many of these undecided voters ultimately do decide to vote for someone, and most decide to support the likely winner (Patterson 1980, 1994).

The bandwagon effect seems particularly prominent in nomination campaigns. Consider, for example, the list of early front-runners who eventually won their party's nomination in recent years: Al Gore and George W. Bush in 2000, Bob Dole in 1996, Bill Clinton in 1992, George Bush and Michael Dukakis in 1988, Walter Mondale in 1984, and Ronald Reagan in 1980. While some challengers did well in an early primary or two (or three)—John McCain in 2000 and Gary Hart in 1984 are two recent examples—very few dark horses ultimately end up being at the top of their party's ballot in November.

Though they rarely win, the tendency of television news to balance coverage through compensatory reporting can give underdogs a chance. Front-runners are subject to heightened media scrutiny as a result of their privileged status as likely winners, and therefore often to negative substantive evaluations. Those negative evaluations may cause a candidate to stumble, as it did for both Clinton (over allegations of draft-dodging and womanizing) and Bush (over allegations of fiscal mismanagement) in 1992, the year with the greatest focus on issues and the least emphasis on the horse race coverage during the primaries. In a few cases, including Ed Muskie in 1972 and Hart in 1984, a campaign may collapse under the weight of questions raised by the intense media scrutiny afforded temporary front-runners. Most of the time, though, horse race reports are more prominent and more numerous than issue coverage on network television. Even in the unusually issue-oriented primary season of 1992, after all, the CMPA content analysis found that more stories focused on the horse race than on candidate issues. Given the "media effects" perspective on agenda-setting, greater coverage of the horse race means that horse race matters seem likely to trump matters of substance in the minds of many network television viewers. Compensatory coverage, in other words, can only go so far. In most contests, matters of substance are likely to be drowned out by the heavy network television emphasis on the horse race aspects of the campaign.

To test this theory that horse race–dominated television coverage helps convince voters to also view the campaign primarily through this same "politics as sports" perspective, we created the most difficult test we could imagine. Our test of media effects and horse race coverage brings us back to New Hampshire, the state that enjoys a special status as the home to the first and most important presidential primary. Many would-be presidents met their downfall in New Hampshire (such as Muskie in 1972, Bush in 1980, and Dole in 1988), and others (including Carter in 1976, Reagan in 1980, and Bush in 1988) owed their eventual victories in large measure to the huge boosts their campaigns received from this tiny and quite unrepresentative jurisdiction. A third group of presidential candidates (most notably Clinton in 1992, Dole in 1996, and George W. Bush in 2000) finished second in New Hampshire, doing well enough in the state's primary to survive to fight another day and to become their party's nominee in the subsequent weeks.

Although we are not among them, some political scientists think highly of the New Hampshire primary and tend to view the state as something out of an old Norman Rockwell print. Candidates do spend years wooing the voters of New Hampshire—a state that, thanks to its antitax fervor and bizarre dominant newspaper, qualifies as eccentric even by New England standards (Farnsworth and Lichter 1999, 2001, 2002; Orren and Polsby 1987; Veblen 1975; see also Buhr 2001 for a different opinion). Supporters of the New Hampshire's first-in-the-nation primary argue that the state is small enough for many voters to meet individuals face to face, at community coffees, town meetings, and church suppers (Sprague 1984; Rueter 1988; Palmer 1997; Vavreck 2001). Other scholars argue that while the state has become more reliant on mass media, mass campaign mailings, and other things common to elections elsewhere, there is still a more direct connection between candidates and voters than is the case in any other part of the presidential nomination and election process (Buhr 2001). In the main, these arguments add up to the conclusion that network television is likely to be less effective in the Granite State than in other primaries, much less a November nationwide presidential election. In other words, mediated images are thought by a number of scholars to be more dominant sources of information used to assess candidates outside the New Hampshire primary.

In New Hampshire during its jealously guarded primary, network television may face its toughest agenda-setting test. In the weeks before the 1996 Republican primary, about 20 percent of those polled in a WMUR–Dartmouth College survey said they had met a candidate running for president or had at least seen one in person, a figure far higher than would be found in most other primary states, where candidates spend less time and where there are many more voters to reach (Buhr 2001). The personal encounters involving presidential candidates and New Hampshire voters before the state's primaries—which along with meetings with Iowa caucus-goers are the closest things to unmediated personal contacts in American presidential politics—give those voters more of a chance than voters elsewhere to reach their own conclusions about candidates and issues (Vavreck 2001). Above all, the New Hampshire contests offer an opportunity for citizen evaluation of potential presidents more removed from the video screen than is the case elsewhere in television-hungry America.

We obtained tracking poll statistics provided by the American Research Group, Inc., a Manchester, N.H., polling firm, for three separate New Hampshire primaries—the 1992 and 2000 Democratic contests and the 1996 Republican contest—and compared them to network news coverage as measured by the content analysis used throughout this project (Farnsworth and Lichter 1999, 2001, 2002). Tracking polls chart the daily course of the campaign, indicating—on a day-by-day basis—which candidates are gaining ground and which ones are losing. Although tracking polls, like all polls, have the potential for a significant amount of error, these polls are the best tools available to help identify the sudden changes in a particular candidate's fortunes during the course of a campaign. Tracking polls, used widely by academics and by political practitioners, are the most effective measures of day-to-day changes in voter sentiments in the days leading up an election or primary.

Conceptually, the test we applied to check for the significance of horse race agenda-setting in New Hampshire is simple. We looked at what the evening news programs on the Big Three networks said about each candidate on each of the days in the month before that year's New Hampshire primary. We divided the comments into positive and negative statements about each candidate as those statements related to the horse race and to more substantive matters like character and issue positions. We then compared the content of the daily newscasts to the daily tracking polls that started surveying state residents that evening. Our research considered two basic questions: (1) Did what was said about the candidates on network television appear to affect their popularity with New Hampshire voters in subsequent surveys? and (2) If so, did network television's focus on the horse race aspects of the campaign mean that voters took horse race matters more seriously than matters of substance in their evaluations of candidates?

In all three primary contests we studied, the answers to these two questions were yes and yes. We could predict effectively in all three elections whether a candidate's fortunes would rise or fall based on what was said about that candidate on the three network newscasts aired shortly before the polls were taken. Also, in a state other scholars have seen as particularly resistant to the messages offered by network television, matters of the horse race trumped matters of substance in all three New Hampshire primaries we studied. These findings do not indicate that New Hampshire is more media-dominated than other parts of America, only that the facts do not support the claim that New Hampshire is a special place where network television has little influence. Voters in the Granite State are moved by network television's drumbeat of horse race coverage just like voters elsewhere in America (Farnsworth and Lichter 1999, 2001, 2002; Patterson 1980, 1994; Robinson and Sheehan 1983). These findings speak volumes about television's influence, as one is hard-pressed to imagine a political environment in the United States less hospitable to network news influences that the flinty, insular voters casting ballots in the New Hampshire primary.

Conclusion

Journalists, especially network television reporters, love to talk about the horse race aspects of presidential campaigns, and they do so at every stage of the process: the general election, the primary campaigns, and even the primary preseason. For the four presidential election cycles subject to the CMPA content analysis, horse race news has been heavily emphasized on network television, usually at the expense of stories that focus on the policy proposals of the candidates. This trend has intensified despite the fact that the candidates for president in 1988, 1992, 1996, and 2000 have been a very diverse and an often articulate bunch—ranging from Pat Robertson and Pat Buchanan on the ideological right to Ralph Nader and Jerry Brown on the ideological left. The "politics as sports" focus of network television news does little to raise the quality of candidate discourse nor does it give citizens the information they need to evaluate which candidate would make a better president. And the data show that this trend has gotten much worse over the past four presidential elections.

Even in New Hampshire, where presidential candidates spend months trying to meet as many voters as possible in person before these crucial early primaries, network television is a powerful force for setting the campaign agenda. Even in that state, where the opportunities for face-to-face issue discussions with would-be presidents abound, the dominant network message—that the horse race is the most important thing to know—is being heard and that message is registering with voters.

Ours is not a naive argument that horse race matters have no place in news coverage of presidential elections. Of course horse race concerns are important. Campaigns, after all, are about winning elections, and presidential campaigns spend hundreds of millions of dollars every four years attempting to win control of the White House. While the network news audiences have been shrinking, tens of millions of Americans vote with their eyeballs and continue to tune in to hear Dan Rather, Peter Jennings, and Tom Brokaw and their reporters talk about the horse race. In other words, the "politics as sports" message is at least acceptable to many news consumers.

While horse race matters are clearly part of the story, they are not all of it. Simply put, horse race–dominated coverage shortchanges candidates who are trying to talk about issues, and voters who are trying to talk about issues, too. The questions citizens ask of candidates and—as we will discuss in subsequent chapters—the comments of the candidates themselves are about a lot more than who is gaining or losing ground in the latest poll or in the latest assessment of reporters and pundits. The movement in recent years toward increased citizen use of cable television and even the Internet suggests that increasing numbers of voters are hungry for the issue-oriented coverage that network television is becoming less and less able and/or willing to provide. Of course, not all people have equal access, or equal ability to use, these alternative sources of information about candidates and campaigns.

Despite considerable ferment and reform efforts by mainstream journalists in recent years, public perceptions seem to echo scholarly studies that find little improvement in broadcast television election news. Meanwhile, the network news departments struggle to redefine their role in a rapidly expanding media landscape that already includes such new venues for election news as talk radio, cable news networks, Internet sites, and entertainment formats that range from *Oprah* to late night comedy monologues. Twenty years ago the broadcast network news departments had the field virtually to themselves among electronic media in setting the campaign news agenda. Today they struggle to remain primus inter pares. Campaign 2000 marked the first time voters were more likely to rely on the wide-ranging offerings of cable rather than broadcast networks for election news, even as various talk show formats were also becoming purveyors of information about the candidates (Pew Center 2000c, 2000d).

Of course the broadcast networks are staking their own claims in the new media landscape. For example, NBC reaches voters through the cable networks CNBC and MSNBC, along with their associated web sites, not to mention other news programs like "Dateline" and Jay Leno's regular attempts to skewer politicians in his nightly monologues. The information at each network outlet is increasingly integrated with the others by cross-promotions that encourage viewers to learn more by visiting the appropriate web site. But the fact that a web page address occurs at the bottom of the screen does not, in our opinion, relieve network newscasters of the responsibility of doing a better job of covering the campaign on air.

This chapter has demonstrated that the amount of campaign coverage overall has fallen, even as the proportion of horse race coverage has increased. In chapter 3, we turn more directly to issues of mediation, the struggles among reporters, candidates and voters to define the matters of most importance in a campaign, and the "framing" of the candidates themselves.

Note

1. Some stories contained discussions of both substantive issues and the horse race, so their respective percentages do not sum to 100. To ensure that the

results were not distorted by the use of story-level variables that were not mutually exclusive, we also examined message units that evaluated the candidates on their policies and proposals as opposed to their standing and prospects in the horse race. The results strongly reinforced the story-levels coding, with individual horse race evaluations far exceeding policy evaluations.

CHAPTER 3

WHO ELECTED YOU?
Candidates versus Reporters

Recent presidential candidates have been hit with a double whammy in getting their messages out via network news. Not only is campaign news airtime shrinking, but the candidates' share of it remains quite small. As a result, today's candidates have little opportunity to speak for themselves on network television, where they can reach by far the most voters of any news genre.

This diminished coverage forces candidates to reduce their ideas to the simplest and most media-friendly descriptions if they expect to receive media attention. Moreover, because reporters love conflict, candidates get more airtime when they provide some. These trends toward more conflict and ever briefer televised snippets encourage candidates to pepper each other with harsh and pithy one-liners, rather than engaging in reasoned argument on the campaign trail. They have little alternative. Candidates who do not appear regularly on television, particularly at the primary election stage, quickly become ex-candidates.

Media consumers look to network television for a clear indication of what the most important issues are in the presidential campaign. As we saw in chapter 2, television reporters tend to present presidential election campaigns—whether in general elections, primaries, or even primary preseason periods—as being mostly about the horse race, the daily line on who is winning and losing. This dominant media "frame" of the campaign as a contest, together with the trend away from coverage of more substantial matters, has become particularly pronounced in network television's coverage of recent presidential elections. This does not mean that television viewers do not want to learn about substantive issues. It means that citizens are told over and over again by the networks that elections are more about polls than policies.

Fortunately, many hardy, thoughtful citizens are resistant to network television's trivializing paradigm. As campaigns become increasingly open to citizens—the proverbial man and woman in the street now have opportunities to ask questions in at least one presidential debate as well as during the course of talk shows and other call-in formats—important issues are still being discussed. With these new venues, citizens do not have to rely on reporters to bring issues of substance to the forefront. In recent elections, citizens have stepped up during debates and call-in shows to ask questions about policy matters, reminding everyone watching that issues matter more to many voters than reporters seem to think they do.

Mediated Coverage and the Shrinking Sound Bite

To be sure, the horse race frame offered up by network television has the potential to degrade our democratic debates. A less visible, but perhaps equally dangerous frame is one that is the result of news media narcissism. Perhaps as a result of the high salaries and pampered lives enjoyed by network television political reporters, these correspondents increasingly seem to believe that elections are largely about themselves as reporters and as interpreters of political events. In the eyes of reporters, their own difficulties on the campaign trail all too often trump the issues raised by the candidates who are actually running for office and who will end up shaping the country's future.

In his seminal work *Out of Order* (1994), political scientist Thomas Patterson presented election news as a zero-sum game in which candidates lose out as journalists increasingly set the tone of reportage. This proved increasingly true for print as well as for television reporters. In a study of front-page presidential election news stories from the *New York Times*, Patterson (1994:114) found that candidates and other partisan sources set the tone of an article nearly two times out of three in 1960 and more than 70 percent of the time in 1964 and 1968. The trend reversed itself in 1972, when reporters set the tone about 60 percent of the time. Since 1972, candidates and other partisan sources never again set the tone even 40 percent of the time, and by 1992 reporters were setting the tone of a story about 80 percent of the time. Patterson attributes the reversal to the weakening of norms that once worked against such advocacy by reporters.

Patterson's critical findings have been both echoed and amplified by other students of recent presidential elections. In his analysis of the differences between news programs on ABC and CNN during the 1992 presidential election, Matthew Kerbel found few differences worth noting between the two networks with respect to who tells the story. On both networks, Kerbel found that "better than three quarters of all statements were attributed to news personnel—correspondents, anchors, or analysts solicited by the networks to make observations about the election" (1998:22). The candidates, he found, were rarely heard in their own words. Kerbel found that the networks were also limited in their selections of independent voices, as few remarks came from nonpartisan individuals.

In her analysis of the 2000 presidential election, political scientist Diana Owen (2002) observed that network television reporters sometimes tried to focus attention on average citizens and their views, which was one of the key differences between broadcast news and cable news in some recent elections. But she found that they abandoned the practice as the campaign progressed, returning to the reporter-centered perspectives relatively quickly.

Reporters know better than to leave citizen perspectives behind entirely. They have seen how effective voter input can be elsewhere, such as on the call-in shows favored by CNN. Consider the remarks of two highly respected and influential journalists: Tim Russert, NBC's Washington Bureau chief and host of its Sunday political show *Meet the Press*, and David Broder, long-time columnist for the *Washington Post* and the dean of America's political reporters.

> There is not a program I've watched [during Campaign 1992] where I've not learned something new about the candidates. It exposes people to politics who wouldn't normally be exposed to politics. It's healthy as hell for the media and the political process. (Russert, quoted in Kurtz 1992d)

> Politics has become—and has been treated by the press [as]—largely a sport for a relative handful of political insiders. . . . It is no longer meaningful to a great many of our fellow citizens . . . because there is no real connection between their concerns in their daily lives and what they hear talked about and see reported by the press in most political campaigns. (Broder, quoted in Meyer 1993:91)

Such comments by highly visible media practitioners notwithstanding, most reporters do not do nearly as much as they might to integrate the concerns and the views of ordinary citizens in their reporting. This is documented in previous research and is demonstrated through the new, expanded findings we present in this book.

Not surprisingly, a number of politicians have joined media scholars in concluding that reporters could do a better job of focusing on citizen interests and opinions. At one particularly frustrating moment during the 1992 primary campaign, for example, Bush White House spokesman Marlin Fitzwater tried to force reporters outside to see for themselves the enthusiasm that Bush was generating at a March 1992 campaign rally at Oklahoma Christian University. This rally occurred during a period of very negative media coverage of Bush, at a time when reporters were attacking the president over his management of the economy and when Bush was being challenged for re-election from within the Republican Party by Pat Buchanan, a conservative television commentator.

> When I opened the door to go out, the crush of the noise and excitement almost forced me back inside. It was like a grenade of excitement had gone off, with nearly 20,000 people straining at the barriers, covering the hillside under a bright and warm winter day. It was spectacular. I walked back into the press filing center, a lecture hall located not twenty feet from that magical crowd. There sat thirty to forty reporters, in an auditorium setting, listening to the president's speech on the public address system. I appeared at the top of the seats, which formed a well in front of the professor's podium, with Ron Kaufman, the White House political director. My blood pressure was surging. . . . "It's a great day," I screamed. "C'mon. Off your asses and outta here." They thought I was laughing, but I was mad. . . . When I saw Rita [Beamish, of Associated Press] and Kathleen [DeLaski, of ABC News] in that Oklahoma Christian hallway I blurted out, "I'm sick of you lazy bastards. Go out and cover the events." (Fitzwater 1995:332–33)

Fitzwater was not able to convince reporters to focus on the enthusiastic crowd. Instead, his own complaint provided them with the story of the day, which was that of a troubled campaign's spokesman lashing out at the White House press corps. As Brit Hume, then of ABC News, reported on March 6, 1992:

> Stung by news stories characterizing Mr. Bush's campaign events as lackluster, Press Secretary Fitzwater ordered the press room loudspeakers turned off, to force reporters—lazy bastards, he called them—to go outside and see the cheering crowds for themselves. (quoted in Kerbel 1998:35)

The real significance of this event, like other reports about the struggles between campaigns and reporters, is that network television reporters and anchors found this recounting of their personal interactions with political figures to be sufficiently compelling to deserve precious network airtime. However much they retreated behind third-person pronouns, the story was usually told by and about the reporters themselves. In fact, Kerbel (1998) found that one in five stories on ABC and CNN during the 1992 campaign referred explicitly to the media.

> One of the preeminent stories of the 1992 campaign was the reporters' own story: the interactions with candidates; the experiences on the road; the frustrations of covering a national campaign; and other similar items about the process of reporting a presidential election and the place of the press in that process. The experiences themselves were not new, but their appearance in a running miniseries deemed worthy of valuable news time represented a significant development in television's political role. (Kerbel 1998:36)

Kerbel, a leading early cataloguer of this important trend of the "story-about-the-story" coverage, observed that media reports about how tough life was for reporters or how close reporters were to the campaigns they covered frequently were reports that ordinary citizens could have lived without. "Often the viewer is told things of dubious importance to the audience but of great interest to the reporter, such as the frustration or unhappiness the correspondent feels toward the campaign" (Kerbel 1998:42).

Kerbel (2001) found the same self-referential coverage in Campaign 2000 as well, even in leading print outlets, like this T. Christian Miller story in the May 21, 2000, issue of the *Los Angeles Times*:

> Take the chaos of a circus, the conversation of C-SPAN and the silliness of World Wide Wrestling. Throw in a ringmaster who enjoys discussing things like the Antiballistic Missile Treaty, a particularly unruly herd of reporters and lots of lost luggage. This, pretty much, is the world of presidential campaign travel. A typical day involves moving more than 100 people, including the candidate, his staff, dozens of reporters and security through stops in as many as six states per day. . . . But for all its complexity, the punishing demands of campaign travel are probably lost on voters. (quoted in Kerbel 2001:112)

These media-centered trends in coverage are not trivial. Kerbel (2001), citing the Vanishing Voter Project at Harvard University, reported that large numbers of citizens exposed to such self-referential media fodder predictably described the fall campaign as "boring." This was an astonishing assessment, given the down-to-the wire (and even past the wire) nature of the November 2000 general election. By any reasonable standard, our most recent presidential general election clearly was far more lively than that of 1996, 1992, or 1988. But if the reporters talk a lot about their troubles on the campaign trail rather than the candidates' future plans for the country, it is no wonder many citizens don't find the campaigns interesting.

Even when candidates are given an opportunity to speak for themselves on network television, they had better be quick about it. The locus of the election narrative, and the heavy mediation it reflects, was first brought to public attention by Kiku Adatto (1990), who found that the average duration of network news sound bites by presidential candidates had decreased from 42 seconds in 1968 to only 10 seconds in 1988. Despite the widespread controversy that ensued (Kurtz 1992b), CMPA content analyses have since revealed a steady decline in the average length of on-air candidate statements from 9.8 seconds in 1988 to 8.4 in 1992, 8.2 in 1996, and 7.8 in 2000. Thus, the average amount of time that a candidate speaks on-air without interruption seems to have stabilized. But the shrunken—and still shrinking—sound bite we now take for granted is about 20 percent below the figure that caused a furor when it was reported by Adatto four presidential elections ago. The overall decline is massive, as the average candidate statement on network news during Campaign 2000 was about 80 percent below the 1968 level.

TABLE 3.1 General Election News: Amount of Coverage, 1988–2000

	2000	1996	1992	1988
Candidate airtime (minutes)	98	102	168	n/a
Average sound bite (seconds)	7.8	8.2	8.4	9.8
Total time (minutes)	805	788	1,402	1,116

Expressing an idea, even a relatively simple one, in eight seconds or less is a considerable challenge. The standard television commercial, which usually has a single, simple message along the lines of "buy these pants," uses twenty to thirty seconds to make its case—about three to four times as much time as a presidential candidate has to say "here is why you should vote for me" or "here is why you should support this policy" (these sentences can be said in about three seconds each, so each would be close to half an average sound bite by itself). Making the case as to why one should be president by speaking for eight seconds or less at a time is a massive—perhaps an impossible—challenge. After all, Old Navy wouldn't try to sell a pair of jeans that fast.

Of course, the television networks, not the candidates, control the airwaves. This can be seen clearly in table 3.1, which shows the amount of coverage received by candidates during recent presidential elections. In addition to documenting the shrinking sound bite, it shows that the combined candidate airtime was 98 minutes during the 2000 election (this figure refers to the time the candidates' voices were heard during network television reports). The 2000 total fell below the 102 minutes the candidates' own words were heard on network news programs in 1996, the Clinton-Dole-Perot election.

Cumulative speaking time for the entire 2000 general election campaign was 53 minutes for Gore, 42 for Bush, and 3 for Ralph Nader. By contrast, cumulative speaking time for journalists was 9 hours 56 minutes during the roughly two-month general election campaign season. The total speaking time for presidential candidates dropped from 168 minutes in 1992 to 98 minutes in 2000, a 40 percent decline that represents a loss of more than an hour of direct communication with viewing audiences on the three networks.

Moreover, the numbers are even worse than they appear at first glance. To start with, those figures represent the cumulative candidate airtime on all three major networks. Since very few people (at least few people outside the Washington Beltway) watch more than one nightly newscast, the effective total amount of time even the most faithful one-news-show viewer would see these candidates would be one-third of the above figures. So, on average, a viewer watching his or her favorite network's evening news program every single night during the period from Labor Day to Election Eve would have heard Gore make his case in his own words for a total of less than 18 minutes and Bush make his case in his own words for exactly 14 minutes. Since each newscast lasts 30 minutes minus commercials, if all the Gore quotes aired on any one network had been spliced together and broadcast one right after another they would not have been long enough to fill a single nightly newscast from which they were drawn. Had the same been done for the Bush, there would barely have been enough verbiage to make it just past the midpoint of that same newscast.

Now imagine a person who uses three VCRs to tape each network's nightly newscast and then spends ninety minutes a day between Labor Day and Election Eve watching each of those newscasts. If all the Gore comments this obsessive (and hopefully hypothetical) news consumer had seen were spliced together and aired one after another, they would take about as much time to air as a single night's episode of *ER* or two episodes of *Friends*. The weather segment on your local news station would have to be added to a similar tape of Bush's remarks in order to get an hour's worth of direct material from two months of nightly newscasts on these three broadcast networks.

Of course a third party candidate without the vast personal fortune of a Ross Perot faces an impossible challenge when it comes to getting his or her message out on network television (Nader 2002). Ralph Nader's three minutes of sound bites during this period averages out to just sixty seconds per network—the length of two commercials over the course of a two-month general election campaign. If the Green Party candidate's sound bites had been strung together just like those for Bush and Gore, you could have listened to everything Nader said on a single network three times in the length of time it would take to listen to a single song on the radio. The nearly total absence of Nader on network television evening news programs was particularly ironic, given his crucial influence in the final outcome of the 2000 presidential election.

Even in presidential primaries, when there are often a large number of lesser-known candidates clamoring for citizen attention, network television news retains its small-sound-bite rule. In fact, a CMPA study of the 1996 Republican primary season found an even shorter average sound bite than in the general election that year. The average sound bite in the 1996 primary campaign was 7.2 seconds, more than 10 percent shorter than the 8.2-second average sound bite in the general election that year. There was a total of 1,066 minutes of network campaign news between January 1, 1996, and the March 26 California primary, and only 129 minutes of candidate airtime. Because primary elections generally involve less well-known figures, and because partisanship does not work as a voting cue in Republican-only or Democrat-only contests, many voters would need even more information about a primary election candidate than a general election one.

These snippets of unmediated commentary from Gore, Bush, and Nader in the 2000 election and from other candidates in previous elections are hardly sufficient for a viewer to get a full sense of a nominee and his or her policies. Of course, interested viewers can go beyond the nightly newscasts for other information, including the more thorough coverage found in most newspapers or on cable outlets like CNN and MSNBC. In fact, the declining overall coverage of the campaign, coupled with the tiny share of that coverage that allows the candidates to speak in their own words, practically invites citizens to look elsewhere. And more and more citizens are accepting the invitation, as the downsizing of campaign coverage has been accompanied by a decline in the viewing audience (Norris 2001; Pew 1996, 2000a, 2000b). But the network news audience remains substantial (Kurtz 2002b).

Lessons for Candidates

Some candidates learned too late about the consequences to their own campaigns of network television reporters' self-referential approaches and the shrinking candidate sound bite. Michael Dukakis, the Democratic presidential nominee defeated by Republican George Bush in November 1988, observed after the campaign's end:

> I said in my acceptance speech in Atlanta that the 1988 campaign was not about ideology but about competence. . . . I was wrong. It was about

> phraseology. It was about ten-second sound bites. And made-for-TV backdrops. And going negative. I made a lot of mistakes in the '88 campaign. But none was as damaging as my failure to understand this phenomenon, and the need to respond immediately and effectively to distortions of one's record and one's positions. (quoted in Butterfield 1990)

Indeed, Dukakis had ample opportunity to learn during his ill-fated presidential campaign how not to run a presidential campaign. In an effort to make the rather soft-spoken Massachusetts governor appear tough on defense, the Dukakis campaign offered a "made-for-television moment" where the candidate peered out the top of a moving tank. Unfortunately this ridiculous image reminded many voters more of the "Peanuts" cartoon character Snoopy than U.S. Army General George S. Patton. "Reporters present at the scene laughed so hard they could be heard on the film soundtrack," observed political scientist Herbert Parmat (2002:42–43). Bush attacked Dukakis over and over again with television ads lamenting pollution in Boston Harbor and for not being sufficiently tough on defense, for not being adequately supportive of the Pledge of Allegiance, for not being protective enough of the U.S. flag, and for allegedly coddling criminals (Butterfield 1990; Hershey 1989). To the end of his 1988 run for the White House, Dukakis failed to mount an effective counterattack. "At his core, Dukakis was a cautious man, a reformer trained in the good government tradition of Brookline, Massachusetts. He opposed negative campaigning and he was committed to running on his own issues" (Hershey 1989:87). He also lost forty states.

Other candidates learn much more quickly how little network television news time will spend on them and how mediated that presentation will be. In that same 1988 campaign, George Bush consolidated his campaign message into six famous—later to become infamous—words: "Read my lips, no new taxes." It took the president a little less than four seconds to say those words, so this brief snippet was clearly made for television with time to spare. In fact, he said this slogan at nearly every campaign stop (Hershey 1989:79). Further, the tough guy, confrontational approach conveyed by this motto helped the Bush campaign present the then vice president as something other than the indecisive "wimp" that he had been labeled by the news media in the past (Hershey 1989:77). An editorial cartoonist of the time portrayed Abraham Lincoln in front of a television crew offering up the 1860s version of a sound bite: "Read my lips. No more slaves."

Governor Bill Clinton, the Democratic presidential nominee who faced Bush four years later, was a quick study. During the 1992 campaign, Clinton responded to attacks quickly, in a way that Dukakis did not. Clinton made Bush the issue, in a way that Dukakis did not. Clinton, who dubbed himself "the comeback kid" after his second-place finish in the 1992 New Hampshire primary, also knew the value of a sound bite in a way that Dukakis did not. Clinton attacked Bush for what the Arkansas governor described as a reckless promise not to raise taxes. This promise was broken by Bush, Clinton went on to observe, when the president signed the 1990 Budget Act. Perhaps most importantly, Clinton won the battle of the sound bites with a terse motto of his own: "It's the economy, stupid."

But the real master of the news media in 1992 may not have been Bill Clinton but rather Texas billionaire Ross Perot, who turned to the wide-open and relatively unmediated discussion format of *Larry King Live* as he tested the waters for an independent presidential run in 1992. As King subsequently observed of his highly visible guest, "Perot showed you could start a national campaign on a prime time TV talk show" (quoted in Kerbel 1998:213).

Of course someone of Perot's visibility couldn't keep a campaign going solely through appearances on *Larry King Live*. After enduring negative network media coverage over such memorable sound bites as Perot's "you people" remark before an NAACP convention and criticism over his midyear decision to abandon his 1992 campaign, the Texan returned to the presidential election campaign later that year with an enhanced commitment to reach the voters through paid television specials (Lichter and Noyes 1995). Perot did little public campaigning during the second phase of his 1992 campaign, and he undertook few media appearances after his early experiences that year. As CNN reporter Chuck Conder observed of Perot in 1992: "If he wasn't available—and he never was—then you couldn't ask him any questions about what was in the news on a given day" (quoted in Kerbel 1998:181).

Perot's infomercial campaign offered this independently wealthy candidate a chance to reach the voters in an unmediated way. And reach them he did. The down-home Texan's first infomercial—"Plain Talk about

Jobs, Debt, and the Washington Mess"—aired on CBS and drew 16 million viewers. According to Nielson ratings, Perot's infomercial finished first in its time slot, beating out *Quantum Leap* on NBC and *Full House* on ABC (Lichter and Noyes 1995:156).

Tom Shales, a television critic for the *Washington Post*, observed that the success of Perot's dry charts-and-pointer seminars demonstrated the error of network television's belief that citizens would not stay tuned to hear sophisticated discussions of policy alternatives (Lichter and Noyes 1995:156–57). But as we have seen, television news nevertheless continued to shrink candidate sound bites and to cut its campaign coverage after 1992.

Perot's efforts to keep reporters away from his message earned their anger. Reporters jealously guard their perogatives as interpreters-in-chief of campaigns and elections, and when a candidate like Perot tries an end run, he does so at his peril.

> What mattered after the TV revolution is what went on the evening news, not what happened on the campaign itself. Perot, who seemed not to care what went on the evening news, decided not to participate in the charade. He aimed his campaign at voters, using television to reach them in their living rooms. Such a strategy, however, cut out journalists' mediating roles, and they didn't appreciate it. As the Perot experience showed, the further candidates maneuvered away from the media's reach, the more determined the media effort to block them became. (Lichter and Noyes 1995:160)

The reverse is also true. In 2000, Sen. John McCain (R-Ariz.) was the anti-Perot, at least as far as dealing with reporters was concerned (Maisel 2002). The senator waged a very media-oriented campaign aboard his "Straight Talk Express" campaign bus and received very positive media coverage for his trouble—the most positive coverage of the four major candidates seeking the Republican or Democratic nomination that year. CMPA content analysis of the 2000 primary season showed that McCain received a total of 63 percent positive substantive evaluations during the primary season, edging out the 62 percent positive evaluations for Bill Bradley (whose campaign was relatively receptive to the news media). The more cautious and media-wary front-runners, George W. Bush for the Republicans and Al Gore for the Democrats, received 53 percent and 40 percent positive substantive evaluations, respectively, during the primary season. The more one sought to cozy up to reporters, the more he tended to receive positive evaluations from network television, at least in 2000.

Although he received very little network news coverage himself, consumer advocate Ralph Nader, the 1996 and 2000 Green Party presidential nominee, was able to see close-up how this media and campaigning process works for major party candidates who get the volume of airtime of which an independent candidate can only dream.

> The media is the message. When George W. Bush nuzzles up to two little schoolchildren, his handlers make sure that the AP [Associated Press] and other photographers on his campaign have good positioning. When Al Gore stands near some national park in his L.L. Bean attire, his handlers know they succeeded only if the image and a few choice words are played throughout the country. There are very few rallies anymore. Instead there are carefully orchestrated photo opportunities that often leave locals resentful, feeling they have been used. And, of course, they have been used, just as the candidates use journalists for their poses, or try to, and just as journalism uses them. (Nader 2002:155)

Locus of Coverage

The viewing audience's experience of the campaign depends not only on the focus of coverage—which topics are highlighted and which are ignored—but also on the locus—the on-camera sources who convey the information. This is analogous to the "voice" of a literary work, in which an author's decision to tell a story in the first person or through an omniscient narrator will produce very different experiences for the reader. Television news can adopt a style of presentation that either transmits the behavior and ideas of the candidates as much as possible in their own words and those of their surrogates, or one that emphasizes the role of journalists who summarize, contextualize, and evaluate this material on-camera. Most news stories fall somewhere along the spectrum anchored by these two poles, interspersing the statements of political actors with comments by anchors and reporters that frame the story and provide its narrative flow. The placement of the coverage along the spectrum itself represents the level of mediation.

The phenomenon of the "shrinking sound bite" is one example of the

TABLE 3.2 General Election News: Locus of Coverage, 1992–2000 (percentage speaking time)

	2000	1996	1992
Journalists	74	73	71
Candidates	12	13	12
Other sources	14	14	17

limitations presidential candidates face as they try to connect with viewers of network television. An even more important measure is the proportion of overall airtime that is allocated to various speakers. During the 2000 campaign, about three-quarters (74 percent) of all speaking time was allotted to journalists, with the remainder split about evenly between candidates (12 percent) and other on-air sources (14 percent) such as voters, pundits, and policy experts. Thus, more than six times as much campaign talk came from anchors and reporters as from the candidates themselves. The truncated appearances and utterances of presidential candidates on the evening news shows made it difficult for voters to take their measure as individuals, thereby abrogating a great advantage that television has over print as a transmitter of information. In short, little of what the voters heard *about* the candidates actually was *from* the candidates.

The distribution of airtime between candidates and journalists during Campaign 2000, shown in table 3.2, was virtually identical to that of the 1996 and 1992 campaigns, despite the spark Ross Perot added to those races. (We do not have this information for 1988.) In 1996 the totals were 73 percent of speaking time for journalists, 13 percent for candidates, and 14 percent for all others. In 1992 the comparable figures were 71 percent, 12 percent, and 17 percent. Moreover, since these percentages are based on declining amounts of overall campaign airtime, they understate the full decline of candidate visibility. This trend also helps to explain the increasing tendency of candidates to bypass traditional news venues in favor of talk shows from *Larry King Live* to *Late Night with David Letterman*. Along with the presidential debates, they represent rare televised opportunities for candidates to address audiences for more than a few seconds at a time.

This pattern of mediated discourse is not limited to general elections. A detailed content analysis of the locus of coverage of network news reports conducted by CMPA on the 1996 presidential primary season found a very similar pattern to that found in the three general elections presented in table 3.2. Journalists also dominated network news coverage of the 1996 Republican primaries, which we analyzed from January 1, 1996, to the California primary on March 26, 1996. Reporters took 74 percent of the 1,066 minutes of network airtime for themselves, leaving only 12 percent of the airtime for the candidates. Other voices, including voters and independent analysts, took the remaining 14 percent of campaign airtime.

In sum, viewers of Campaign 2000 continued to learn about presidential campaigns mainly through the words of journalists, rather than hearing either the candidates or voters speak for themselves. The trend has been clear in the past three presidential elections, as well as through our analysis of the 1996 Republican presidential primaries. Relatively speaking, sad to say, this is the good news. Many other measures used in this book to assess network television news finds the quality of coverage has declined. Here we see yet again that the network news coverage is unsatisfactory—an overwhelming coverage bias in favor of reporters rather than candidates hardly seems desirable—but here we can say that the network news coverage of presidential elections does not seem to be getting worse.

Media Framing: Past Research

In 1944, as World War II raged, a desperately ill Franklin Delano Roosevelt ran for an unprecedented fourth term as president. Thomas Dewey, the Republican presidential nominee that year, charged that Roosevelt was not doing enough to guard against communist infiltration into the U.S. government, particularly through New Deal programs (Burns and Dunn 2001:481). During that 1944 campaign, a Republican congressman from Michigan complained that the president's dog Fala had been retrieved at taxpayer expense by a destroyer sent to collect the wayward pet, which had mistakenly been left behind during a presidential trip.

This line of partisan attack contained a number of things FDR did not want to talk about in mid-1944. The last thing the White House needed as Allied forces made their way across France was domestic pressure on the alliance with the Soviet Union against Nazi Germany or a "Red Scare" in the U.S. government. Doubts about the New Deal programs were not an optimal subject for discussion, either, as the administration clearly had been devoting more energy to the war than anything else throughout Roosevelt's third term (Goodwin 1994). The GOP attack also subtly planted doubts regarding the president's vigor—perhaps even raising indirectly questions of the long-serving president's obviously failing health (Burns and Dunn 2001; Goodwin 1994). And questions regarding the judicious use of taxpayer funds during wartime also were explicit in the reference to the Fala incident.

What's a president to do? When facing trouble in American politics, talk about the family dog.

> Then came his rebuttal of the Fala story, his dagger lovingly fashioned and honed, delivered with a mock-serious face and in the quiet, sad tone of a man much abused. "These Republican leaders have not been content with attacks on me, or my wife, or on my sons. No, not content with that, they now include my little dog, Fala. Well of course I don't resent attacks, and my family doesn't resent attacks, but Fala—being Scottish—*does* resent them!" Some reporters saw this as the turning point of the campaign. (Burns and Dunn 2001:482, emphasis in original)

In mid-1952, with his Republican vice presidential nomination in jeopardy over charges of political corruption, then Sen. Richard Nixon gave a nationally televised statement, known as the "Checkers speech," to defend himself and salvage his place as Dwight Eisenhower's running mate. Like Roosevelt eight years earlier, Nixon had sense enough to reframe the controversy around the family dog.

> One thing I should probably tell you, because if I don't "they'll" probably be saying this about me too: we did get something—a gift—after the election. A man down in Texas heard Pat mention on the radio the fact that our two youngsters would like to have a dog. And believe it or not, the day before we left on this campaign trip we got a message from Union Station in Baltimore saying they had a package for us. We went down to get it. You know what it was? It was a little cocker spaniel dog that he sent all the way from Texas. Black-and-white spotted. And our little girl—Tricia, the six year old—named it Checkers. And you know, the kids love that dog and I just want to say right now that, regardless of what they say about it, we're going to keep it. (Nixon, quoted in Aitken 1993:216–17)

In agenda-setting, reporters—sometimes with the intervention of politicians—tell citizens what to think about. In framing, the subject of this next section, reporters—sometimes with the intervention of politicians—tell citizens *how* to think about a subject (McCombs and Shaw 1993). In the two examples above, savvy politicians deftly changed the focus of discussion in ways that suited them. In both instances, reporters knew a good story when they heard one and went along for the ride (Aitken 1993; Burns and Dunn 2001). By trying to frame allegations of communist infiltration into government, an ailing president's health, and careless war spending into a joking tale of a dog defending the family honor, FDR was able to dissipate with a laugh potentially troubling issues. By converting charges of political corruption into a story of how Nixon's enemies will not be satisfied until they take away a young girl's dog, efforts to have the nominee stricken from the second spot on the GOP ticket evaporated. In a battle where partisan politicians stand on one side and a dog stands on the other, man's and woman's (and girl's) best friend is going to win every time.

Normally, though, politicians don't have that much influence over how an issue or controversy or even their own character will be framed by the media and ultimately in the public consciousness. Roosevelt and Nixon (at least until Nixon's Watergate cover-up) demonstrated considerable abilities as media "spinners" (Aitken 1993; Gellman 1999; Goodwin 1994; McGinniss 1969), and both men operated in a time of a far less assertive press than that covering today's politicians (Sabato 2000). The CMPA content analysis of more recent presidential campaigns demonstrates that journalists have a great deal more control over the content of campaign news stories than do the subjects of those stories, the politicians. If presidents (or their advisers) have a good sense of how to package their messages, they can sometimes influence the framing process (Hertsgaard 1989; Jamieson 1996), but clearly the majority of the control over news content on the news programs and in the news columns is in the hands of reporters and editors.

Framing, that is, the process of putting the information given into a logical order or context, is not a trivial source of media influence. Reporters can choose not to cover a political actor or a particular actor's comments on a certain topic, they can reduce the influence of a given actor's comments by increasing the attention given to alternative voices on that topic, and they can even investigate the claims and find them to be transparent symbols or even false (Bennett 2001). All of these can contribute to the way the story is told, which may be as important to political conceptualizations of the issue as the fact that the subject is worth being talked about in the first place.

> The news is not just an information bulletin board, but more importantly a story-telling operation. Stories become pegged to or summarized around central ideas or categories of meaning, such as sex scandal, government waste, natural disaster, election horse race, or world crisis, just to name a few. These frames are shorthand reminders or placeholders about the central meaning of an ongoing story. (Bennett 2001:123–24)

Context can be decisive for a politician's fortunes, as it was for President Clinton during the controversies over the Clinton/Lewinsky matter. If Republicans had succeeded in their efforts to frame Clinton's cover-up as a criminal matter of perjury—that is, the felony of lying under oath—they might have had greater success in their efforts to drive him from office. Instead, the media frame of the Clinton scandal was largely that the president's alleged lies were of a less sinister nature, that of covering up an extramarital affair. This latter perspective generated far less public pressure for the president to resign or be forcibly removed than would have been the case had the public embraced the "criminal Clinton" frame offered by the Republicans on the House Judiciary Committee (Bennett 2001; Klein 2002; Owen 2000; Sabato et al. 2000).

> Framing is often used to analyze how news stories emphasize or de-emphasize different aspects of reality, which both shape and reflect the cognitive categories politicians, journalists, and citizens use to make sense of the political world. . . . The fundamental premise of framing is that people generally cannot process information without (consciously or unconsciously) using conceptual lenses that bring certain aspects of reality into sharper focus while relegating others to the background. Frames are the basic building blocks with which public problems are socially constructed. (Lawrence 2001:93)

If information is presented absent a context, as news often is presented through the fragmentary, brief stories that are the norm on America's evening newscasts, the contents of those stories are not likely to be recalled or to play to play a significant role in citizen evaluations of political figures and issues (Graber 1988; Postman 1985; Iyengar and Kinder 1987).

> Media frames, largely unspoken and unacknowledged, organize the world both for journalists who report it and, in some important degree, for us

> who rely on their reports. Media frames are persistent patterns of cognition, interpretation, and presentation, of selection, emphasis and exclusion, by which symbol-handlers routinely organize discourse, whether verbal or visual. (Gitlin 1980:7)

Network news' disjointed, horse race–oriented campaign coverage is particularly likely be presented in a decontextualized manner (A. Simon 2001). Addressing this issue more systematically, Shanto Iyengar (1991) divides media framing of political issues into two categories: episodic and thematic. The first type of framing undermines citizen evaluation of issues, the second type helps place matters into context.

> The episodic news frame takes the form of a case study or event-oriented report and depicts public issues in terms of concrete instances (for example, the plight of a homeless person or a teenage drug user, the bombing of an airliner or an attempted murder). The thematic frame, by contrast, places public issues in a more general or abstract context and takes the form of a "takeout" or "backgrounder" report directed at general outcomes or conditions. Examples of thematic coverage include reports on changes on government welfare expenditures, congressional debates over the funding of employment training programs, the social or political grievances of groups undertaking terrorist activity, and the backlog in the criminal justice process. (Iyengar 1991:14)

Because episodic stories tend to have better pictures, can be told more briefly, are easier to prepare, and are less susceptible to charges of bias—four items that dramatically improve a story's chances of being aired on the half-hour evening newscasts—far more story's are episodic than thematic, according to Iyengar (1991). Society may be worse off if citizens receive episodic-dominated media coverage, because voters will not be as inclined to recognize the importance of key policy issues—including such topics as education, gradual environmental degradation, and the consequences of budget deficits. Such controversies, though clearly important matters for public discourse, do not lend themselves to brief discussions and good visuals.

> The premium placed on episodic framing means many issues of significance have not received and will not receive the news coverage necessary to permit the public to become critical observers of national affairs. Many social problems tend to be invisible because they lack immediate or readily traceable symptoms. (Iyengar 1991:141)

This episodic framing, in the context of president elections, is yet another reason why reporters may give short shrift to issues and instead focus on more simply told stories, like horse race matters, character traits of the candidates, and other matters than can be discussed in less than two minutes and offer the potential for good visuals. This approach likewise reduces political pressure on candidates to try to respond to problems, as few people who rely on media cues to determine the most important matters would conclude that issues are all that important.

The frame of politics as sports has serious consequences in citizen perspectives on politics, consequences above and beyond the earlier concerns that issues are given short shrift. Citizen knowledge is also affected, according to past research on the consequences of framing. In his study of the 1984 Democratic presidential nomination struggle, Larry Bartels (1988:42) observed that 581 of 583 Democrats in a 1984 American National Elections Study poll who recognized Gary Hart's name could give an estimate on his chances of securing the nomination, while 149 of the 583 refused even to guess on a basic policy question, such as whether he favored cutting government services. This horse race frame so quickly picked up by citizens is not likely to go anywhere soon, as it is particularly easy for reporters to use because poll numbers change over time and those standings provide a shorthand estimate of the success of the overall campaign, according to Bartels (1988).

Defining Candidate Character through Media Frames

Perhaps the best general example of media framing can be seen through the news media's focus on the horse race, as discussed in chapter 2. But equally important to individual candidates are the ways they are defined through media frames regarding character. Unfortunately for some of them, every now and then a candidate seems to attract an extra measure of ridicule from the campaign press pack. Ideology does not seem to matter much, as both liberals and conservatives can be presented by reporters as a given campaign's court jester. Although dark horses are often the butt of reporters' campaign humor, they are sometimes lionized. On the other hand, even viable candidates can get this dismissive treatment. Although there is no consistency over who gets the extra helping of ridicule in a given campaign, it is a serving that no candidate should desire.

Former California governor Jerry Brown, a candidate for the Democratic presidential nomination during the 1980s and 1990s, is a liberal candidate who sometimes was portrayed within an unflattering frame. One could certainly have envisioned Brown as a credible national candidate in a nomination contest that in recent years was won by less well-known governors of the much smaller states of Georgia, Massachusetts, and Arkansas. But the media consensus was formed early: Brown's various presidential campaigns were frequently reported as comic relief rather than as sources of serious policy alternatives. Although Brown regularly suffered from little coverage as a presidential candidate, the sporadic coverage he did receive could be dismissive.

> His rhetoric was unconventional. Whatever the specific content of his proposals, the language and the concepts he used—his talk of colonizing space, of holistic health—were alien to most reporters, who responded with barely concealed derision. His scant coverage consisted largely of snide swipes at his asserted typical California weirdness. (Paletz and Entman 1981:42)

The alternative approach, of course, would be for reporters simply to report Brown's issues without the sarcasm and leave it to the voters to evaluate the candidate through his own words. The general unwillingness to do so represents a pattern of media bias that is applied to candidates of varying ideological stripes.

Conservatives, liberals, and centrists are all framed in one fashion or another by network news. As reporters move ever more deeply into the world of analyzing presidential candidates and their psyches rather than just reporting on the campaign, journalists increasingly rely on shorthand ways to describe candidates—in 2000 Al Gore was seen as a "serial exaggerator" who would say just about anything to be elected, while George W. Bush was presented as an amiable dunce (Abramson et al. 2002). Anytime something happened consistent with these perspectives, a claim about inventing the Internet here or creating the word "subliminable" there, reporters jumped on the story (Ceaser and Busch 2001). This was a chance to replay the candidate's theme song—a song the reporters themselves had penned. The more evidence there was in support of a given candidate's media-created frame, the more savvy reporters seemed to be for having developed the perspective for that candidate in the first place. Most candidates have little choice but to endure such media-created frames, particularly given the fact that reporters get to say a sentence for every word uttered on air by a candidate.

The character frames of candidates—even of the same candidate—can vary from year to year. In 1988, for example, Democratic nominee Dukakis was seen as a cold technocrat while Bush struggled to get beyond his "wimp" image. In 1992, Bush was portrayed as a clueless blue blood, while Clinton was seen as "Slick Willie," the sleaziest politician ever to ooze out of Arkansas. We will have more to say about this general network news negativity, an important form of media bias, in chapter 4. Here our discussion of framing is designed to provide another instance of the many ways in which reporters take it upon themselves to expand their role beyond simply reporting on campaigns.

The frame that reporters developed for Jerry Brown, of course, was that the former governor of the nation's largest state was a flake who was little more than a sideshow attraction in the primaries. Consequently he rarely was taken seriously by reporters and received virtually no coverage, particularly during the critical early phase of the 1992 primary season (Farnsworth and Lichter 1999). Brown, who eventually emerged in 1992 as the strongest challenger to the well-financed Clinton primary operation, was featured or mentioned in only seventeen network news stories during the month before the New Hampshire primary, as compared to sixty-eight features and mentions for Clinton; thirty-nine for Sen. Tom Harkin of Iowa; thirty-five for Paul Tsongas, the former senator from Massachusetts who won the primary; and thirty-one for Sen. Bob Kerrey of Nebraska (Farnsworth and Lichter 1999). The lack of an image during the early part of the 1992 campaign was every bit as damaging to the former governor's ability to convince voters to support him as the media's rough handling of Dan Quayle, Michael Dukakis, and President George H. W. Bush.

When Brown did become a focus of media coverage in the 1992 primaries, it had nothing to do with his policy positions on taxes or international trade. Although Brown's overall coverage in 1992 was more positive than it had been in his previous nomination campaigns, an important area of media coverage of the former governor that year had to do with a personal scandal that tended to reinforce the former governor's media-defined reputation as offbeat. The most commonly reported personal matter on ABC and CNN regarding Brown in 1992 was allegations that he had been smoking marijuana while California's governor. Kerbel (1998:64–67) found that that issue, the subject of 103 references during a one-week period in April 1992, ranked third among the scandals on network news during the primary season that year, behind only Clinton's top two scandals: questions over his relationship with Gennifer Flowers and over whether he tried to evade the military draft during the Vietnam War. ABC was the network that broke the story of the drug allegations against Brown and pursued it aggressively for several days. The charges eventually fell away as Brown's angry denials were soon followed by doubts regarding the source of the network's original report of gubernatorial "pot parties" in Sacramento (Kerbel 1998:68).

For Brown, at least, the story does not have an entirely unhappy ending. Although he lost the 1992 Democratic nomination to Clinton and subsequently fell even farther below the national media's radar screen, Brown soon thereafter was elected mayor of Oakland, one of California's largest (and most troubled) cities. Clearly some California voters viewed this politician with greater seriousness than did the national media. In fact, the job of being a big-city mayor in America is probably one of the most challenging political positions out there. Citizens of Oakland could hardly trust the operation of their particularly challenging city to a flake or a joke.

Of course, Democrats are not the only source of media merriment. A leading Republican target has been former vice president Dan Quayle, often portrayed as a half-wit who could not win a spelling bee even if he competed against elementary school students. Consider as well the media frame of President George H. W. Bush as so out of touch that he didn't understand the economic troubles of ordinary citizens. In fact, he was presented by the *New York Times* and other media outlets as someone who in 1992 was stunned to see a department store's price scanner in action.

The objective truth of the matter used to construct these media frames is sometimes beside the point, at least to the reporter involved. The *New York Times* report of Bush's alleged amazement at seeing a price scanner in operation failed to mention that the president was actually being shown new features about the price scanner's technological advancements. Bush's amazement was over the scanner's ability to reassemble a universal product code ripped and jumbled into five pieces, not over the existence of price scanners themselves (Fitzwater 1995:329).

> The [*New York Times*] story indicated that the president didn't know how a scanner worked and was out of touch with American life. Other newspapers and TV stations picked up the story, all suggesting that the president was out of touch. It was one of those stories where the truth never catches up with the lie. No other reporter at the event wrote the story that way. Reporters started arguing about what actually happened. I urged all reporters to go view the pool videotapes of the episode. Then we contacted NCR [the manufacturer of the device] and asked them to give interviews about what really happened. NCR also sent a letter to the president, confirming that it was brand new technology involved. (Fitzwater 1995:329)

Marlin Fitzwater, Bush's press secretary, said that Bush eventually received his due, not from the *New York Times*, where the story originally appeared, but from the Associated Press and Charles Osgood of CBS Radio (Fitzwater 1995:331).

President Bush, in a 1994 interview, also pointed to that checkout scanner story as one of the most frustrating news reports of his presidency:

> Even though [the *Times* reporter] wasn't there, he wrote a piece that said I was startled to find out there was a checkout counter that recorded prices when a package was swept across it. The fact was, I had been shown something else, some mind-boggling new technology, and that was what I referred to, not a routine checkout scanner. The company that displayed the technology pointed that out, and a CBS reporter looked into the facts and reported that what I'd said was true. But the myth had been created by the *New York Times*. I wrote the publisher, Mr. Sulzberger—one of the few instances when I complained to a publisher—and I pointed out the facts and said their coverage was inaccurate and grossly unfair. And other reporters who were there pointed that out. But the *Times* refused to correct it, and it was picked up by my opposition. So it became not a report but an attack story. (quoted in Gold 1994)

The image that this story conveys of Bush, framed by reporters as an out-of-touch president, was hard to shake and was seen by the former president as one of the reasons he lost his 1992 bid for re-election (Gold 1994).

Gary Bauer, a candidate at the opposite end of the ideological spectrum from Brown and at a substantial ideological distance from President (and GOP moderate) George H. W. Bush, nevertheless got this same abusive treatment. Bauer, a long-shot Republican candidate for the 2000 presidential nomination, was another candidate who, like Brown, received little media coverage except when a scandal was alleged. Bauer first drew substantial media attention in September 1999, when he denied allegations of an alleged affair with a member of his campaign team. The story was not even so much about Bauer as about the culture of scandal that the story represented, as demonstrated by the September 30, 1999, *Los Angeles Times* article by Geraldine Baum and Mark Z. Barabak quoted below. Bauer's troubles were another self-referential story about news created and reported by the media.

> The real news was the wall-to-wall press throng that showed up to listen [to Bauer's denials]. Most Americans probably had never heard of Gary Bauer, a Republican White House wannabe, let alone the allegations he vociferously denied. Still, it was standing room only for 45 minutes of question-and-denial, as 50 journalists—including eight TV crews—chronicled the latest turn in Washington's Wheel of Scandal. Just last week, when Bauer delivered a 15-page address about his views on U.S.-China policy, a measly five print reporters and three local TV crews showed up and the event garnered scarcely a line in most newspapers. (quoted in Kerbel 2001:117–18)

Bauer disappeared from Campaign 2000 about as quickly as did the allegations of an extramarital affair, which were never substantiated. Had reporters thought more about Bauer's issue concerns, however, they would have provided coverage that would have proven quite prescient. One of Bauer's signature issues was his deep concern over U.S. relations with China. He argued that we were not being tough enough with the totalitarian Asian superpower. One of the first international crises the new Bush administration faced involved a U.S. surveillance plane that was attacked by a Chinese jet fighter and forced to land in China, with its crew taken hostage. Of course the often-prickly relations between the two nuclear-armed nations, like the impending crisis the United States would soon face in Afghanistan, barely registered on the media's radar screen during the nomination and general election phases of Election 2000.

Framing candidates, then, has great appeal for reporters. Media-manufactured frames allow reporters to tell a story about a candidate in simple terms: this guy is dumb, that guy is out of touch, this guy has a zipper problem, and that other guy is just plain from another planet. Reporting and recycling such simplistic characterizations does not require a great deal of homework or initiative from the reporter. Revisiting the campaign frame is particularly appealing for television news, when the amount of time spent on politics during a newscast is in decline and a newer theme would take longer to introduce. These media frames of candidates tend to be self-reinforcing, as the reporters use examples of these individual themes to tell a continuing story. Returning to these themes also can be used by reporters to justify the images (or stereotypes) they have bestowed upon candidates in the first place. Framing also allows reporters to practice the sort of "gotcha" journalism that they can substitute for the more time-consuming, less glamorous, and more expensive investigative reporting. Framing represents a chance to go negative without having to work too hard or say too much. Returning to established frames also offers reporters ample opportunity to talk about themselves, since they created the frames in the first place. In these ways, candidate framing is the news media's gift to itself, and it is a gift that keeps on giving.

Given the convergence of media opinion regarding how much time reporters should spend talking about themselves and to each other in news reports, it is impressive how many voters rebel and try to redirect campaign discourse in the direction of more substantive matters. This trend, of course, is consistent with the media effects model discussed in chapter 1. During a 1992 Clinton campaign appearance on his show, for example, Phil Donahue became the target of criticism from Melissa Roth, a 25-year-old member of the show's studio audience—who later said she was a Republican.

> I think really, given the pathetic state of most of the United States at this point—Medicare, education, everything else—I can't believe you spent half an hour of air time attacking this man's character. I'm not even a Bill Clinton supporter, but I think this is ridiculous. (Roth, quoted in Rosen 1992:35)

Even though Donahue ran a talk show rather than a network newscast, the woman's comments produced cheers and applause from the audience. This offers yet another example of the gap between the way the media cover a candidate and the way voters would like to see a campaign covered (Rosen 1992). Donahue was, after all, pressing Clinton for answers about the same character issues the network reporters had been stressing throughout the primary season.

Polls verify that the electorate has begun to agree with many reporters that campaigns are largely about the journalists, though perhaps not in a manner that reporters would find encouraging. In the wake of the 1988 campaign, for example, only 17 percent of the voters blamed the candidates for the deplorable nature of campaign. Instead, the *Newsweek* poll found that 40 percent of those surveyed believed that the "news organizations covering the campaign" were the real problem (Lichter and Noyes 1995:136).

Events seen as pivotal by reporters do not have to be rooted in an established frame to generate intense, self-referential media coverage. One of the major dust-ups reported in the media's portrayal of the 2000 elections was George W. Bush's ill-advised assessment of a newspaper reporter at a campaign rally. This incident was another example of how reporters love to report about themselves. In front of a live microphone, the Republican nominee observed *New York Times* political writer Adam Clymer in the audience and described him as a "major league asshole" (Sabato 2002). Dick Cheney, the Republican vice presidential nominee who was sharing the stage with Bush, readily agreed: "Yeah, big time," he replied. Both comments clearly were not intended for the audience. Nevertheless, they were carried by that live mike and were heard by reporters and viewers around the country as the tape of the incident was broadcast and rebroadcast (sometimes with the offensive word excised) on the evening news. This "major league" story was hardly that, particularly when compared to the scandals that plagued Clinton from 1992 onward (Klein 2002; Sabato et al. 2000).

What Bush said was hardly novel. Many political figures have an abiding distrust if not outright contempt for the press, so Bush probably expressed what many political figures say privately about reporters in even stronger terms. President Clinton's unguarded moments likewise show a profound contempt for—and frequent rage against—reporters. But he did not make accidental remarks in front of live microphones. Instead, insight into Clinton's personal views of the media comes indirectly, through leaks from and books by administration insiders (Morris 1997; Reich 1998; Stephanopoulos 1999; Woodward 1994).

Media apologists may point to this "major league" incident as evidence that Bush was ill prepared to be a national candidate, and perhaps even that his private thoughts were at variance from his public persona as a

Christian conservative. The incident might even be shoehorned into the "Bush as dim bulb" media frame. But however revealing a reporter might consider this incident to be, it would be difficult to argue that the attention paid to this scandal would not have been better spent on the consequences of tax cuts or on foreign policy, both of which have preoccupied the new president ever since his inauguration.

A damaging facet of the media's self-referential nature of reporting is that journalists are inclined to determine the newsworthiness of an event by the extent to which it conforms to the previous media consensus regarding the candidate. Marjorie Hershey (2001:68) observed, for example, that Bush received "a free pass" from the media when he mistakenly claimed in the first debate that he had been outspent by Gore. Fortunately for the Texas governor, the media's postgame focus on that debate concerned Gore's audible sighs and aggressive demeanor. Gore's supercilious behavior fit into a news frame that the then vice president was a major-league know-it-all, a vision of the vice president that was frequently used in *Saturday Night Live* parodies of Gore (Paletz 2002). During the debates, Bush made a second significant error when he said that Texas was going to execute three people for the racially based murder of an African American in the state. (Actually, only two of the three men were to be executed.) The man was dragged behind a pickup truck until his body broke apart, a horrific image that generated national media coverage of the murder and the passage of a hate-crimes law in Texas. But that capital punishment misstep by Bush received less media attention than Gore's misstatements regarding the pricing of canine medications and the length of time a student in Florida had to stand up in a crowded classroom (Ceaser and Busch 2001; Sabato 2002). The latter two were seen as more newsworthy because of the "serial exaggerator" news frame that haunted Gore and worked to Bush's advantage throughout the 2000 campaign. It is hard to avoid the conclusion that these media frames were used throughout the fall to hold Gore to a higher standard on factual matters. In the world of media expectations, it is sometimes an advantage to be seen as not too smart.

Bush should have known the facts better in both cases. His team had raised and spent record amounts of money during the 2000 campaign, an issue that had come up repeatedly during his primary campaign battles with John McCain, long a leading proponent of campaign finance reform. As governor of Texas, Bush had presided over the state perennially ranked first in number of executions, and Bush himself had aggressively defended the state's capital punishment operations against many critics during his years as the state's governor. Gore's behavior, so consistent with the "serial exaggerator" frame, simply proved more tempting to reporters who may have tired of the "Bush as dim bulb" media frame this late into the election year. A one-trick pony, after all, can only get a showman so far. Reporters had many opportunities to use this Bush frame during the Republican Party's much more contentious nomination process during the first third of 2000. Gore had a comparably easy time disposing of his Democratic rival in the 2000 primaries, and so was out of the news throughout the spring of 2000. This may have made Gore particularly vulnerable to more aggressive media framing when the general election campaign began in earnest.

The propensity of reporters to reflect in their reports about themselves and their troubles not only tends to make the campaigns less interesting for voters, it also deprives citizens of the information they need to evaluate candidates effectively. The search for the latest confirmation of an existing media frame takes precious media time away from discussion of more substantive matters. In fact, policy proposals tend to be interesting to journalists mainly when reporters can attack them as unrealistic. When a candidate offers a new idea to the public policy debate—be it George McGovern's plan in 1972 to develop a new income assistance program, Ronald Reagan's "Star Wars" missile defense plan in 1984, Walter Mondale's observation in 1984 that the massive federal deficits of the Reagan years would require new taxes, or Bob Dole's 1996 tax cut plan—reporters always seem to find sources who will bury the idea or, in some cases, do the grave-digging themselves (Patterson 1994:158–59). Such a "kill on sight" media approach to new initiatives hardly encourages candidates to offer new ideas to try to solve old problems. This may help explain why the federal deficit grew dramatically in recent decades and, after a few years of balanced budgets, the nation's finances appear as of this writing to be on the verge of heading back into the red for quite some time. It may also help explain why few subsequent presidential candidates followed President Clinton and tried to deal with a vitally important issue—the tens of millions of Americans who lack health insurance (Skocpol 1997).

As poet Robert Frost once observed, the world may end in fire, or in ice. "Either," Frost wrote, "would suffice." This is how candidates must feel about media treatment of their new policy ideas. Reporters may tear apart a new policy idea like hungry jackals, or they may ignore it entirely, until it dies for lack of exposure. Although journalists often claim that candidates are shirking substance, an extensive CMPA content analysis of campaign speeches during 1992 shows that exactly the opposite is true. The journalists themselves, not the politicians, were the ones doing the shirking. Fully 44 percent of the 1992 campaign speeches made by Clinton, Bush, and Perot focused on policy issue stances, and another 33 percent focused on policy records. These speeches were divided roughly equally between economic matters (key lines of attacks on Bush by both Clinton and Perot during the economically lumbering 1992 campaign season) and other domestic policy issues, including Social Security and health care. Television newscasts and elite newspaper stories focused mostly on candidate assessments and candidate viability, which together comprised 35 percent of the media coverage. These topics were the focus of only 7 percent of the candidates' speeches that year. Issue stances and candidate records were the focus of 77 percent of the speeches made by the three candidates, but they were only the focus of 24 percent of the media coverage (Lichter and Noyes 1995:111). With results like these, it is no wonder that candidates forced to campaign before network television cameras eight seconds at a time, and largely forced to reach voters through those same cameras, may question whether they should debate issues. We'll talk more about this topic in chapter 5, when we compare what the candidates actually said to what the reporters said the candidates said.

Conclusion

Viewed from a variety of perspectives, it seems evident that reporters and editors increasingly believe that they have much more to say about elections than do the candidates whose names appear on the ballot. Candidate sound bites in recent elections have shrunk to about one-quarter the length of a Gap ad, making the direct dissemination of even the simplest message problematic. Candidate comments represent only a tiny fraction of the total time spent covering the campaign. In fact a whole election season of one candidate's comments on the three nightly network newscasts could fit in a single hour-long entertainment show's time slot.

Reporters could respond to these time pressures by spending more time on the candidates and the issues that the candidates—and, as we have seen, that the voters—think are important. Less time could be spent trying to demonstrate how smart reporters are and on placing candidates in oversimplified frames to telegraph the cast of characters appearing on the campaign trail. More time could be spent on issues, particularly those issues that the next president will likely face. These are not revolutionary ideas. In fact, reporters and anchors say much the same thing every four years. The networks could follow their own assessments of where their newscasts fall short, particularly with respect to expanding issue coverage and increasing the length and number of unmediated candidate remarks. In other words, reporters could just plain do better.

But they do not. In election after election, network television news offers up horse race–dominated coverage in which even policy discussions are often framed in terms of a candidate's election strategy or prospects. When reporters do step away from horse race reporting, much of what remains is self-referential reporting. That reporting does little to illuminate the differences among candidates. Thirty minutes of news goes by very quickly—and without much public benefit—if the time is spent talking about such things as how many reporters came to hear Jerry Brown deny unsubstantiated allegations of marijuana use while governor of California.

As might not be surprising for people who seem to think campaigns are largely about them, reporters often give themselves high marks for their role in campaigns. A 1992 postelection survey of reporters, for example, found that four out of five rated their own 1992 coverage as "good" or "excellent" and nearly all considered it far better than the coverage of 1988 (Lichter and Noyes 1995:225). This is an illustration of why professors do not let students grade their own exams.

Ordinary citizens, who might be considered more objective evaluators than the journalists themselves, reach very different conclusions. Only 36 percent of those surveyed after the 1992 election were willing to give the press an "A" or a "B" grade (Lichter and Noyes 1995:226). CMPA data demonstrate repeatedly that network television news is getting worse, and the grades are falling along with the networks' performance.

> Why didn't the public appreciate the press' efforts? According to [a 1992 postelection study by] Times-Mirror, a majority (54 percent) believed the press had too much influence on which candidate becomes president. During the primaries, nearly three in five voters (58 percent) thought that the media had too much influence on the selection of a Democratic nominee. Moreover, most of the electorate believed journalists "often" (49 percent) or "sometimes" (35 percent) let their own political preferences influence the way they report the news. (Lichter and Noyes 1995:226)

The next chapter addresses other important areas to consider when assessing the Big Three's nightly newscasts: questions of media negativity, accuracy, and fairness. It is here that many of the candidates and the campaigns make some of their loudest criticisms about the performance of network television news. Using content analysis, we will consider whether those complaints—or whether the networks' protestations that they are objective chroniclers of campaigns—have merit.

CHAPTER 4

A PLAGUE ON ALL YOUR HOUSES
Negativity, Fairness, and Accuracy

Network television coverage of Campaign 2000 was a textbook example of how network television should not cover an election, an even more powerful indictment of television news than the networks' generally weak performances in 1988, 1992, and 1996. The CMPA content analysis of the evening network newscasts throughout the 2000 primary and general election periods showed high levels of negativity against both major party candidates, a pattern consistent with network coverage of the presidential candidates in 1988, 1992, and 1996. To make matters worse, reporters also often select candidates' sound bites and comments that are particularly negative, giving viewers the erroneous impression that campaigns are conducted far more negatively than they actually are. This pervasive negativity can discourage citizens from tuning in to news and make them too frustrated and discouraged to vote for anyone. After the presidential contest of 2000, we recognize all too well the significance of the adage that "every vote counts."

Another major problem with the news coverage in recent elections, and in particular in the presidential contest of 2000, is the media's sometimes cavalier approach to accuracy. The astonishing series of media blunders that marked Election 2000 is the latest of the errors of judgment in a process that has hurt the credibility of the news media—the key vehicle by which candidates and governing officials connect with citizens—and made a bad situation in Florida far worse. The race among reporters to be first, which has intensified as media technologies have improved and as use of the Internet has increased—has led to a growing recklessness in the calling of elections. The Florida blunder was not the only mistake the networks made in their rush to report winners and losers on November 7, 2000, although it was by far the most visible and important. And the 2000 election was not the only time that the networks had erred in reporting results based upon the less-than-reliable Voter News Service.

The Rising Tide of Media Negativity: Past Research

More than a quarter-century ago, Americans generally and journalists in particular were rocked by twin scandals of governmental deceit: Vietnam and Watergate (Gergen 2000; Halberstam 1979; Haldeman 1994; Lowi 1985; Neustadt 1990; Sabato 2000; Woodward 1999). In a televised moment eerily similar to President Bill Clinton's finger-wagging denial of any sexual relationship with Monica Lewinsky more than twenty years later, President Richard Nixon boldly declared that he was "not a crook," while the Watergate scandal swirled around him (Gergen 2000; Haldeman 1994). President Nixon, and President Lyndon Johnson before him, repeatedly misled the country about the ultimately failed U.S. military intervention in Vietnam. When the magnitude of their deceit became apparent, investigative reporters who doubted the government, such as Bob Woodward and Carl Bernstein of the *Washington Post*, became folk heroes and best-selling authors (Bernstein and Woodward 1974; Woodward and Bernstein 1976). The brightest of Hollywood's stars—Robert Redford and Dustin Hoffman—portrayed these enterprising reporters in a hit film on Watergate (Ryan and Kellner 1988). Reporters ever since have viewed government pronouncements with suspicion and governmental figures with contempt. For two generations now, reporters have resolved that they won't be fooled again (Kurtz 1998; Sabato 2000).

Or maybe it has been more than two generations. Some political scientists argue that today's aggressive reporting is a continuation of the "muckraking" journalistic trends of a century ago. "If television newspeople have any prevailing political outlook, it is not the liberalism of Edward Kennedy or the Americans for Democratic Action, but rather a revised and updated version of the 'progressive' outlook that dominated American politics from the 1890s to the 1920s" (Ranney 1983:52).

However old the journalistic antecedents, it is clear that in today's political environment reporters are not the only ones who think the worst of politicians. Citizens became similarly cynical of government as the events of the 1960s and 1970s unfolded, and they remained negatively disposed in the years that followed (Craig 1993, 1996; Farnsworth 1999a, 1999b, 2000, 2001; Hibbing and Theiss-Morse 1995). In the 1964 American National Elections Study, 78 percent of the people surveyed said they believed that the government in Washington could be trusted to do the right thing just about always or most of the time. That percentage fell to 54 percent in 1972, when the magnitude of the government's deceits in Vietnam had become quite apparent. That percentage fell even further, to 34 percent, in 1976, two years after Nixon had resigned over his illegal cover-up of the Watergate break-in. Four years later, in 1980, only 26 percent of citizens surveyed believed the government did the right thing at least most of the time, an increased cynicism that followed President Jimmy Carter's struggles with the economy and with the Iranian hostage crisis (Farnsworth 1997; Woodward 1999). Not until after the terrorist attack on the United States on September 11, 2001, did this trust-in-government measure fully rebound. This gain in trust in government in late 2001 probably had more to do with a "rally 'round the flag effect" that often occurs in times of political crisis than with any long-term renewed faith in governmental officials (Adams et al. 1994; Lowi 1985; Nincic 1997). As of this writing it is too soon to say whether the dramatic rebound in this key trust-in-government measure will remain in the years ahead.

Campaign news coverage was not exempt from the growing media negativity of the post-Watergate years. A content analysis of news coverage of the 1980 presidential campaign found that all four major candidates that year—President Carter, Sen. Edward Kennedy (D-Mass.), Ronald Reagan, and John Anderson—received more negative than positive press on CBS, the television network that was the subject of extensive scrutiny that year (Robinson and Sheehan 1983). Despite allegations of a liberal media bias, in 1980 there was no evidence to indicate that the most conservative candidate of the four—Reagan—received more negative press than the other leading candidates.

> In 1980, frontrunners and the incumbent consistently experienced the least balanced, least favorable news coverage. Being at the head of the pack almost always means lots of access but lots of bad press as well; being the incumbent may almost inevitably mean the toughest press of all. Remarkably enough, a candidate's press was most easily predicted by his position in the polls than by his party or his philosophy. As far as we could determine, a candidate's ideology had little to do with his press score, at least not over the long haul of a year's campaign. (Robinson and Sheehan 1983:138–39)

In his study of favorable and unfavorable references to major party nominees in *Time* and *Newsweek*, Thomas Patterson (1994) found a dramatic trend toward negativity in recent decades. The study, which excluded horse race evaluations, found that, in 1960, 75 percent of the references in America's two leading weekly news magazines were positive and that as late as 1976 over 60 percent of the coverage was positive. A majority of references were negative in 1980, and by 1992 reporters' evaluative references of the candidates were negative 60 percent of the time (Patterson 1994:20).

Struck by this negative coverage, political scientist Patterson asked reporters why the candidates are so often portrayed as liars. "'Because they are liars,' was the most common response, which was usually followed by an example, such as Bush's 1988 pledge not to raise taxes ('Read my lips') and Clinton's description of his marijuana experience ('I didn't inhale')" (Patterson 1994:8).

Once a few reporters develop a frame that is negative with respect to the candidate being covered, a media consensus may soon develop over how an event should be portrayed or a character presented (Fitzwater 1995; Kurtz 1993, 1998). Our content analysis of recent presidential elections has shown that reporters for the Big Three television networks consistently approach news stories from very similar perspectives. So when the news is good for a candidate on one network, it is usually good on the other networks as well. And when the news is bad, the candidate faces a simultaneous barrage of criticism from many news outlets, as this example from the 1992 Bush campaign suggests:

> On ABC, President Bush is in the cabinet room, dismissing "crazy rumors" that he is about to drop Vice President Quayle from the ticket. Democratic nominee Bill Clinton is addressing a huge crowd in St. Louis, drawing cheers when he contrasts his choice of Sen. Albert Gore with Bush's selection of Quayle. On CBS Dan Rather says Bush "had to put down talk that his reelection campaign is in retreat and in disarray," while Richard Threlkeld announces that "Bill Clinton's campaign is now off to the best start of any Democrat in 16 years." On NBC, Tom Brokaw says Bush is "a distant second and fading," while Andrea Mitchell says Clinton's crowds have "exceeded anyone's expectations." (Kurtz 1992c)

Howard Kurtz, media critic for the *Washington Post*, said that reporters tend to avoid writing stories that are very different from what other reporters are writing. When the poll numbers are good, as they were for Clinton in mid-1992, there are a flood of positive stories. When the poll numbers are bad, as they were for President George H. W. Bush throughout the year, there are a flood of negative stories, Kurtz (1992c) observed.

Previous research suggests that tonal coverage alternates in different years between balanced coverage and more favorable treatment of Democrats, a pattern detected by comparing the presidential campaigns of 1980 and 1984. Michael Robinson and Margaret Sheehan conducted the first large-scale content analysis of print and broadcast election news, which focused on the tone of coverage during Campaign 1980. By controlling for horse race evaluations, this landmark study provided the template for later studies of this type. They concluded that in 1980 Ronald Reagan and Jimmy Carter "both did about equally badly on television" (Robinson and Sheehan 1983:138). When Maura Clancey and Michael Robinson reprised this study four years later, however, they found that Walter Mondale received balanced coverage, while Reagan's was predominantly negative: "Our measure of candidate spin shows that [Reagan and Bush] lost the battle for the network news and lost it badly" (Clancey and Robinson 1985:27). This finding was replicated by Doris Graber (1987), who pioneered the use of content analysis to code pictures as well as words in television newscasts. She concluded, "In both words and pictures, the Democrats were favored" (Graber 1987:137–38). In an analysis of the words and images found in media coverage of the 1992 presidential campaign, the pictures tended to be kinder than the words for all candidates (Just et al. 1996).

Overall, the evidence from content analysis in recent decades suggests there has been more bad news than good news for most presidential candidates on the nightly newscasts and elsewhere in the world of journalism (cf. Germond and Witcover 1989, 1993; R. Simon 2001). As Jack Germond, a longtime political writer for the Baltimore *Sun,* remarked after the 2000 election:

> You couldn't find anybody who would walk through a wall for Al Gore. Bush was even more superficial. His candidacy was based primarily on the money he raised for his campaign. . . . George Bush has a lack of knowledge of the world around him and Gore was too programmed. I find it very hard to describe why I was spending my dotage on these two people. (quoted in Owen 2002:129)

The Tone of Presidential Campaign Coverage

If academic criticism has concentrated mainly on the superficiality and negativism of campaign news, the candidates and their supporters are most attuned to the fairness issue. Historically this complaint has been raised most often by Republicans, who see the national media as presenting the perspectives of liberals and Democrats (Bozell and Baker 1990; Rusher 1988; Dionne 1992). The Democratic voting patterns and relatively liberal personal perspectives of national media journalists are well documented, particularly on social and cultural rather than economic issues (Lichter 1996; Schneider and Lewis 1985). In recent years, however, Democrats have increasingly joined the chorus of media criticism. President Clinton's resentment of the media for its treatment of his personal life, beginning in the 1992 campaign, is well known. And in the waning weeks of the 2000 campaign, several prominent liberal commentators charged that the media coverage was favoring George W. Bush, stemming either from journalists' personal antipathy toward Al Gore or their efforts to lean over backwards to avoid charges of partisanship (Kurtz 2000b).

In response to such criticism, journalists typically argue that their professionalism prevents their personal politics from influencing their coverage in any overt or systematic fashion (Deakin 1983; Hunt 1985). Some scholars have reached the same conclusion by pointing to economic and social constraints as counterweights to personal opinion in the news product (Epstein 1975; Gans 1979). But this position should be treated as an empirical question rather than an article of faith. CMPA's content analysis system was designed to examine this question with greater depth and precision than it usually receives. The system identified the tone as well as the source and topic of each statement about a candidate or issue, that is, who said what about whom. This procedure allows for a more detailed and nuanced analysis than is possible when the entire story is treated as the unit of analysis.

Our coding procedure differentiated between the source and the object of each evaluative statement. We separated evaluations of candidate viability (horse race assessments) from those of candidate desirability (assessments of a candidate's qualifications, policies, personal character, or conduct). Only the latter were included in our definition of tone or valence, which is concerned with the merit of each candidacy rather than its likelihood of success. (Judgments of candidate viability, of course, have already been addressed in our discussion of network television's horse race focus in chapter 2). Second, we differentiated between evaluations made by (or attributed to) partisan and nonpartisan sources. In this case, "partisan" refers to sources who are identified as being affiliated with a particular candidacy; "nonpartisan" refers to all other sources. In practice, the vast majority of partisan evaluations in election stories come from the candidates and their campaign staffs. Nonpartisan sources of evaluative statements are most frequently journalists themselves, voters, experts (such as an economist commenting on a candidate's economic policies), and various pundits.

We followed the lead of Robinson and Sheehan's pioneering work (1983:94ff.) in restricting our measure of tone to statements by nonpartisan sources. This was done for two reasons. First, they are more influential in the sense of predicting opinion change (Page et al. 1987), presumably because voters give less credence to identifiably partisan opinion. Second, they represent the more discretionary portion of election news, the value-added element of a journalist's (and media organization's) particular news judgment. So news accounts of partisan evaluations are more closely linked to the campaign trail give-and-take, whereas nonpartisan evaluations give more latitude to journalists' own judgments in selecting sources and topics.[1] Examples of "positive" and "negative" evaluations by our definitions are as follows: Positive: "I like [Gore's education] proposals because I feel like he wants to fix the system that's there." (Voter, NBC, September 8, 2000). Negative: "My biggest concern is that Al Gore will say about anything he needs to say to get elected President of the United States" (Voter, NBC, October 5, 2000).

Tone in General Elections

Throughout Campaign 2000, the tone of the presidential campaign coverage was predominantly negative for both candidates. That is, Bush and Gore fared about equally poorly in the battle for good press, which was calculated by tallying every positive or negative on-air evaluation of a candidate's record, policies, personal character, and behavior on the campaign trail by nonpartisan sources. (Evaluations of Ralph Nader and Pat Buchanan were too rare to permit meaningful analysis—only eleven assessments for Nader and none for Buchanan.) Gore's substantive evaluations were 40 percent positive and 60 percent negative, while substantive evaluations of Bush were 37 percent positive and 63 percent negative (analysis of tone excludes horse race evaluations, which are discussed separately). This overall pattern differed little from network to network or according to the aspects of their candidacies that were most frequently addressed—their policies, their political skills, and the way they conducted their campaigns. Comments about their policies and performance, for example, were most positive overall—45 percent favorable for Gore and 39 percent for Bush. Evaluations of their political skills were slightly less favorable, with Gore receiving 41 percent and Bush 34 percent positive comments.

But the main repository of candidate criticism lay elsewhere. By far the most negative on-air judgments were reserved for the ways both men conducted their campaigns. An overwhelming 96 percent of candidate evaluations linked to events on the campaign trail were negative, leaving a mere 4 percent that were positive—fewer than one in twenty assessments. For example, in response to a GOP commercial that briefly flashed the word "rats" on-screen, a voter told CBS on September 15, "When I heard about that 'Rat' thing the first thing that came to my mind was Nixon and

Watergate." Thus, both candidates received almost unanimously bad reviews for their actual behavior on the campaign trail, including the speeches they gave, the ads they ran, and their raising and expenditure of campaign funds.

Although the networks found virtually nothing worthy of on-air praise in the campaign behavior of the candidates, even this finding probably understates the overall negativism of the 2000 election news. In both 1992 and 1996 we coded comments on the election process, apart from evaluations directed toward the candidates. These included commentary on such topics as voter interest, campaign financing, and the overall quality of campaign discourse. In 1996, 86 percent of such evaluations were negative. In 1992 the proportion of critical assessments was even higher at 93 percent. For example, Tom Brokaw opened the *NBC Nightly News* on October 29, 1996, with the comment, "If this campaign has an unofficial motto, it is this—wake me when it's over."

Winning Streaks, Losing Streaks in Tones of Campaign 2000

The tonal quality of election news varied significantly along only one dimension that we measured—that of the campaign calendar. From Labor Day to the end of September, Gore's coverage was almost evenly balanced between positive and negative evaluations (48 percent versus 52 percent, respectively), while the negative judgments of Bush outweighed the positive by a two-to-one margin (33 percent versus 67 percent). During the latter half of the campaign (October and early November), however, this pattern was reversed. Gore's proportion of positive comments dropped to 36 percent during this period, while Bush's evaluations improved to 39 percent positive. Prior CMPA election studies had never shown such a midcourse turnaround in good press. In 1988, 1992, and 1996, the tonal pattern that was established by Labor Day prevailed with only minor variations throughout the entire campaign. For example, in 1992 Bill Clinton got better press than President George H. W. Bush during sixteen out of the seventeen weeks between the Democratic convention in July and election day in November.

By contrast, our studies had uncovered no instances of the stars being aligned to favor all three components of any candidate's media image during the three previous general elections. Indeed our search of the content analysis literature uncovered no such instance during the past two decades. In Campaign 2000, however, both nominees had time to enjoy the glow of the media spotlight without being singed by it. If we combine both categories of evaluation—desirability (good press) and viability (horse race evaluations)—into a single "global" measure of tone, the mid-course turnaround in the candidates' fortunes stands out in even sharper relief. In September Gore received 65 percent favorable comments in both dimensions combined, compared to only 25 percent favorable for Bush. In October and November Bush's proportion of positive comments rose to 51 percent, compared to 39 percent for Gore. Thus, each candidate's temporary surge in support may have been reinforced and magnified by the interactive effect of news content variables that are usually inversely related.[2]

Such reversals of fortune have been far more characteristic of primary campaigns than of general elections. During the frenetic primary season, it is not unusual for a dark horse to receive a burst of favorable attention after either a surge in the preference polls or a better-than-expected showing in a primary. Meanwhile, the media's heaviest fire is often concentrated on the front-runner. However, such bursts of good press are usually self-limiting, as the media begin to treat the new contender's presidential prospects seriously enough to warrant closer scrutiny, which usually brings more criticism (Lichter et al. 1988; Noyes et al. 1993; Arterton 1984; Orren and Polsby 1987). Thus, Gore experienced a wave of good press as he surged ahead of Bush in the preference polls during and after the Democratic convention. Having replaced Bush as the front-runner, however, he fell victim to the build-them-up-break-them-down cycle of election news that is so familiar from primary contests. The next turning point corresponded almost precisely with the first presidential debate on October 3. Thereafter, most polls showed an increase in voter support for Bush. However, Bush's relative advantage in the race for good press during the second half of the campaign owed less to his own slight increase in favorable notices than to Gore's sharp decline in supportive sound bites.

Our overall finding of negative but balanced coverage also bears on the long-standing debate over media bias. The charges of partisan bias coming from Democrats in 2000 were the exception. Ever since Vice President Spiro Agnew complained publicly about "nattering nabobs of negativism" in 1969, Republicans and conservatives have voiced the loudest complaints of bias by the "liberal media." *Los Angeles Times* political reporter Robert Shogan (2001:171) reported that Richard N. Bond, a former Republican Party national chairman, said that GOP attacks on the news media were designed to be like coaches yelling at umpires, "in the hope, as Bond put it, that 'maybe the ref will cut you a little slack on the next one.'"

In Campaign 2000, journalists would seem justified in treating complaints from both parties as evidence of balanced coverage. On the charge of negativism, the networks are on shakier ground. Their evaluations of both candidates' ideas and behavior were consistently downbeat. But they can at least lay claim to being equal opportunity naysayers.

Tone Imbalances: Changes from Year to Year

If the results of Campaign 2000 represented a typical year with respect to tonal coverage, we would agree with those journalists who dismiss charges of partisan bias as selective perceptions (and perhaps cynical posturing) by partisan observers. But CMPA studies from the three previous elections caution against the outright dismissal of such criticism. In the presidential elections of 1988, 1992 and 1996, CMPA studies twice found a significant imbalance in the tone of network news toward the major party candidates.

As table 4.1 shows, the roughly equally negative assessment of Gore and Bush in Campaign 2000 was not consistently found in previous campaigns. In 1996 Democrat Bill Clinton enjoyed 50 percent positive evaluations versus only 33 percent positive commentary for Republican Bob

TABLE 4.1 General Election News: Tone of Coverage, 1988–2000 (percentage good press)

	2000	1996	1992	1988
Democratic Nominee	40	50	52	31
Republican Nominee	37	33	29	38

Note: Based on campaign news stories from ABC, CBS, and NBC between September 4 and November 6, 2000; September 2 and November 5, 1996; September 7 and November 3, 1992; September 8 and November 8, 1988, respectively.

Dole. In 1992 Clinton bested then President George H. W. Bush by an even wider margin of 52 percent to 29 percent positive evaluations (Perot's coverage that year was 45 percent positive). Thus, during his two campaigns for the presidency, a slight majority of Clinton's on-air evaluations were positive, while over two out of three evaluations of his Republican opponents were negative. Clinton's advantage in election news coverage has also been independently replicated by other media scholars (Just et al. 1996; Kerbel 1998).[3]

Neither the 1992 nor the 1996 imbalance can be interpreted as an accurate reflection of the loser's inferior political skills, that is, the reality of the campaign trail. Even after controlling for this subset of evaluations, Clinton enjoyed significantly better press notices for his policy stands than his opponents did. (For all four elections, the tonal directionality of policy judgments mirrored the overall pattern of candidate evaluations.) The only time the Republican candidate fared better than his Democratic opponent was in 1988, when coverage of Bush, who was then vice president, was slightly more positive than that of Michael Dukakis, by the margin of 38 percent to 31 percent favorable assessments. Bush's slight advantage in 1988 and Gore's in 2000 can be treated as effectively balanced (or as canceling each other out). If we accept a ten-percentage-point difference as the threshold for a clear advantage, then the Democrats' scorecard in this battle for better network news coverage reads two wins, no losses, and two ties in the four presidential elections between 1988 and 2000. (A ten-point difference seems a minimal standard for a difference significant enough to be detected by viewers, but even that may be akin to asking a baseball fan to distinguish between hitters with batting averages of .260 and .280.)

Of course, in both instances of unbalanced coverage over the past four presidential campaigns, the advantage went to the same individual. Although it is difficult to imagine that this finding reflects a generalized pro-Clinton tilt to the news, we controlled for this factor by examining all evaluations of Democratic and Republican candidates during the two off-year elections of 1994 and 1998, from Labor Day through Election Day (we did not collect these data for 1990). The results were consistent with the pattern that we observed for general elections: In 1994 Democratic candidates fared better, collectively receiving 43 percent positive evaluations, compared to 31 percent for their GOP counterparts. In 1998 the tone was more balanced, with 43 percent positive judgments of Democrats and 40 percent positive for Republicans.

The CMPA findings demonstrating tonal advantages that favor neither party in some years and favor the Democrats in others are consistent with the results of the tonal analysis of the two presidential elections that occurred before our four-presidential-election research period (1988, 1992, 1996, and 2000). Content analysis revealed relatively evenhanded tonal news coverage of Campaign 1980 (Robinson and Sheehan 1983), while analysis of the media messages in Campaign 1984 found the tonal news discussion favored Mondale over Reagan (Clancey and Robinson 1985).

Clancey and Robinson (1985) accounted for the good-press gap between Mondale and Reagan by positing a general antifront-runner bias termed "compensatory journalism." With this bias, reporters are thought to be toughest on the candidates who are most likely to become president, in effect compensating those who are trailing with better press than the leaders. However, this hypothesis has since been contradicted by data from subsequent general elections. Clinton got far better press than both Bush in 1992 and Dole in 1996, despite his wire-to-wire leads in the polls. And Bush led Dukakis in good press in 1988, albeit by a slight margin, despite his front-runner status in preference polls throughout the fall.

In sum, a general pattern of negativism on network news has coincided with an intermittent tendency toward more favorable press for Democrats than Republicans. In four of the past eight elections for which exhaustive systematic content analysis data are available (1980, 1988, 1998, and 2000), both sides received mainly negative notices. In the other four (1984, 1992, 1994, and 1996), Democrats fared substantially better on the evening news programs than did the Republicans.[4]

It appears that negativity and political ideology represent separate dimensions that contribute independently to the tone of election news. Patterson (1994) has traced the rise in network negativism back to 1960, based on changes in the aggregate tone of both parties' coverage. To paraphrase George Orwell, however, journalists may see all candidates as evil, but some as more evil than others. Democratic candidates did not always get better press than Republicans, but Republican candidates never got much better press than Democrats. To be sure, any difference in tone seems far less pro-Democratic than anti-Republican. Nonetheless, these data suggest that allegations of ideological tilt in election coverage cannot be dismissed entirely as the special pleading of partisans. At the same time, neither negativity nor partisanship alone can fully account for the variation in the valence of campaign news.

It is important to note that positive media coverage during the general election does not always help the candidate who receives it. For the four elections in which the Democrats received significantly better coverage (the presidential election years of 1984, 1992, and 1996 and the midterm congressional elections of 1994), the party was only two-for-four at the polls. Bill Clinton won his two presidential campaigns, but Democratic presidential nominee Walter Mondale was trounced in 1984, winning only his home state of Minnesota and the overwhelmingly Democratic District of Columbia. In 1994, the off-year election in this group, the Republican candidates for the U.S. House and Senate scored extraordinary victories on their way to taking majority party status away from the Democrats in both chambers (Jacobson 2001a).

The four elections where the coverage was about equally negative for the two parties and their candidates (1980, 1988, 1998, and 2000) also offer mixed results. Ronald Reagan won easily in 1980, and the Republican Party took control of the Senate that year. George H. W. Bush won the presidency in an easy victory in 1988, securing nearly 54 percent of the popular vote and the electoral votes of forty states (Pomper 1989). In the midterm election of 1998, when the air was thick with the presidential impeachment controversy, the Republicans broke even in the Senate and suffered a net loss of five seats in the House (Jacobson 2001a). In 2000, of course, the presidential election ended in a virtual deadlock that was settled by the U.S. Supreme Court after a five-week struggle involving partisan activists, lawyers, and Florida ballot counters. Although the Republicans took back the White House that year, the party lost four Senate seats and two House seats (Jacobson 2001b).

The mixed results demonstrate that the fear of an all-powerful media is overblown. In cases both of equally negative media and of more one-sided coverage, the results offer no evidence in support of the hypodermic effects model of media influence. The media don't tell us, or at least they don't tell us in a consistently decisive and effective way, for whom we should vote. After all, positive media coverage didn't help Mondale in 1984, nor did it help the congressional Democrats in 1994.

But this doesn't mean television news coverage is unimportant. The media have powerful agenda-setting effects, particularly that of framing the story, which tell us what issues to think about and in what ways those issues should be thought about. The evidence here does not demonstrate that the media tell us what to think: otherwise we would be talking about a President Mondale, a President McCain, and a House Speaker Dick Gephardt (D-Mo.). The media negativity of our content analysis reveals that what we are told to think about by television—the horse race, candidates who seem to be scheming at every opportunity, and the human failings of those candidates—are not matters likely to make us informed citizens or congenial voters. Nor does the declining amount of coverage we have found on all networks remind us about the importance of presidential elections for us as citizens. We will return to these issues later in this chapter.

Tone in Primary Elections

The tone in coverage of presidential candidates during the nomination stage has varied far more widely than has been identified during the four presidential elections subject to the CMPA content analysis. In 2000, the Democratic candidates again received somewhat fewer positive assessments than did the Republicans. When combined, the two candidates for the Democratic nomination received a total of 43 percent positive reports. But that figure masks a very distinct difference: Bill Bradley's network news coverage was 62 percent positive in tone, as compared to Al Gore's coverage, which was only 40 percent positive. This is powerful evidence of the compensatory coverage identified in past media research. As table 4.2 shows, Bradley won the battle for the press, but Gore won the Iowa caucus, the New Hampshire primary, and every nomination contest that followed. Not all candidates are listed, as some did not receive sufficient network news coverage (a minimum of ten evaluations) to allow for meaningful content analysis.

The compensatory coverage so apparent in 2000 was also found in 1992, the year Bill Clinton won the Democratic nomination and ultimately the presidency, after overcoming scandals involving Gennifer Flowers and questions over how he evaded military service during the Vietnam War (cf. Farnsworth and Lichter 1999). Coverage of Clinton was

TABLE 4.2 Primary Election News: Tone of Coverage for Democratic Candidates, 1988–2000[a] (percentage good press)

2000	
Bill Bradley	62
Al Gore	40
Democratic candidates	43
1996	
Democratic candidates	n/a
1992	
Jerry Brown	82
Paul Tsongas	56
Bob Kerrey	52
Tom Harkin	52
Bill Clinton	37
Democratic candidates	50
1988	
Bruce Babbitt[b]	91
Jesse Jackson	70
Al Gore	48
Michael Dukakis	45
Richard Gephardt	43
Gary Hart[b]	38
Paul Simon	36
Democratic candidates	49

[a]Through the eve of the Super Tuesday primaries on March 7, 2000; March 12, 1996; and March 10, 1992. The 1988 data are through the eve of the Illinois primary on March 15, 1988. Only candidates with ten or more evaluations are reported individually.
[b]Through February 26, 1988.

far more negative in tone than the coverage of his four major rivals for the Democratic nomination that year. (Table 4.2 does not contain Democratic results for 1996, as Clinton was renominated by his party without opposition that year.)

In 1988, the most favorable evaluations of candidates were also saved for those candidates who had no realistic chance of being their party's nominee. In the 1988 Democratic nomination contest, for example, former Arizona governor Bruce Babbitt received an amazing 91 percent positive substantive evaluations, and civil rights activist Jesse Jackson received an extraordinarily high 70 percent positive substantive evaluations. Both were far ahead of the 45 percent positive substantive evaluations received by Massachusetts Governor Michael Dukakis, the eventual nominee.

Candidates who were seen as having a reasonable chance of securing the nomination received scores similar to that of Dukakis. Rep. Richard Gephardt (D-Mo.), who won the 1988 Iowa caucus, received a 43 percent positive tone. Sen. Al Gore (D-Tenn.), who emerged as a serious contender when he won five Upper South and border states on Super Tuesday, received 48 percent positive press.

Of course, being unlikely to win did not guarantee a positive tone to one's coverage. Sen. Paul Simon (D-Ill.) finished second in Iowa but third in New Hampshire, all but dooming his nomination hopes. (All eight major party nominees of the four presidential elections examined in this book finished either first or second in the pivotal New Hampshire primary.) But Simon's coverage was only 36 percent positive in tone, lower even than Gary Hart. Hart, who had waged a strong but ultimately unsuccessful campaign in the 1984 Democratic contest against Walter Mondale, was an early casualty in the race for the 1988 nomination following reports of infidelity and the subsequent derision he faced from the press pack and from the late-night comedians—Johnny Carson of NBC joked that the new Hart campaign motto should be "back in the saddle again" (quoted in Pomper 1989:37).

Table 4.3 shows the tone of network news coverage received by candidates for the Republican presidential nominations in 1988, 1992, 1996, and 2000. John McCain, who was something of a media darling throughout the 2000 primary process, received 63 percent positive press, while the tone of George W. Bush's media coverage was 53 percent positive. While no other primary candidate received the ten or more substantive evaluations necessary to be evaluated individually, the various negative evaluations of some of the other Republican candidates pushed the party average down to the 50 percent mark during the 2000 Republican primary season.

In some cases, the media's positive treatment of the Arizona senator in early 2000 did not seem entirely well-founded. CBS anchor Dan Rather, for example, described McCain as "a reformer and a hero" and "a shrewd politician . . . stirring up voters [with] his style and a heroic bio"

TABLE 4.3 Primary Election News: Tone of Coverage for Republican Candidates, 1988–2000[a] (percentage good press)

2000	
John McCain	63
George W. Bush	53
Republican candidates	50
1996	
Richard Lugar	88
Phil Gramm	67
Bob Dole	44
Pat Buchanan	43
Lamar Alexander	39
Steve Forbes	36
Bob Dornan	0
Republican candidates	43
1992	
Pat Buchanan	34
George H. W. Bush	24
Republican candidates	27
1988	
Bob Dole	60
George H. W. Bush	49
Pat Robertson	48
Jack Kemp[b]	46
Republican candidates	52

[a]Through the eve of the Super Tuesday primaries on March 7, 2000; March 12, 1996; and March 10, 1992. The1988 data are through the eve of the Illinois primary on March 15, 1988. Only candidates with ten or more evaluations are reported individually.
[b]Through February 26, 1988.

on March 1, 2000. Although McCain, a former prisoner of war in North Vietnam, is unquestionably a hero, Rather's comments about his political savvy seemed ill-timed. The night before Rather's comments, McCain had finished second to Bush in both the Virginia primary, by 53 percent to 44 percent, and the Washington primary, by 58 percent to 39 percent (Stanley 2001). A few days before those contests, McCain had criticized the "evil influence" of the Christian conservative movement on the Republican Party, a curious approach to take in Virginia, the home state of two leading Christian conservatives: Pat Robertson and Jerry Falwell (Mayer 2001). Several days later, on March 7, the allegedly politically savvy McCain lost crucial contests in California, New York, and Ohio to Bush, though he did win four less significant New England primaries (Stanley 2001). At other times, though, the media's more positive treatment did not depart so clearly from ongoing campaign events. Shortly after the New Hampshire primary, a South Carolina voter appeared on *ABC World News Tonight* to say: "Intellectually, my heart tells me I am a Democrat. And yet, my heart tells me I like McCain a lot better than I like Al Gore" (February 17, 2000).

In 1996, the most positive tone again was lavished on the candidates with little chance of winning the GOP nomination. Sen. Richard Lugar (R-Ind.), a soft-spoken foreign policy–oriented moderate unlikely to appeal to the conservative Republicans who dominate the party's primary electorate, received 88 percent positive coverage. Sen. Phil Gramm (R-Texas), who basically committed nomination suicide by suggesting that some state other than New Hampshire should hold the first primary, received 67 percent positive press. Sen. Bob Dole (R-Kans.), the eventual nominee, was further back, with 44 percent positive press. Pat Buchanan, who emerged as the leading challenger to Dole after the conservative commentator won the New Hampshire primary, received similarly lukewarm press, as his coverage was only 43 percent positive in tone. Political novice Steve Forbes, a wealthy magazine publisher who could remain in the race thanks to his willingness to spend down his immense personal fortune, received the lowest rating of any remotely viable candidate, with 36 percent positive press.

The 1992 Republican nomination contest was remarkable for its very negative media tone. The average for the two candidates was the lowest average in presidential nomination campaigns since 1988, and President George H. W. Bush's 24 percent positive evaluation was one of the lowest recorded for any candidate. Buchanan's more positive showing—34 percent positive—was not a great deal better, but the relative advantage enjoyed by this outsider candidate is consistent with the idea of compensatory journalism.

The tone of Bush's campaign coverage was more favorable in 1988, when the then vice president won his party's presidential nomination. Dole, the main Republican obstacle to Bush's plan to succeed Ronald Reagan, received the most positive press that year, again consistent with compensatory journalism. The GOP field received an average of 52 percent positive press that year, which by a narrow margin was the highest average score on the network news during the primary season.

Tables 4.2 and 4.3 can be used to compare the tone of coverage of the two parties' candidates during the nomination stage. If we use the 10-percentage-point-difference standard that we used to compare general election coverage earlier in the chapter, the score here is one win for the Democrats (1992), when the GOP faced a 50 percent to 27 percent positive coverage deficit. There were two years of less significant differences, years that favored Republicans by a less than ten-point margin: the Republicans had a 50 percent positive to 43 percent positive advantage in 2000, and a 52 percent to 49 percent advantage in 1988. There was also one year (1996) in which there can be no comparison because there was no Democratic competition to President Clinton's renomination. The pattern seen here with respect to primary coverage is consistent with that found for network news tone in general elections, where some years are virtual ties and other years favor the Democrats. The results here are also consistent with general conclusion that 1992 was a particularly good year to be a Democrat running for president, at least as far as the tone of network news coverage was concerned.

Blaming the Victim?

Reporters often criticize candidates for being too tightly managed and too uninteresting. Many journalists, like political writer Jack Germond of the *Sun* of Baltimore, say that the candidates, not the reporters, are responsible for many of the complaints over coverage that end up directed at the press. Reporters say they are only reporting the facts, warts and all (Shogan 2001). If readers and viewers have a problem with what they see and read, the politicians are largely to blame. "The politicians provide us with a campaign that's superficial, deceptive, dishonest. It's hard for reporters to change that," lamented Robert Shogan, long-time political correspondent for the *Los Angeles Times* (quoted in Owen 2002:129).

News routines create certain unavoidable demands on reporters. The first of these, a particularly powerful one for television reporters, is the need to condense available information into a brief news segment. A day's campaigning cannot and should not be repeated verbatim on the evening news. The whole program lasts only half an hour—and just over 20 minutes once the commercials are subtracted. Reporters who want their stories to make it past the producers will choose the most interesting, exciting, controversial, and revealing material for their segments, which usually run two minutes or less. Presidential candidates and their campaigns hire media experts who can help their candidate get on the air, and if they are lucky, sometimes even convince a reporter to portray candidate in a way the candidate wishes to be portrayed. The central question here is how well the picture that emerges reflects the campaign.

To examine this question, we analyzed televised candidate interviews during the 1996 campaign and compared them to network evening news presentations of the candidates. This involved 164 nationally televised interviews with presidential candidates during the primary season (January 1 through March 26) and the general election (September 2 through November 5). The interviews were broadcast or cablecast on more than twenty different programs, including the morning, evening, and Sunday news shows for all three major networks, the *NewsHour* on PBS, and a variety of CNN programs, including *Larry King Live*, *Late Edition with Frank Sesno*, *Talkback Live*, and *PrimeNews*. These 164 interviews totaled 26 hours 38 minutes of questions and answers, led by *Larry King Live*, which had 5 hours 19 minutes of interviewing and twenty-two interviews.

In the 1996 general election, Bill Clinton received 50 percent positive tone on network television's nightly newscasts during the general election period and Bob Dole received 33 percent good press (reported in table 4.1 above). Dole had far more positive reviews in the talk show interviews, with 62 percent positive evaluations. In contrast, Clinton fared worse, with only 37 percent positive evaluations in the interviews. Clinton's low score resulted from his decision to give only one TV interview during the entire fall campaign. During a September 23 interview on PBS's *NewsHour*, Clinton was asked a series of questions about Susan

McDougal's imprisonment for her refusal to cooperate with Kenneth Starr, the Whitewater independent counsel. Clinton's intimation during the interview that he believed Starr had a personal vendetta against him led to considerable media criticism from normally friendly media sources. In the wake of this experience, Clinton did not schedule another interview during the remainder of the 1996 campaign.

Dole also did not grant many interviews, apparently because of concerns that he would face allegations (which first surfaced in the *National Enquirer*) that he had committed adultery during his first marriage. Dole granted just four television interviews in the fall. A Dole aide told a *Washington Post* reporter after the election that the allegations "froze our ability to do a number of things, most importantly to have the candidate commit to television interviews" (Kurtz 1996b). Despite his positive treatment in these venues during 1996, Dole's reluctance to participate in more interviews demonstrates that the media's search for scandal can discourage candidates from participating in communication environments that are both friendly to them and useful to citizens. By sometimes scaring candidates away from these more open venues, journalists take away from voters a useful source for policy information that citizens are not likely to receive through a sound bite– and horse race–oriented evening newscast.

Most Republicans did not do badly on these interview shows during the 1996 primary campaign either. Overall, the Republican candidates in the 1996 primaries received 43 percent positive press on the network news, and three of the four leading candidates had far more positive evaluations on the interview shows. Lamar Alexander received 85 percent positive coverage on the interview programs, Pat Buchanan 74 percent, and billionaire publisher Steve Forbes 61 percent. The tone of the coverage on the evening news programs for these three candidates was 39 percent, 43 percent, and 36 percent positive, respectively. Only Dole, the GOP front-runner who stumbled in New Hampshire and struggled to win his party's nomination, faced particularly negative treatment on the interview shows, with only 31 percent positive evaluations there. The tone of his network news coverage was 44 percent positive, the only one of the four leading candidates to do better on the evening news shows than on the interview shows.

What sets these interview shows apart from traditional television news coverage, of course, is that the candidates themselves control large portions of the discussions. Nearly nine out of ten evaluative statements (88 percent) from these 164 interviews came from the candidates rather than the hosts or callers. Of course, candidates would not be expected to undermine their own campaigns, but they concentrated far more on their own virtues than on their opponents' vices. These much-less-filtered venues also allowed for far more discussion of issues than the more horse race–dominated coverage of the network nightly newscasts.

CMPA also analyzed campaign speeches given and campaign ads aired nationally by Clinton and Dole from Labor Day to Election Eve, a total of 131 speeches and 110 different commercials. Clinton's top four campaign issues were (in order) education, children, the state of the economy, and crime. Dole's leading campaign issues were taxes, drugs, the state of the economy, and Medicare. The news media agenda, however, focused on (in order) Dole's strategy, taxes, Clinton's strategy, and the state of the economy.

This comprehensive analysis shows clearly that both candidates ran issue-dominated campaigns in both their speeches and their advertisements. But their issue-dominated campaigns were heavily mediated—and distorted—by reporters, who focused far more intensely on campaign strategy than did the candidates themselves. In their ads and speeches, both the front-running incumbent and the increasingly desperate challenger offered voters far more valuable information with which to evaluate their candidacies than did the reporters covering them.

Journalists often express dismay over the negativity of candidates during the primaries, when a candidate needs to distinguish himself or herself from the pack clearly and quickly. Yet our content analysis of speeches and ads during the 1996 Republican primaries again found a positive and issue-oriented message. Contrary to the conventional wisdom, the 1996 primaries, like the general election that followed, were marked by positive and informative candidate messages that were undermined by network news coverage that selectively focused on the most negative elements. Despite Dole's overwhelmingly positive stump speeches during the primaries (78 percent positive, to be precise), a majority of Dole's sound bites (56 percent) that ran on the evening news were negative. Similarly, Dole was 56 percent positive in his advertising during the primary campaign, but reporters portrayed his advertising as being positive only 11 percent of the time. A dominant media frame for Dole was that he was somewhat ill-tempered, and that may account for these dramatic gaps between what Dole said and what the networks said Dole said (Kerbel 1998).

Buchanan saw somewhat less dramatic but nevertheless significant gaps between what he said and what the network reporters said he said. The CMPA content analysis found him to be 70 percent positive in his speeches and 45 percent positive in his advertising, but he was portrayed in the media as only 46 percent positive in speeches and a mere 13 percent positive in his advertising during the primary. Both Alexander and Forbes were also more than 70 percent positive in their speeches, though the media portrayals of their speeches fell to 48 percent and 51 percent positive, respectively.

Once again, the news media were equal-opportunity naysayers. The pattern here is clear: network news portrayed the 1996 primary and general elections far more negatively, and as far less issue-oriented, than they actually were. The 1996 results here raise general questions about the accuracy of the mediated "reality." The evidence in chapter 1 demonstrates that voters want issue-oriented campaigning and the evidence in this comparative content analysis indicates that candidates try to give citizens just that. But the reporters choke off much of that substantive and desired communication through shrinking sound bites, negativity, reduced coverage overall, and their focus on the horse race rather than substance. You can't help but wonder why candidates continue to offer up hearty portions of positive, issue-oriented campaigning when they will be served to so few people. Perhaps the candidates eventually will stop trying so hard (Kerbel 2001). Even some reporters are starting to realize they may be getting in the way of issue-based public discourse during campaigns, as demonstrated by Cathleen Decker's article in the June 11, 2000, edition of the *Los Angeles Times*.

> It is one of the strange ironies of politics: candidates expound on issues and people assume they are angling for votes. Politicians try hard, only to have people believe them less—even when they are speaking from the heart. Rarely does a candidate emerge with that trait that neither charm nor money can buy: the assumption that one wholly means what one says. (Decker, quoted in Kerbel 2001:125)

The results here again point to the utility of the media effects model. As reporters present their cynical views of candidates, citizens are being encouraged to consider candidates in that same negative light.

Poll Coverage Miscues during Campaign 2000

Of course, distortion is one thing, and simple inaccuracy is quite another, as an examination of network television's treatment of campaign polls during the 2000 general election campaign shows. Ironically, since network television coverage is dominated by horse race concerns, their reports of campaign polls suffer from an apparent confusion over proper sampling techniques, effective question design, or the uncertainty represented by the polls' margins of sampling error (Larson 2001; Owen 2002).

> The wide variation in the type of polls made it difficult for news consumers to gauge the quality of information. Polls were being conducted in quick succession, and many did not use proper sampling techniques and question design. "Instant polls" conducted overnight to gauge people's reactions to dramatic events, such as the announcement of vice presidential candidates, proliferated. These polls, often fielded using auto-dialers with recorded messages, are notoriously inaccurate, as they average a 2 percent acceptance rate of homes dialed. (Owen 2002:128)

In her study of network evening news coverage of polls during the 2000 election, media scholar Stephanie Larson (2001) found that fewer than one-quarter of the 192 network news stories that included reports of public opinion showed or mentioned the surveys' margins of error, a key component of the reliability of any survey. The stories that did include some reference to the margin of error often mangled the discussion, Larson observed:

> Word choice indicated that reporters were not sure how to talk about sampling error. On November 3, Peter Jennings claimed, "It's as close as ever. Take a look—Mr. Gore and Mr. Bush are within *shall we say* the margin of error—48 percent support for Mr. Bush and 45 percent for Mr. Gore." Dan Rather also seemed confused when he reported on September 12: "The latest CBS News/*New York Times* poll out tonight suggests Al Gore may have a very narrow edge over George Bush, but it's so small it is within the poll's *possible* margin of error." (Larson 2001:12, emphasis in original)

When results are within a survey's margin of error, as any student of public opinion knows, the determination of who is ahead or behind cannot be determined with any acceptable level of confidence. If the poll numbers for the two candidates are close enough to be within the survey's margin of error, it is appropriate to describe the results as "a statistical dead heat" or "too close to call" or some other way of saying that we do not know for sure who is actually ahead (or, more precisely, that we are not 95 percent certain that the candidate with the higher number in the poll actually is ahead of the candidate with the lower number).

If television reporters do not understand such things as margins of error (and, in fairness, reporters cannot be expected to know everything), they could turn to public opinion professionals or academics to explain such matters. Reporters often do so when reporting on other complicated issues, including economic reports, health issues, and military matters, to name just three. But reporters rarely turn to polling experts, at least not on-air. Larson (2001) found that 87 percent of network news stories featuring poll results did not use experts to interpret the polls on-air, an obvious way for reporters to provide viewers with an interpretation for something that the reporters themselves apparently do not understand.

Further, some of the experts who were used to answer questions of public opinion were not always being fair and objective. NBC was censured by the National Council of Public Polls for using Republican pollster Frank Luntz as an allegedly objective public opinion analyst (Owen 2002:128). "This stuff is rough and ready, and would hardly pass anyone's test of gauging a representative sample of voters. I don't know what purpose it serves journalistically or in terms of research," Andrew Kohut, director of the Pew Research Center for the People and the Press, said of Luntz's appearances on NBC (quoted in Owen 2002:128).

In a finding consistent with the horse race orientation of network news coverage, Larson (2001) found that few news reports included references to questions other than who was ahead and who was behind—only 1 percent of the reports she examined included discussion of responses to a question relating to which candidate would make a better leader, for example.

The difficulties network news programs had in interpreting the polls during the fall campaign should have made network news reporters and editors doubly concerned about how their limited ability to make sense of survey research might be further compromised in the high-pressure, uncertain, and anxious environment of highly competitive Election Night reporting. Indeed, there was some concern early on that evening that television reporters should be careful. But that concern was soon brushed aside in the rush to be first to "call" a state for one of the candidates. The result was the most irresponsible and error-ridden night in the history of television news.

The Election Night 2000 Mess

For months, the national surveys had moved back and forth between George W. Bush and Al Gore. For part of Campaign 2000, Bush was ahead; at other times Gore held the lead. The surveys conducted in the final days before the first presidential election of the twenty-first century indicated that the contest had become too close to call. Pundits began to speculate that one candidate might win the popular vote, while the other would win in the Electoral College, something that had not happened in more than a century. Election Day was marked by early-morning campaign rallies and feverish get-out-the-vote drives in closely contested states. As the polls began to close in the Eastern states, the network news teams settled in for what many expected would be a long night. But no one expected that the hours of uncertainty would ultimately stretch into days and then weeks (Ceaser and Busch 2001).

Rather than wait for the votes to be counted, a process that can take many hours to determine a winner under normal circumstances, many news organization rely on exit polls to forecast winners. Workers ask people in selected precincts whom they voted for as a way of perceiving larger trends in a state. Every state has towns or counties that are overwhelmingly Democratic, others that are overwhelmingly Republican, and still others that could tip either way, depending on the candidates and the issues in a given election. In Florida, for example, Democratic candidates are likely to prevail in places like those that have become part of American political lore, including Broward and Palm Beach counties. Republicans are likely to do very well in many of the northern tier counties of the Florida Panhandle, jurisdictions like Okaloosa and Clay counties (Fiedler 2002). Still other counties are "swing" counties, as they swing back and forth from one party to another, depending on the particulars of a given election.

By sampling precincts in counties with different voting patterns, exit pollsters can get an indication of such things as whether turnout is high in normally Democratic jurisdictions, whether a Republican candidate isn't keeping pace with past Republican patterns in overwhelmingly GOP counties, and whether groups of swing voters, like the so-called soccer moms, are tending Republican or Democratic. Put a number of these factors together, combine them with early official returns, and polling experts may be able to predict a winner in an election several hours before all the votes are counted.

Of course, making a prediction is not the same as making a correct one. There are things that exit polls cannot do, such as determining the significance of the absentee ballots (which in Florida in 2000 need not even have arrived at state election offices by Election Day), or whether voters actually cast their ballots in a valid, countable manner. Both of these matters turned out to be highly significant to the outcome of the presidential election in Florida. Large numbers of absentee votes for Bush were received by election officials in the days following the election, primarily from military personnel on duty outside the United States on November 7. In fact, a *New York Times* investigation subsequently concluded that some of the absentee ballots were counted as legitimate despite having no postmark and in some cases despite having been cast after Election Day, circumstances in violation of Florida law (Barstow and Van Natta 2001). In addition, thousands of voters in Palm Beach County—a county with large numbers of African Americans and Jewish Americans—apparently mistakenly invalidated their ballots or accidentally cast a vote for Reform Party nominee Pat Buchanan, whose opposition to affirmative action, criticism of U.S. aid to Israel, and expressed skepticism concerning U.S. involvement in World War II against Hitler would hardly have made him an appealing choice to large numbers of voters in that jurisdiction. Experts believe most of the 3,400 votes Buchanan received in Palm Beach County were almost certainly the result of a poorly designed "butterfly ballot" that generated considerable attention in the days following the election (Fiedler 2002; Pomper 2001).

In addition to the bizarre factors that undermined the legitimacy of the exit polls in Florida in 2000—factors that even cast doubts in many minds about the legitimacy of the actual vote count in the state—exit polls are not immune from the normal sources of error that are a fact of life for any survey. No matter how carefully designed, a survey that asks some people how they will vote or did vote as a proxy for determining how everyone in a group voted will always have risks: one side may be oversampled and the other side may be undersampled. This basic factor should lead to caution on the part of anyone calling elections on the basis of exit polls, as is done routinely in American news programming. Exit polls may be particularly prone to bias because of who would and would not participate—it may be much easier to answer questions over the phone at home in the evening than to fill out a survey while rushing back to work or to pick up the kids at day care. Finally, voters who refuse to cooperate may skew the sample.

During the afternoon of Election Day, while the entire country was still voting, the first early and erroneous returns were trickling in to the television networks affiliated with the Voter News Service (VNS). Before 2 P.M., network executives had in their hands exit poll results suggesting that Gore was going to lose Pennsylvania, a key state in Gore's Electoral College strategy. Those results, soon to be discovered as erroneous, were withdrawn by VNS before 5 P.M. (Greenfield 2001; Mnookin 2001). Although not released to the public that day, those results offered a powerful, early warning sign to journalists that the VNS models had major problems, as Jeff Greenfield of CNN noted:

> At 4:47 P.M., VNS sent out a reassuring alert to subscribers: "The problems with the [Pennsylvania] survey weighting are cleared up. We have cleaned out the bad precinct problems." This was not all that reassuring to CNN co-anchor Judy Woodruff, who was openly uneasy about a vote-gathering operation—the only vote-gathering operation—deciding in the middle of Election Day that its model might have a bug or two in it. It was, said another colleague, like looking out the window of a jumbo jet ten minutes before departure time, and noticing a group of mechanics huddling around engine number 4 shaking their heads and flipping through the maintenance manual. (Greenfield 2001:56)

Gore, by the way, ended up winning Pennsylvania by a 51 percent to 47 percent margin, with a plurality of more than 204,000 votes (Nelson 2001).

When the evening campaign coverage began, the network anchors promised to be very careful as they sorted through the exit polls and the election returns that would be coming in during the subsequent hours. As Dan Rather of CBS offered: "Let's get one thing straight from the get-go. . . . We would rather be last in reporting returns than to be wrong. . . . If we say someone has carried a state, you can pretty much take it to the bank" (quoted in Sabato 2002:112).

The Voter News Service was hired by ABC, CBS, NBC, CNN, Fox News, and the Associated Press to be their collective exit pollster in the 2000 election. Dozens of other media outlets, including some of the nation's largest newspapers, also pay to use the VNS data. Ironically, the networks pooled their resources in the 2000 election, as they had in the 1992 and 1996 presidential contests, to improve the quality of the exit polling beyond a level that would have been affordable for any one news outlet (Sabato 2002). What actually happened was that this collective arrangement, together with the normal journalistic fears of being beaten to the story by competitors, led all the networks to make the same mistakes at the same time. The limitations of polling may not make much difference in one-sided elections, but there is a world of difference between a first place finish of 51 percent and a second place finish of 49 percent.

There was one other reason for the reporters to be highly cautious in their use of VNS estimates. The networks had already learned that the Voter News Service can make mistakes. In 1996, for example, the VNS provided exit poll data that indicated that Sen. Bob Smith (R-N.H.) had been defeated in his bid for re-election. Television anchors called the contest in favor of Dick Swett, but when the votes were counted, Smith emerged victorious (Greenfield 2001; Mnookin 2001).

Everyone expected Florida to be one of the most important states in the close presidential contest, and an early call that one candidate had won Florida's 25 electoral votes would have a dramatic impact on the overall election. Early on, Clinton adviser-turned-media-pundit George Stephanopoulos told ABC's viewers to watch three states: Pennsylvania, Michigan, and Florida. "Whoever wins two of those three states should be in the driver's seat tonight," Stephanopoulos said (quoted in Sabato 2002:112).

By 8 P.M. all six media outlets behind the VNS had officially placed Florida's electoral votes in Gore's column. All relied on the same faulty VNS data, which seemed more and more questionable as the actual precinct-by-precinct returns came in (Owen 2002). During the next two hours, a number of Republicans started criticizing the networks for what they claimed were faulty calls on the state (Greenfield 2001). By 10 P.M. or so, all the networks reported computer problems, returned this crucial state to the "undecided" column and said they were sorry. "To err is human, but to really foul up requires a computer," Rather said during one of his election night mea culpas on CBS. "If you're disgusted with us, frankly, I don't blame you" (quoted in Owen 2002: 123). Humility was likewise the order of the day in the following CNN exchange over Florida.

> *Bernard Shaw:* Stand by, stand by—CNN right now is moving our earlier declaration of Florida back to the too close to call. . . .
> *Jeff Greenfield:* Oh waiter. . . .
> *Shaw*: Into the too close to call column.
> *Greenfield:* One order of crow.
> *Bill Schneider:* One order of crow, yes. (quoted in Mnookin 2001:150)

In the undecided column was where the state remained until shortly after 2 A.M. Wednesday morning. At that time, a cousin of George W. Bush, the Republican nominee, working as a vote counter at Fox News, declared that the Republicans had taken that crucial state, the state containing the electoral votes that would decide the next president. The other television networks followed suit immediately, with the same sense of security with which they had proclaimed a Gore victory in the state several hours earlier. The networks' sense of certainty was back, despite having been so powerfully humbled a few hours before. As Rather said shortly before 2:30 A.M.: "Bush wins. . . . That's it. . . . Sip it. Savor it. Cup it. Photostat it. Underline it in red. Put it in an album. Hang it on a wall" (quoted in Sabato 2002:113).

The networks' certainty during those early morning hours were sufficient to trigger a telephone call from Gore to Bush to concede. The dejected Gore team began to make their way to a campaign rally to deliver a concession speech. But something happened on the way to the rally: the supposed Bush lead in Florida vanished, and VNS and the networks were shown to have missed the Florida call once again. Gore then called Bush to retract his concession and canceled his planned public appearance (Owen 2002).

Over at the networks, doubts also began to resurface. As the minutes ticked by, the actual returns continued to show that Gore and Bush remained locked in a neck-and-neck race and Gore was not making the concession speech that everyone had been told to expect. "Good grief," Tom

Brokaw said on NBC at 3:27 A.M. on November 8, as the returns suggested no one had clearly won Florida. "That would be something if the networks managed to blow it twice in the same night" (quoted in Sabato 2002:113).

As the hours of uncertainty passed, and as Florida was pulled back once again into the undecided column, the comments from the weary and repeatedly humbled anchors become increasingly strange. "Frankly, we don't know whether to run, to watch, or bark at the moon. We just don't know what to do under these circumstances," said CBS's Rather at 4:10 A.M. on November 8 (quoted in Mnookin 2001:98).

Things were even more bizarre at the ABC News studio an hour or so later, as Peter Jennings and Stephanopoulos had the following "heated" exchange at 5:30 A.M. on November 8:

> *Jennings:* Okay, I hate to tell you, we're also on fire here at the moment. . . . Yes, please, go ahead. We're not always right, but we're very efficient. Thanks, gentlemen, very much. You know, it's a very—I mean I realize at this late hour of the night we're probably broadcasting to ourselves in many respects, but it's a very good time for me to say thank you to the local fire department.
>
> *Stephanapoulos:* Wow, the smell.
>
> *Jennings:* You talk, I'll check the fire. (quoted in Mnookin 2001:98)

There actually was an early morning fire in the ABC studio, one that was put out relatively quickly. But what Election Night 2000 actually incinerated was the networks' credibility, their most precious but highly flammable asset. Television news was not alone in its media malpractice, however. Overall, the media's handling of this story was a widespread "Dewey Beats Truman" failure, to quote the famously erroneous 1948 *Chicago Tribune* headline that Truman never tired of ridiculing (Karabell 2000). The *New York Times* released 100,000 papers stating that Bush "appears to have won," while the *New York Post* boldly proclaimed "Bush Wins!" (Owen 2002:141). Many other newspapers also prematurely called the election for Bush, including the *Miami Herald*, *San Francisco Chronicle*, and *Atlanta Journal-Constitution* (Owen 2002:141).

Although the morning-after focus was on the miscalls in Florida, VNS and the networks also bobbled a number of other projections on Election Night. Early reports that Virginia—a reliably Republican state that has not given its electoral votes to a Democrat since 1964—was too close to call proved terribly wrong as Bush ultimately carried the state by a comfortable 52 percent to 45 percent margin (Owen 2002; Sabato 2002). VNS and the networks also called New Mexico for Gore too soon, and the networks had to recall that early finding as well (Sabato 2002). They also prematurely called the Washington State U.S. Senate race for Democrat Maria Cantwell, even though the race was finally decided by absentee ballots that took several days to count (Mnookin 2001). Although Gore did in the end win New Mexico by a narrow margin—well under 1,000 votes—and although Cantwell was eventually found to have defeated incumbent Slade Gorton narrowly, these contests clearly were too close to have been called on Election Night (Owen 2002; Sabato 2002). That, after all, is why the calls based on insufficient evidence were retracted later on during that chaotic evening.

Media analyst Seth Mnookin, who surveyed the wreckage of network television news on Election Night for *Brill's Content*, concluded:

> These mistakes combine to paint of picture of VNS' model as seriously flawed. On the basis of about 30 close races nationwide—senatorial, gubernatorial and statewide presidential races that were decided by 5 percentage points or less—VNS fumbled three calls, or 10 percent of those it was hired to make. (Mnookin 2001:151)

In fact, Mnookin was generous in his analysis, counting only Florida, New Mexico, and the Washington Senate race as clear mistakes. He did not include the early afternoon mess in Pennsylvania, nor does he count the erroneous first reports of "too close to call" in the races in Virginia, North Carolina, and Ohio (all easy Bush wins) as mistakes. Nor did Mnookin count Florida as two separate mistakes, which he could have done since VNS and the networks called the presidential race in the state incorrectly twice in the same night.

We should probably mention, in passing, that political scientists who try to determine presidential election outcomes on the basis of macroeconomic statistics also turned out to be poor prognosticators in 2000. The average forecast for a Gore victory among the seven most cited academic models predicted Gore would get 56.2 percent of the two-party vote; in the end he received 50.2 percent of the votes cast either for himself or Bush. Political scientists tended to blame Gore's campaign blunders, not the mathematical models themselves, for the poor predictions (Campbell 2001; Lewis-Beck and Tien 2001; Wlezien 2001).

As the day after Election Day dawned, armies of campaign lawyers and partisan activists were making plans to go to Florida to monitor recounts and perhaps prepare legal arguments. Even in the early morning hours of "the day after," it was clear that this was going to be a postelection like no other in American history (Klain and Bash 2002; Terwilliger 2002; Tapper 2001, 2002). What came next in the presidential election saga, the five weeks of recounted ballots and legal maneuvers, has been described extensively and from a variety of perspectives in the many books that have examined the 2000 election and the postelection process (Bugliosi 2001; Ceaser and Busch 2001; Greenfield 2001; Pomper 2001; Sabato 2002; R. Simon 2001; Sunstein and Epstein 2001; Tapper 2001; *Washington Post* 2001). Ironically, network television's coverage of the weeks that followed deserves considerable credit, particularly in comparison to the election night (and morning after) fiasco. Reporters immediately recognized the magnitude of this story: the Election 2000 deadlock produced 183 network newscasts during the first week (November 8–14, 2000) alone. That exceeded the first week's coverage of such megastories as the 1999 death of John F. Kennedy Jr. (148 stories), the 1995 Oklahoma City bombing (146 stories), the 1999 Colorado high school killings (142 stories), and the Clinton/Lewinsky scandal (142 stories).

The resources devoted to the postelection allowed for extensive network news coverage of the complicated and rapidly changing scandal. Without a full-fledged horse race to report upon—though there was of course some jockeying for an advantage in public opinion—the coverage moved in a more responsible and factual direction in the weeks following Election Night. It may come as no surprise that the 2000 election was the top network news story of 2000, with 2,420 stories on the evening news programs of the Big Three networks. But who could have predicted that the coverage *after* Election Day (812 stories) would be higher than that of either the primary season (550 stories) or the general election (462 stories)?

In a February 14, 2001, Congressional hearing called to examine the networks' performance on November 7 and 8, 2000, television executives pronounced themselves deeply embarrassed by their Election Night coverage (Kurtz 2001a). They said they would continue to use exit polls in their coverage, but they would try to fix the problems before the next election. The executives called for a law that would require all national polls to close at the same time, in part to reduce the possibility that the early returns reported from early poll-closing Eastern states would depress turnout in Western states, which have later closing times (Kurtz 2001a).

Fox News came under considerable criticism from Democratic lawmakers at that hearing for allowing John Ellis, a first cousin of both George W. Bush and Florida Governor Jeb Bush, to make Fox's pro-Bush call in Florida, a move rapidly followed by the other networks in those early morning hours. Ellis, who talked to both of his cousins on Election Night, was also harshly criticized by political writer Robert Shogan of the *Los Angeles Times:*

> The opportunity he eagerly granted his cousin to influence his judgment was a manifest betrayal of those Americans who watched Fox on election night in the innocent belief that its projections would be made by someone who was not personally involved with one of the protagonists. (2001:264)

Ellis, and the network's decision to place him in such a prominent role, was defended by Fox News President Roger Ailes, who described Ellis as "a consummate professional" who acted "as a good journalist talking to his very high-level sources" (quoted in Kurtz 2001a:C8).

The hearing offered one final caution to network news organizations who plan to rely on exit polls in the future. Whatever limitations in terms of reliability these surveys now have may increase in the future, at least if citizens follow the advice of Rep. Billy Tauzin (R-La.), chairman of the House Energy and Commerce Committee. "Americans don't like exit polls," Tauzin remarked at the hearing. "Perhaps they ought to adopt a simple strategy and that's to lie about how they voted" (quoted in Kurtz 2001a:C8).

Consequences of Negativity: Cynicism and Apathy

It is clear from past research that today's television and newspaper reports concerning government and politicians are far more negative than they were in the past (cf. Kerbel 1995; Patterson 1994; Sabato 2000; Sabato et al. 2000). The research in this chapter likewise documents considerable negativity in the media coverage of recent presidential elections.

But scholars disagree over what this increased negativity means for American government and politics. A key problem is the inability to demonstrate consistently that media impacts are as powerful or as destructive as many scholars expect. As political scientist Larry Bartels observed: "The scholarly literature has been much better at refuting, qualifying, and circumscribing the thesis of media impact than at supporting it" (1993:267). But Bartels attributed many of the problems to measurement error and research design difficulties, not to a lack of media effects. He was not advocating a return to the days of minimal effects. Instead, he was worried that scholars would try to morph the "more-than-minimal" media effects model back into the "hypodermic effects" perspective, the highly influential model that is not supported by most contemporary research.

The pervasive media negativity found in coverage of recent presidential elections can trigger dire consequences for the polity, cutting to the heart of our democratic traditions, according to some media researchers.

> For most men [and women] most of the time, politics is a series of pictures in the mind, placed there by television news, newspapers, magazines, discussions. The pictures create a moving panorama taking place in a world the mass public never quite touches, yet one its members come to fear or cheer, often with passion and sometimes with action. (Edelman 1985:5)

Media scholar Michael Robinson (1976), a leading early researcher into questions of how news programs related to public opinion change, developed the concept of "videomalaise" to describe how media exposure can increase citizen cynicism and negativity. Subsequent researchers also found that the downbeat coverage offered by jaded post-Vietnam, post-Watergate reporters leads to heightened citizen frustration, which can bring about an increase in the number of citizens "tuning out" from news and perhaps even politics (cf. Putnam 2000; Jamieson 2000).

Thomas Patterson (1994) found that rising citizen dissatisfaction with candidates tracks the increasingly negative coverage those candidates have received from journalists. In the 1960s, a period of far more positive press evaluations of candidates, the only major party nominee who received negative public marks was Barry Goldwater, the highly controversial 1964 GOP nominee. By 1980, half the people polled said that they were unhappy with the major party nominees; in 1988 more citizens said they felt negatively than positively about Michael Dukakis and George Bush; and in 1992, 40 percent of those surveyed wished they had someone else to choose from besides presidential candidates Ross Perot, Bill Clinton, and Bush (Patterson 1994:21–24). "Politicians are not saints, but when the balance of coverage tilts so strongly in the negative direction, the election cannot serve as it should to raise the quality of public life," wrote Patterson (1994:202).

Political scientist Russell Neuman (1986) said that the news media—particularly television—contribute to a fragmentary, haphazard understanding of issues through their generally entertainment-oriented (and superficial) coverage. Media critic Neil Postman (1985) agreed, saying we are "amusing ourselves to death" as we watch what he considered to be the insultingly trivialized reporting found in television news programming. The harsh and sometimes simplistic news reports, these scholars (and others) have concluded, leads to increased citizen cynicism with politicians and may trigger greater alienation with respect to the government as well.

Experimental evidence supports this proposition. Citizens exposed to a heavier diet of strategic, or horse race, campaign news generated higher levels of cynicism than those exposed to coverage that was less focused on the "game schema" of politics (Cappella and Jamieson 1997). When they consumed news about as policy-oriented a matter as health care reform, citizens exposed to more strategic-oriented news showed greater cynicism about the political process than they had previously possessed. Indeed, the evidence that news activates cynicism is so strong that the researchers raise the possibility that at least some citizens exposed to years of negative coverage of government and politics are perceiving politics and policy though an overall negative frame that dominates one's thoughts about politics:

> A public that has accepted the belief that officials are acting in their own self-interest rather than in the interest of the common weal can be easily primed to see self-promotion in every political act. When journalists frame political events strategically, they activate existing beliefs and understandings; they do not need to create them. (Cappella and Jamieson 1997:208)

Above all, says political scientist Roderick Hart, today's negatively oriented media coverage of politics tends to suggest that elections and politicians are not worth much respect. "We tower above politics by making it seem beneath us," Hart (1994:8) wrote. But he noted that this erroneous public impression of politics as just another form of gossip is dangerous to us all:

> [Democracy is] imperiled (1) when its people do not know what they think they know and (2) when they do not care about what they do not know. Television miseducates the citizenry, but worse, it makes that miseducation attractive. (Hart 1994:12)

The very act of watching television has come under suspicion of undermining democracy, according to Robert Putnam (1995a, 1995b, 2000), who is one of the best-known researchers on how citizen discontent may be undermining any sense of community in this country. In his widely read *Bowling Alone* (2000), Putnam blames the mass media for much of the disintegration of our sense of common purpose. He also blames the media for much of our declining interest in interacting with each other to achieve any collective end, even a relatively modest activity like operating a community bowling league. To illustrate the magnitude of this media-abetted change, Putnam contrasts the sacrifices of the World War II generation—a group some have called "the greatest generation"—with today's greater self-centeredness. Sixty years ago those on the home front bought bonds, saved scrap metal, and accepted food and gasoline rationing to help defeat Hitler. Today, in contrast, many people cannot even be civil on the nation's highways and take the time to cast a ballot for president once every four years. Of course, the surge of patriotism that followed the September 11, 2001, attacks on the World Trade Center and the Pentagon may have revived, at least temporarily, the public-mindedness last seen in America more than a half century ago.

Some scholars think that media critics like Putnam have gone too far in their condemnations. Studies show that high consumers of television news tend to have high levels of interest in politics and actually are more likely to vote than those who do not consume news (Norris 1996). Researchers have also found that critical coverage of specific issues, even of the highly charged Vietnam War, does not necessarily trigger declines in support for the political system (Hallin 1984).

> Television news may be objective, but it is far from neutral. The production of news takes place within boundaries established by official sources

> and dominant values. . . . We see television news as a cautious and conservative medium, much more likely to defend traditional values and institutions than attack them. (Iyengar and Kinder 1987:133)

Along the same lines, these researchers argue that media effects actually add up to system-building activities, even as reporters may criticize individual politicians through episodic coverage (Iyengar 1991). Citizen reactions depend on the ways a given issue is framed. Television and newspapers can, for example, act as boundary-maintaining institutions that declare certain types of criticism off-limits, too threatening for mass dissemination (Ginsberg 1986). For example, the way scandals are framed can actually help political leaders remain in power. Although the nation's media outlets severely criticized President Clinton throughout the Clinton/Lewinsky scandal and the subsequent impeachment trial, many reporters and citizens came to view the incident as a personal failing, not as a reason to throw a still-popular president out of office (Owen 2000). The same incident could have been presented quite differently. It could have been used as evidence against the political system itself, for the system allowed such a self-centered, ambitious, and ultimately self-destructive man to rise to the pinnacle of power in America (Owen 2000; Sabato et al. 2000).

Election Coverage, Cynicism, and Apathy

Returning to the network's treatment of recent presidential elections, we see certain embedded messages in news coverage that relate to citizen cynicism and apathy. As network television cuts back on coverage and devotes less time to matters of substance and to the candidates themselves, the voters may be learning an important lesson, one that is not particularly appealing for a democracy. The embedded message contained in these network news trends is simple: presidential campaigns are not worth much of our attention, and the candidates themselves are worth only a tiny fraction of that concern. While there are many, many factors that affect voter turnout in presidential elections—education, income, intensity of partisanship, and age are among the key issues—it is nevertheless interesting to note that voter turnout has declined along with the reduced network news coverage of presidential elections. Table 4.4 shows the per-

TABLE 4.4 Network Coverage and Voter Turnout, 1988–2000

	Campaign as Percentage of Network News				*Voter Turnout (%)*	
	ABC	CBS	NBC	Total	of Registered Voters	of Voting-Age Population
Campaign '00	23	18	22	21	68	51
Campaign '96	20	20	19	20	66	49
Campaign '92	40	39	40	40	78	55
Campaign '88	27	30	26	28	72	50

Source: U.S. Federal Election Commission and CMPA data.

Note: TV news data from CMPA content analysis of ABC, CBS and NBC evening newscasts during general election campaigns. 2000 data based on 462 stories from September 4 to November 6, 2000; 1996 data based on 483 stories from September 2 to November 4, 1996; 1992 data based on 727 stories from September 7 to November 3, 1992; 1988 data based on 589 stories from September 5 to November 7, 1988. CBS was preempted more often in 2000 due to NFL coverage on Sundays.

Calculations for 1988, 1996, and 2000 based on 64-day period/192 possible newscasts; calculations for 1992 based on 57-day period/171 possible newscasts.

centage of campaign news in the last four presidential elections and the voter turnout in those same elections.

Voter turnout is measured in two ways in table 4.4. The far right column considers voter turnout as a percentage of the entire voting-age population, and the second column from the right measures voter turnout as a percentage of registered voters. While only registered voters can vote, passage of the Motor-Voter law in the early days of the Clinton administration led to an increase in the number of registered voters for the 1996 and 2000 presidential contests. But having more people registered did not lead to a commensurate rise in the number of ballots cast. In fact the increased number of voters signed up under the Motor-Voter law is an important reason why the percentage of registered voters who actually voted fell so far between 1992 and 1996. The voting age population number, therefore, is the more useful measure for comparison. The lowest-turnout presidential election year by either measure, 1996, was also the year with the least amount of campaign news. Both the percentage of time on the nightly newscasts and the percentage of the voting age population bumped up slightly in the 2000 election. The 1992 campaign, which had by far the largest amount of news coverage of the four elections considered here, also had the highest turnout of these four elections.

Of course, correlation does not demonstrate causality. Just because two measures move in the same direction—and with roughly the same magnitude—does not mean that one causes the other, or even that they are related to each other in any way. Obviously many factors are at work in these elections. The relatively high turnout in 1992—relatively high for American elections, that is—was at least partly the result of the aggressive independent campaign waged by Ross Perot. Perot's presence in the 1992 race gave Americans an unusually strong third option in that presidential election and that drew some people to the polls who would otherwise have been nonvoters. On the other hand, Perot's campaign was a media-driven one, starting with the friendly treatment he received on *Larry King Live*, continuing through his positive early news coverage, and finally through his own widely viewed paid network television infomercials. While Perot clearly struck an appealing chord to some voters, do not forget that it was television—and $60 million of his own money, much of it spent to purchase television time—that allowed his song to be heard.

In addition, researchers at Harvard University's Vanishing Voter Project found a correlation between media coverage of the campaign and public interest in the contest.

> The Vanishing Voter Project (VVP) discovered that public interest in and discussion of the campaign peaked when press coverage was high and diminished when it was low. Key campaign events, such as heated primary contests, conventions and debates can drive up civic engagement. (Owen 2002:130)

These results can be coupled with the work of a number of other researchers who suggest that recent trends in media coverage have exacerbated public cynicism (Jamieson 2000; Putnam 2000). Veteran *Washington Post* political writer David Broder, who often spends a great deal of time interviewing ordinary citizens as he prepares his reports, likewise has long argued that media (and candidate) cynicism leads voters to turn away from civic involvement, and he has urged journalists to become more "partisan . . . on behalf of the process" (Broder 1990).

These results suggest that more network television coverage of campaigns would not hurt, and might even help, overall voter turnout, one of the most important ways that America falls short of its ideals of a highly participatory democratic society. Low turnout is also a major way in which America lags far behind other Western democracies. Just over half, 51 percent, of the voting age population in the United States voted in the tight 2000 election, as compared to over 60 percent turnout in national elections in Canada, France, Mexico, and Russia; over 70 percent turnout in Britain and Israel; and over 80 percent turnout in Denmark, Germany, and South Africa (Lowi et al. 2002:425).

Conclusion

Over the past several chapters, we have demonstrated that the evening network news broadcasts do a poor job of telling the electorate what they need to know to evaluate candidates for president effectively. The amount of coverage has fallen during every phase of recent elections, including the primaries, the general election, and even the primary "preseason." The smaller amount of coverage that remains is increasingly focused on handicapping the horse race, rather than considering matters of substance. Even in those instances when issues are discussed, they are often discussed in terms of their political impact. In Patterson's words, the "game" frame dominates, leaving viewers with a sense of politicians as scoundrels. Candidates get little opportunity to speak for themselves, as the average length of a sound bite has fallen to less than eight seconds. Anchors and reporters hog the reduced airtime that remains, even though they aren't running for anything, and they spent a lot of that time talking about themselves. In addition, reporters and producers air far more negative than positive assessments about candidates, and reporters and anchors have a very unsatisfying record on that cardinal journalist matter of just plain getting the facts right.

Several decades ago, media theorist Marshall McLuhan argued that "the medium is the message." But the evidence shows that in presidential campaigns the message matters a great deal to candidates and voters. So what messages do network television news programs offer us? The short sound bites and shrinking amount of news coverage of elections tell us that presidential candidates aren't worth listening to for long, and that presidential campaigns don't deserve much of our attention. The horse race–dominated coverage tells us that issues don't really matter much either. The embarrassing way the networks made mistake after mistake on Election Night 2000 raises questions about how seriously they really take their central mission of being responsible, fair, and accurate transmitters of critically important information. The heavily mediated and negative coverage of Campaign 2000 told us that neither the Democratic liar nor the Republican lightweight deserved to be president. And the lack of coverage of third-party candidates like Ralph Nader and Pat Buchanan tells us they don't even exist. (Ironically, the votes of both of these candidates turned out to be decisive in Florida. Gore would have won Florida with a fraction of either Nader's 97,000 votes in the state or less than one-quarter of the 3,400 apparently mistaken votes recorded for Buchanan in Palm Beach County.)

This multicount indictment of network news is particularly troubling in light of the central role that the news media play in linking citizens to candidates. Since few of us ever meet presidential candidates in person, our views of Gore, Bush, Clinton, Dole, and the rest develop largely from what we learn about them from the mass media. And if we rely on network television's evening newscasts, the flagship public representation of some of the world's largest companies—General Electric (NBC), Disney (ABC), and Viacom (CBS)—we are not in a position to learn much beyond the basic fact that candidates are not nearly as important as reporters, that the candidates' positions and records don't matter much, and perhaps that neither major party candidate deserves our vote. Of course, the networks' Election Night 2000 inaccuracies might also send an unintended message that the networks don't deserve our confidence any more than the candidates do.

Although the performance of network television leaves much to be desired, it is by no means impossible to do better, either in print or on television. We examine alternative media approaches in chapter 5, which compares network television's news coverage of presidential elections to that of PBS, the *New York Times*, the *Wall Street Journal*, the *Washington Post,* and CNN. We also compare network news coverage to the campaign discourse of the candidates themselves in the next chapter.

Notes

1. Additional data analysis showed that the inclusion of partisan evaluations did not significantly alter the tonal balance between Bush and Gore. However, we could not make longitudinal comparisons, because only nonpartisan source evaluations were coded for all four elections.

2. These factors help to explain why our results run counter to those of a study released during the campaign by the Committee of Concerned Journalists (2000), an organization whose goal is to improve the quality of news coverage. Because the committee's study was reported as demonstrating more favorable coverage toward Bush, it may be useful to catalogue the sampling and methodological constraints that prevent this conclusion from being sustained by the evidence. First, the CCJ study was based on a story-level analysis that conflated comments about viability and desirability. Second, the sample from which the findings were drawn was a collection of local and national news outlets, along with web sites and opinion journals, such as *Salon* and *National Review*, and local and network television. By releasing the marginals from this heterogeneous sample, the committee mixed apples and oranges. Third, and most problematic, the study's time frame consisted of three nonconsecutive weeks in late September and October. Unfortunately, these weeks turned out not to be representative of the tone for the entire campaign. Our study found that the coverage shifted in Bush's favor during most of this period, and his positive desirability ratings were reinforced by even more positive viability ratings. When we re-analyzed our data to replicate the sample and method used in the CCJ study, we too found a tilt in Bush's favor. But this tilt was an artifact of the committee's methodology, rather than an accurate reflection of overall general election coverage.

3. Just et al. (1996) found no clear tilt in terms of visual images in 1992. CMPA coded shot-by-shot visuals during the same contest and similarly found no clear pattern. We also concluded that few images could be reliably categorized for tone in a fashion that met the criteria of reliability and validity, that is, replicable judgments that were substantively meaningful.

4. Hofstetter (1976) found negative but balanced network news coverage in the 1972 race between Nixon and McGovern. Unfortunately his coding system conflated what we have termed the viability and desirability dimensions of evaluative content. Robinson and Sheehan (1983:311) cite this problem as a major drawback of this study, which "relied almost totally on references to success or failure as a measure of good press or bad." This convinced them to separate the two dimensions in their analysis of the 1980 campaign.

CHAPTER 5

"*NOBODY* DOES IT BETTER"?
The Networks versus Other Campaign News Sources

After every presidential election, the television networks promise to do better next time. They vow to offer coverage that is more substantive and less devoted to the horse race, coverage that will educate the public about what the candidates would do if elected. The networks intend to provide more detailed coverage on what the candidates stand for and give them more of a chance to make their cases to the country in their own words. So they say, every four years.

Unfortunately, when these promises are put to the test of systematic analysis, we find that they have been broken just as regularly as they were made. On Election Night 2000, as we discussed in chapter 4, the networks failed even on the central journalistic concern of being accurate. By nearly every measure, evening news coverage of Campaign 2000 was at best no better, and sometimes worse, than the coverage of the 1996, 1992, and 1988 campaigns. The declines were most evident in general election coverage, but were echoed in the primary season as well.

We are far from the first researchers to find fault with television's election coverage. But our empirical analysis is based on one of the deepest and most wide-ranging quantitative critiques ever applied to network news. By basing our analysis on each individual sound bite rather than entire stories, and by examining every story during an election season rather than looking only at samples, we can determine in a far more extensive and precise way just how poor and how much worse a job television news has done in campaign coverage in recent elections. Our comparisons, using the same measures across several elections, allow us to plot a clear trajectory of network television's coverage of presidential campaigns since the 1988 contest. The resulting trends are not encouraging for either television's potential or its past performance. The television networks do such a poor job on these important issues that even the self-interested candidates offer more information about their policies, and provide that information with a far more positive orientation, than do the reporters' accounts of those same campaigns. As this chapter demonstrates, we have come to a point in American journalism where the campaign speeches and advertisements of candidates—so widely disparaged as the self-interested pleadings of the desperately ambitious—compare favorably to news media accounts.

Despite the explosion of mass information sources in recent years, the broadcast evening news programs remain the industry leaders during presidential campaigns, attracting a vastly larger news audience than any other news genre. To the extent we have a national discussion about the future of the country during a presidential contest, it occurs largely on these network evening news programs. The poorer the performance of television news, the poorer our polity. Citizens with better information can make more meaningful choices among the candidates and their issues. As it is now, television offers little more than warped portraits of horse race coverage framed by cynical media carping regarding candidates' hidden motivations. In fact, the negative coverage may drive people away from political participation altogether (Jamieson 2000; Patterson 2000).

While the Big Three television networks are vital links between citizens and presidential candidates, they are not the only politician–citizen links involving the news media. In this chapter, we ask whether any other source of news or information does the job better.

In addition to network news, we examined the reports of other major sources of news and information, including the *NewsHour* on PBS: leading newspapers like the *New York Times*, the *Washington Post*, and the *Wall Street Journal;* and CNN's *PrimeNews*. For 1996, we even analyzed the messages disseminated by the campaigns themselves. By examining different media sources in different election years, we can make broader comparisons than would have been possible if we had looked at a smaller number of news providers in every election or a larger number in only one election.

The Networks versus the *NewsHour* in Campaign 2000

For Campaign 2000, we applied the CMPA method of content analysis to the *NewsHour,* the nightly evening newscast of the Public Broadcasting Service. While public television does not have the commercial breaks throughout the broadcast found on the Big Three networks, the news hole (i.e., actual airtime apart from commercials or promotions) of the *NewsHour* is slightly less than that of the three commercial network evening news shows combined. This is because the *NewsHour* lasts one hour, less underwriter statements and promos, as compared to the three thirty-minute—less commercials and promos—network newscasts. Comparisons on many of the measures we have discussed in previous chapters are found in table 5.1.

Despite the somewhat smaller news hole when compared to the combined coverage of ABC, CBS, and NBC, PBS devoted 31 percent more airtime to election news during the 2000 campaign than the Big Three did, by a margin of 16 and one-half minutes to a combined total of 12 and one-half minutes per night. Moreover, the PBS coverage included far more substantive discussion, with a substance rating of 67 percent for *NewsHour* stories to a 40 percent rating for the networks. Horse race coverage was far less concentrated on PBS, appearing in only 32 percent of all *NewsHour* stories versus 71 percent for the networks (if a story contained both horse race and substantive elements it was included in both groups). The tone of PBS coverage was as balanced as that of the networks but far more positive overall—59 percent positive for Bush and 60 percent positive for Gore, for a combined 59 percent positive, compared to only 39 percent positive combined candidate evaluations on the networks.

Most striking of all the findings found in table 5.1 was the difference in mediation. The *NewsHour* reversed commercial television's journalist-centered presentation style. Only 24 percent of airtime on PBS went to journalists, one-third the level of reporter discourse at the networks. Can-

TABLE 5.1 PBS versus the Networks, 2000

	PBS	Networks
Amount of Coverage		
Minutes per day	16.5	12.5
Candidate airtime (minutes)	191	98
Average sound bite (seconds)	52	7.8
Locus (percentage)		
Journalists	24	74
Candidates	21	12
Other	55	14
Focus (percentage)[a]		
Horse race	32	71
Substantive	67	40
Tone (percentage positive)		
Bush	59	37
Gore	60	40
Combined	59	39

Note: News media based on 639 campaign news stories on ABC, CBS, NBC, and PBS between September 4 and November 6, 2000.

[a]A news story may have discussed substantive topics or the horse race, both topics, or neither topic. Thus percentages do not sum to 100 percent.

didates accounted for 21 percent of the coverage, and other sources provided the remaining 55 percent. Total speaking time for the candidates on the *NewsHour* more than doubled the combined total of the three commercial networks (3 hours 11 minutes versus 1 hour 38 minutes).[1]

Other measures of mediation also showed that viewers can learn more of the candidates' perspectives directly on PBS. The average candidate sound bite on the *NewsHour* was 52 seconds, nearly seven times the average length allowed on the network newscasts. This is just shy of a minute, or about twice the length of an average commercial advertisement on network television. PBS's more candidate-centered and issue-oriented focus reflects a format in which an initial taped "package" allowed the candidates to speak at length on a campaign issue, followed by an in-studio live discussion by their surrogates or independent experts.

These findings are consistent with those found by most other researchers. Political scientist Marjorie Hershey is among those who are bothered by the consequences for democracy of inadequate network news coverage of issues:

> The emphasis on game and personality frames serves to construct a comforting illusion, just as entertainment programs usually do. In this case, the illusion is that an American presidential election in the twenty first century—which has the potential to determine matters ranging from the composition of the Supreme Court to the state of our nuclear arsenal—*can be* about nothing more weighty than whether the gregarious chairman of the Inter-Fraternity Council will beat the earnest leader of the Science Club. (Hershey 2001:70, emphasis in original)

In essence, the *NewsHour* gave voters reasons why they should support one or the other candidate, while the commercial networks gave them reasons to oppose both. Thus, public broadcasting offers a model of election news that is more thorough, more substantive, and more positive in tone than its commercial network counterparts. This is not to say that the Big Three could successfully emulate PBS, whose evening newscast is seen by a far smaller and more elite audience. Indeed, the notion that PBS coverage is relatively substantive and positive in tone might be regarded as a truism. However, this conclusion runs counter to a recent "revisionist" portrayal of PBS election news that depicted the commercial and public television newscasts as fundamentally similar in style, substance, and quality.[2]

Horse Race versus Substance, 1988–2000

For the 1988, 1992, and 1996 elections, we broadened the comparisons to include additional outlets. In the remainder of this chapter we will see what the coverage tells us about the possibility of quality election news in sources other than the networks' evening newscasts. During the 1996 general election, for example, CMPA analyzed 2,360 news and editorial items from a wide range of television and print news outlets, including local as well as national news. To measure local news coverage, we examined campaign news from a sample of fifteen local newspapers, representing cities of varying sizes and from different geographic regions. During each fifteen-day period, a different newspaper was randomly selected for analysis. This sampling procedure, designed by political scientists Ann Crigler and Marion Just, yielded the equivalent of a single "composite" local newspaper without any consistent regional or local bias. The local newspaper composite included the *Las Vegas Review Journal*, *Dallas Morning News*, *Fargo Forum*, *Salem Statesman-Journal*, *Oakland Tribune*, *Manchester Union-Leader*, *Winston-Salem Journal*, *Chicago Tribune*, *Boston Globe*, *Tucson Citizen*, *Flint Journal*, *Shreveport Times*, *Harrisburg Patriot-News*, *Miami Herald*, and *Los Angeles Times*. A comparison of the various broadcast and print sources, including PBS, the networks, *New York Times*, and *Wall Street Journal*, analyzed in recent general elections is found in table 5.2.

Turning first to the 1996 general election results, note that the three broadcast networks stand far above all the other media outlets in their focus on horse race rather than substantive matters. They ranged from 45 percent to 51 percent horse race coverage in the 1996 election, a contest in which President Bill Clinton cruised to such an easy victory over Republican nominee Bob Dole that there was actually very little horse race to report on. The newspapers examined here focused far less on the horse race aspects of the campaign. The *New York Times* led, with 37 percent emphasis on horse race matters, followed by the *Wall Street Journal* and the local newspaper sample with 32 percent each. Once again, there were dramatic differences in 1996 between the networks and PBS. The *NewsHour* carried the lowest proportion of horse race news, only 20 percent of its election coverage, as compared to a 48 percent average for the Big Three.

A heavy diet of horse race coverage not only crowds out more substantive coverage but can also give voters the impression that the outcome is preordained so their own ballot doesn't matter. This isn't a question of accuracy. Most horse race assessments these days are based on scientific polls, which makes them much more objective than many other matters raised by journalists in news accounts. Candidates are far less able to question poll results than other areas of media mistreatment, even though reporters do not always understand the limitations of survey research. It is the consequences for democracy that are worthy of concern. Heavy horse race coverage, particularly in a one-sided campaign year like 1996, can hardly help voter turnout. Nor does an emphasis on the sports aspects of politics encourage citizens to learn more about the candidates, their issue positions,

TABLE 5.2 Horse Race Stories as Percentage of All Campaign News: General Elections, 1988–2000

	1988	1992	1996	2000
Big Three Broadcast News	**71**	**48**	**58**	**58**
ABC World News Tonight	71	51	54	59
CBS Evening News	69	47	58	60
NBC Nightly News	72	45	61	60
PBS *NewsHour*	**37**	**30**	**20**	**30**
Newspapers	**48**	**43**	**35**	**n/a**
New York Times	n/a	37	44	48
Wall Street Journal	n/a	32	35	41
Local newspapers	n/a	n/a	32	n/a
Total General Election	**n/a**	**36**	**45**	**52**
Number of stories	639	2,360	3,633	7,574

Note: Horse race stories are those that provided extensive discussion of the placement or status of one or more of the candidates in the campaign horse race, or of the candidates' campaign strategies or tactics.

Source: 2000 data based on 639 campaign news stories from ABC, CBS, NBC, and PBS between September 4, 2000, and November 6, 2000.

1996 data based on 2,360 campaign news stories and editorials from the *New York Times, Wall Street Journal*, a local newspaper sample compiled from fifteen local newspapers, ABC, CBS, NBC, and PBS between September 2 and November 5, 1996.

1992 data based on 3,633 campaign news stories and editorials from the *New York Times, Wall Street Journal, Washington Post*, ABC, CBS, CNN, NBC, and PBS between September 7 and November 3, 1992.

1988 data based on 7,574 campaign news stories and editorials from the *New York Times, Washington Post, Christian Science Monitor, Wall Street Journal, Los Angeles Times, Newsweek, Time, U.S. News and World Report, National Journal, New York Daily News, Chicago Tribune, Houston Chronicle, Sacramento Bee*, NBC, ABC, CBS, CNN, and PBS between September 8 and November 8, 1988 (Buchanan 1991, 1995).

or their personal characters. In 1996, the media's horse race conclusions were not controversial; even Dole's own supporters expected him to lose. A September 1996 Pew Research Center poll found that only 12 percent of voters believed Dole would be elected, even though 35 percent said they intended to vote for him (Pew 1996).

> The question is not whether these are reasonable judgments, but whether the margin [between Clinton and Dole] has become the message. A con-

> stant media drumbeat that the election is all but over could drown out Dole's attempts to dramatize the differences between himself and President Clinton. (Kurtz 1996a)

Was this pattern of coverage the rule or the exception? To find out, CMPA also analyzed samples of 3,633 television news and prestige press stories from the 1992 general election and 7,574 stories from the 1988 contest. The result was an even greater focus on the horse race, with the heaviest concentration in 1988. In both years, the Big Three networks had by far the greatest horse race focus, followed by the *New York Times*, the *Wall Street Journal*, and finally PBS (the local newspaper sample was analyzed only during the 1996 election). We also saw the same pattern in the 2000 elections (see chapter 2), where network news was unusually heavily focused on the horse race aspects of the campaign. In the most recent presidential election, the percentage of horse race coverage on the networks was double that of the *NewsHour*.

These very clear distinctions among media outlets in general elections disappear when we turn our attention to the 1996 Republican primary campaign. We examined a total of 1,965 news stories and editorials between January 1 and March 26, 1996, by which time it had become clear that Dole would be the nominee. The news outlets bunched together in the proportion of coverage they devoted to the horse race. In fact, by a slight margin, the 62 percent horse race coverage on PBS during this three-month period actually outpaced the 60 percent horse race coverage on ABC, the 59 percent on CBS, and the 58 percent on NBC. The newspapers also offered similar perspectives: the *Wall Street Journal* provided coverage that was 60 percent horse race, as compared to 53 percent in the *New York Times* and 44 percent in the composite local newspaper.

Since the New Hampshire primary is a pivotal point in the nomination process, we also looked at the horse race orientation of leading sources of news in that state during the 1996 primary season (cf. Farnsworth and Lichter 1999, 2001, 2002). We looked at 1,103 stories and editorials in three leading New Hampshire media sources from January 20 to February 20, 1996 (the month before the primary). WMUR, the dominant New Hampshire television station, turned out to be much like the national television news, with 60 percent horse race coverage. During this period, 56 percent of network news campaign coverage was devoted to horse race matters, roughly the same percentage as that for the networks during the entire primary season. In contrast, the state's two dominant newspapers, the *Concord Monitor* (37 percent horse race) and the *Union-Leader* of Manchester (32 percent) were the least horse–race oriented of any of the media outlets studied during the primaries.

The drawbacks of horse race news are more significant in light of the reduction in overall coverage on the network evenings news programs in recent years. When compared to the 1992 general election, the Big Three television networks each cut their coverage by more than 40 percent during the 1996 general election. Further, the 19 hours 39 minutes of general election news on the *NewsHour* was 47 percent more than the 13 hours 8 minutes aired by the three commercial networks *combined.*

So far we have looked at the media's focus on the horse race, as opposed to more substantive coverage. But the candidates had the greatest incentives of anyone involved to concentrate on horse race matters. They are, after all, the people who are winning or losing. Did the candidates also give short shrift to substance, campaigning in bland generalities or attacking opponents' records without offering detailed policy alternatives? To find out, we examined the candidates' campaign discourse, including campaign speeches, advertising, comments in candidate debates, and the campaigns' Internet web sites. We evaluated these forms of campaign communication in 1996 with the same content analysis methodology that we applied to the news reports. In table 5.3, the differences between campaign-generated election discourse and news media–generated election discourse stand out in sharp relief.

Turning first to the 1996 results, the distinctions among the messages the candidates themselves offer and the mediated messages offered by network television could not be clearer. The more control the candidates have, the higher the substance; the less control candidates have over the campaign message, the greater the devotion to the horse race. The candidate-controlled venues, including the free candidate airtime messages, campaign speeches, and campaign advertising, take the top three positions in the substance sweepstakes. All three offer at least 87 percent substance, and all three provide at most 4 percent coverage of the horse race. Another candidate-controlled venue, the campaigns' Internet web sites, finished seventh, behind only one media outlet, the *NewsHour*, which consistently has done

TABLE 5.3 Substance versus Horse Race in the 1996 and 2000 General Elections

	Percentage Substance[a]	Percentage Horse Race[a]	Number of Cases
2000			
PBS *NewsHour*	68	30	171 stories
ABC World News Tonight	42	71	180 stories
CBS Evening News	42	69	137 stories
NBC Nightly News	36	72	145 stories
1996			
Free candidate airtime	100	0	54 speeches
Campaign speeches	99	4	142 speeches
Campaign advertising	87	1	130 commercials
Candidate debates	85	0	50 exchanges
Television interviews	70	43	42 segments
PBS *NewsHour*	68	20	256 stories
Internet web sites	63	6	1,171 files
New York Times	51	37	821 stories
CBS Evening News	49	47	159 stories
Local newspapers	47	32	440 stories
Wall Street Journal	43	32	360 stories
NBC Nightly News	39	45	155 stories
ABC World News Tonight	27	51	169 stories

Note: 2000 news media based on 639 campaign news stories ABC, CBS, NBC, and PBS between September 4 and November 6, 2000. 1996 news media based on 2,360 campaign news stories and editorials from the *New York Times, Wall Street Journal,* a local newspaper sample compiled from fifteen local newspapers, ABC, CBS, NBC, and PBS between September 2 and November 5, 1996.

[a]Percentage of cases. A news story, speech, commercial, etc., may have discussed both substantive topics and the horse race or other topics. Thus percentages do not sum to 100 percent.

well in comparisons with other media outlets. Other venues in which candidates have at least a share of the control over content—the candidate debates and the television interviews—rank fourth and fifth in the percentage of substance. The interviews, which are the most subject to media influence over content among the top five categories, had the greatest amount of horse race coverage.

At the bottom of the rankings is *ABC World News Tonight*, which had less than one-third the percentage of substance found in the free candidate airtime statements and the campaign speeches. Both ABC and the NBC *Nightly News* had less than half the percentage of substance found in the top four candidate-controlled campaign discourse categories. CBS, the best of the Big Three, nevertheless finishes fifth from the bottom, beating out the *Wall Street Journal,* the composite local newspaper, and its two sister broadcast networks. But even the best television network by this measure finished far back in the comparison of substantive content. (The relatively high performance of CBS was the result of the network's decision to include free-airtime statements during their evening newscasts in 1996. NBC aired them at other times in the evening, and ABC did not air them at all.)

Although CMPA did not undertake this massive content analysis for these candidate discourse venues for 2000, the content analysis of network news in the most recent presidential election was even more focused on the horse race than the poor performance found in 1996.

This chasm between the campaign presented by the candidates and the campaign filtered through the media (found in the CMPA's 1996 content analysis) brings back into focus the questions we raised earlier about media fairness and objectivity. When we as news consumers watch the network news shows, we do not receive a fair and accurate representation of election campaigns as they actually take place on the campaign trail and in the materials distributed by campaign staffers. When the politicians talk, the discourse is almost entirely about matters of substance; when the reporters report, it is mostly about the horse race. While the prestige press is not the main focus of our inquiry, the results here suggest that major newspapers do better than the broadcast network newscasts on these matters. But that is cold comfort, since our results demonstrate quite clearly that even the leading newspapers skew candidate discourse in a negative direction. And for the print press to be declared superior to TV news, as is becoming increasingly clear through this content analysis, is not much of a compliment.

The comparisons found in table 5.3 for 1996 open a window onto possible alternatives to improved campaign discourse. Any solution must involve less mediation and more candidate-controlled discourse. If those free-airtime remarks—sometimes in the form of two-and-a-half minute speeches by Clinton and Dole, sometimes in the form of sixty-second remarks—are on network television where they can be seen widely, so much the better. The free candidate remarks in 1996 were carried by CBS, NBC, PBS, CNN, C-SPAN, some Paramount-owned stations, and National Public Radio. CBS put the speeches on the *Evening News* broadcasts, NBC used the news magazine *Dateline*, and CNN used its *Inside Politics* program (Lichter and Noyes 1998). Each of the fifty-four free-airtime speeches, according to the CMPA content analysis, focused primarily on issues, with taxes (15 speeches), children's issues (12), and education policy (11) the most common topics.

The following economic policy exchange, aired on Fox News on October 6, 1996, demonstrates how substantive the candidates can be, even in brief remarks that are unmediated and considerably longer than the average network news sound bite, now under eight seconds.

> *Clinton:* Our strategy is to raise incomes by growing the economy, creating more high-wage jobs, giving people the education they need to hold those jobs. It's working—wages are rising for the first time in a decade, we have the lowest unemployment in seven and a half years, ten and a half million new jobs, a 60 percent cut in the deficit, lowering interest rates on car loans, home mortgages, business loans, a minimum wage increase for ten million families. Now we have to help more people get ahead by balancing the budget without undermining Medicare, Medicaid, education, and the environment. We need targeted tax cuts for child rearing, home ownership, health care, and especially for college costs because education is the key to higher-paying jobs. Our opponents have a risky $550 billion tax scheme that independent experts say would balloon the deficit, slow the economy, raise taxes on nine million families. My plan will keep our economy growing, building our bridge to the twenty-first century.
>
> *Dole:* My economic plan will help millions of Americans who are working harder to make ends meet. We will provide the average American family with a $1,600 tax cut. That's $1,600 to save, spend, or invest as they see fit. We'll also cut the capital gains tax in half, which will increase jobs and opportunities. And I will expand Individual Retirement Accounts to increase savings and investments. My tax relief plan is based on a simple theory—it is your money, not the government's, and you should be able to keep more of it. That's a principle President Clinton simply doesn't understand. The average American family is now spending nearly 40 percent of its income on taxes, thanks to the president's tax increase, the largest tax increase in history. I would also put America on a path to a balanced budget which, with low interest rates, would put more money in the pockets of Americans who borrow money to buy a home, a car, or send a child to college. The president's vetoed two balanced budgets, and he did everything in his power to defeat a balanced budget amendment to the Constitution. (quoted in Lichter and Noyes 1998:96–99)

In these brief remarks, each candidate describes in some detail his economic plan. As would any incumbent presiding over good economic times, Clinton stresses the improvements that occurred during his term, and he offers a clear set of economic policy goals for a second term. He does take a swipe at what he described as "a risky $550 billion tax scheme," but on balance Clinton's remarks are far more focused on what he has done and would do in the economic arena than on negative attacks. Dole, like many Republicans, makes a clear appeal to voters' pocketbooks. His tax cut plan is front and center, and he too takes a swipe at Clinton, whom he intimates is mainly interested in raising taxes.

In both cases, the negative remarks are part of the candidates' efforts to illuminate what they consider to be the substantive differences between their approaches. Attacks on opponents are in the background, not the foreground. Further, the discussion of horse race that is so dominant on the Big Three evening newscasts is not in evidence here. The thoughtful, issue-oriented discussion offered by these competing statements is simply not supported on network newscasts with their constant references to campaign strategy and horse race calculations and with the candidates able to speak in their own words for only eight seconds at a time. Paid candidate advertisements, as well as the major party candidate debates, offer additional venues for citizens to learn about candidate policy preferences and plans, and the evidence suggests that citizens do learn more about candidates' positions in less-mediated formats such as debates (Drew and Weaver 1991).

One of the most interesting new developments in the 1996 election was the increasing use of the Internet by campaigns as a source of political communication (Owen 1997). The numbers of citizens using the Internet remained quite small during the 1996 campaign—78 percent of those surveyed by the Pew Research Center that year said they never went online for news or information about the election, and another 10 percent said they went online no more than once a week (Farnsworth and Owen 2001). But these numbers did not stop candidates, campaigns, news organizations, and other interested parties from developing extensive campaign web sites. The CMPA content analysis of campaign web sites includes all 1,171 files posted on the Clinton, Dole, and Perot sites during the course of the 1996 general election campaign. These web postings are similar to campaign speeches or ads in that the campaigns are free to offer an unmediated presentation of the candidate and of the candidate's issues to interested citizens. On their sites, Dole provided lengthy position papers of at least several pages on twenty-five different issues, while Clinton's site contained thirty-five major issue discussions, and Perot presented his point of view on fourteen major issues. These lengthy position papers provided far more detail than would be provided in a debate response or a 30-second commercial, and of course far more than could be expressed in a network news sound bite.

Two examples—one from each major party candidate—demonstrate just how precisely tailored web-based voter appeals can be. Clinton offered on his page a state-by-state listing of how each jurisdiction benefited from his administration's policies. Dole, on the other hand, told visitors to his web site how much each state had suffered under the Clinton years. As was the case in other candidate-controlled venues, the bulk of the material presented on web pages (71 percent) was devoted to promotion of the host candidate rather than criticism of other candidates. Citizens learning about campaigns through the flagship evening news programs learn mostly about the horse race, rarely about substance, and almost nothing in a candidate's own words. In many ways, candidate-controlled communication is an entirely different campaign than that seen by television viewers, and one that may be more appealing to citizens than the negative, horse race–obsessed, scandal-driven politics of recent presidential elections as presented by network television news.

Campaign Tone, 1992–2000

We found dramatic differences between the candidates' campaigns and the media's campaign coverage in their relative focus on substance and the horse race. Perhaps even more controversial than the focus of campaign news is its tone. When we discussed tone in earlier chapters, we found that network news coverage was usually negative toward both major party presidential candidates. In some years the network news coverage was about roughly equally harsh during the general election period (1988 and 2000), and in some years the networks were more negative in tone with respect to the Republican presidential nominee (1992 and 1996). How do the candidates, and other media outlets, stack up against the networks on this dimension? Table 5.4 compares the tone of candidate-controlled dis-

TABLE 5.4 **Tone of General Election Discourse in the 1996 and 2000 General Elections**

	Percentage Positive	Percentage Negative	Number of Cases
2000			
PBS *NewsHour*	56	44	171 stories
ABC World News Tonight	43	57	180 stories
CBS Evening News	38	62	137 stories
NBC Nightly News	39	61	145 stories
1996			
Free candidate airtime	80	20	54 speeches
Campaign speeches	78	22	142 speeches
Internet web sites	71	29	1,171 files
Candidate debates	66	34	50 exchanges
Television interviews	62	38	42 segments
Campaign advertising	60	40	130 commercials
PBS *NewsHour*	60	40	256 stories
CBS Evening News	46	54	159 stories
New York Times	43	57	821 stories
Local newspapers	43	57	440 stories
NBC Nightly News	41	59	155 stories
ABC World News Tonight	39	61	169 stories
Wall Street Journal	34	66	360 stories

Note: Based on all explicitly positive and negative evaluations of Bill Clinton, Ross Perot, and Bob Dole from all sources in 1996 and all explicitly positive and negative evaluations of Al Gore, George Bush, and Ralph Nader in 2000. Excludes all ambiguous or neutral comments, as well as all references to the candidates' status in the campaign horse race.

News media for 2000 based on 639 campaign news stories from ABC, CBS, NBC, and PBS between September 4 and November 6, 2000. News media for 1996 based on 2,360 campaign news stories and editorials from the *New York Times*, *Wall Street Journal*, a local newspaper sample compiled from fifteen local newspapers, ABC, CBS, NBC, and PBS between September 2 and November 5, 1996.

course venues, including free candidate airtime, campaign speeches, campaign web sites, with news media coverage on the networks and elsewhere, with a particular focus on the 1996 general election.

Once again, the candidate-dominated discourse venues scored well, demonstrating high percentages of positive discourse. The news media outlets dominated the bottom of the table, indicating a far more negative tone to their coverage. When candidates control the campaign discourse environment, as they do with respect to free candidate airtime, campaign speeches, and campaign web sites, the result is an overwhelmingly positive discourse (cf. Alliance for Better Campaigns 1999, 2001). These top three venues in 1996 were all more than two-thirds positive, and in fact the top two were more than three-quarters positive. A fourth venue that involves some candidate control, the campaign debates, was about two-thirds positive. Another venue in which the candidates have some control, the television interview programs, were 62 percent positive in the 1996 general election. Campaign advertising, another campaign discourse environment under campaign control, was 60 percent positive in tone.

The mainstream media sources were again found at the bottom of the table, mired in the depths of negativity. The *Wall Street Journal* was the most negative outlet of all, at only 34 percent positive coverage, somewhat lower than *ABC World News Tonight* and the *NBC Nightly News*, with 39 percent and 41 percent positive coverage, respectively. The *NewsHour* on PBS again finished at the top of the media outlets, with 60 percent positive, followed by the *CBS Evening News* at 46 percent positive. Between CBS and the other networks came the *New York Times* and the composite local newspaper, both with 43 percent positive coverage. (The network television figures for 2000 offer no signs of encouragement: each network was about as negative or more negative in 2000 as it was in 1996).

These findings deepen our concerns regarding the fairness and accuracy of network news coverage. The 1996 findings suggest a campaign that is relatively positive in tone is skewed to its most negative snippets when mediated by television—and even when mediated by the country's leading print news outlets. Since few voters attend campaign rallies or watch lengthy campaign speeches on venues like C-SPAN, the electorate relies primarily on the news media to present the facts. If the news media suggest that the campaigns are more negative than they actually are and that the candidates are more critical of each other than they actually are, then the news media are doing the country a considerable disservice. Many researchers (see chapter 4) suggest that citizen discontent with government is at least partially the result of media negativity, and our findings do little to allay those concerns.

In the 1992 general election, our content analysis into campaign tone considered eight separate media outlets; we did not consider candidate discourse venues in that election. We also divided the results by candidate. In 1992, Clinton received far more positive coverage on the television networks than did George H. W. Bush, the incumbent president, much of whose bad press was focused on the state of the economy. Of the eight media outlets examined in this segment of the CMPA content analysis, Clinton received his highest percentage of positive press in the *Wall Street Journal*, with 68 percent positive coverage (the *Wall Street Journal* is well known for its conservative editorial page, but like most large newspapers the *Journal* places its news and editorial page staffs under the control of different editors). CBS ranked second with 55 percent positive press for Clinton, just ahead of ABC and the *Washington Post*, which tied for third with 54 percent positive coverage. Clinton failed to get a majority of good press at the four remaining news outlets: NBC and the *New York Times* (each at 46 percent positive coverage), the *NewsHour* (45 percent positive) coverage, and CNN (43 percent positive). In our age of media negativism, rarely does a presidential candidate do as well in the media as Clinton did in the 1992 general election.

Bush was treated far more negatively in 1992, as we have discussed previously. As with Clinton, the television networks did not differ markedly in their tone from other leading news organizations. The most positive news outlet for Bush was ABC, where his on-air evaluations were only 36 percent favorable, considerably lower than the 43 percent positive coverage for Clinton at his lowest-rated outlet. Following ABC was the *Wall Street Journal* (33 percent positive coverage), then NBC and PBS (each at 30 percent positive), the *New York Times* (29 percent), CBS (27 percent), the *Washington Post* (26 percent), and finally CNN (22 percent). The closest Bush came to breaking even was on PBS, but even there Clinton had a substantial advantage, with a 45 percent to 30 percent positive margin. In fact, Clinton's advantage in good press exceeded a two-to-one margin with respect to three of these outlets—the *Wall Street Journal* (a 35-percentage-point gap), CBS (28 percentage points), and the *Washington Post* (28 percentage points)—and nearly reached that level at CNN, where Clinton had a 21-percentage-point advantage. The coverage at the four remaining media outlets in this portion of the analysis favored Clinton over Bush by at least fifteen percentage points.

Absent a major personal or political scandal, it seems remarkable that some of America's most prestigious and influential news organizations, who pride themselves on their fairness, could give a challenger twice as much good press as an incumbent in a presidential election. During the

1992 campaign, George Bush often found himself fighting a two-front war, facing Bill Clinton's attacks on the economy on one flank and Ross Perot's attacks on foreign policy on the other. The results here suggest that the Bush team had reason to believe they were fighting on a third front as well, the one facing the mainstream news media. Our content analysis suggests that the 1992 campaign bumper sticker, "Annoy the Media, Re-elect Bush" may not have been entirely without foundation (cf. Fitzwater 1995).

The former president was particularly frustrated with the media coverage he received in 1992, saying several months after leaving office that his re-election prospects were dimmed considerably by negative media coverage of his presidency and the American economy:

> I couldn't cut through the fog, the barrage. I give the Clinton campaign credit for those three famous words: "The economy, stupid." . . . The media would find someone unemployed who would say, "He [Bush] may say things are getting better, but not for me and my family." And I'd sympathize with that individual worker, but the larger fact, as we now see, was the economy was doing far better than the Clinton campaign or the press, particularly the network TV shows, portrayed it. (quoted in Gold 1994)

Bush wished he were more like Ronald Reagan, who was more able to use the news media to his advantage.

> If he had been in my place, he'd have cut through the opposition fog that everything was going to hell. He'd say, "Wait a minute, here are the facts, the reality." And the reality was that the recession had bottomed out in 1991, and the economy had grown not just by the 2.7 percent [annual rate] I claimed for the third quarter, but by 3.4 percent. And in the fourth quarter it grew at a very robust 5.8 percent—not exactly a recession. The last two quarters of 1992 were better than what the economy has done under President Clinton, but I failed as a communicator. (quoted in Gold 1994)

Bush's objections notwithstanding, the notion of a generalized liberal press seems a tough case to make, even with the negative treatment of a Republican incumbent president in 1992. For example, conservative television commentator Pat Buchanan, who challenged Bush from the ideological right in the 1992 Republican primaries, fared far better on the television nightly news programs than did the more moderate incumbent president (48 percent positive for Buchanan in the primaries versus 18 percent positive for Bush) that year. In addition, notwithstanding research showing that about 90 percent of the White House press corps voted for Clinton in 1992, a CMPA content analysis of news coverage of Clinton's first two years in office found that negative evaluations made up 73 percent of network news coverage of his new administration, with only 23 percent positive evaluations. Ironically, these are the same proportions of good and bad press Bush received during 1992 (Lichter and Noyes 1995). Of course, 1993 and 1994 were well before the nation's reporters had ever head the name Monica Lewinsky (Kurtz 1998; Sabato et al. 2000).

In fact, the 1992 election is yet another example of the utility of the "more than minimal" effects school of media research. Under the hypodermic effects model, Bush would have been lucky to get even a few votes from regular consumers of such pervasively anti-Bush media fare. Although he lost in 1992, Bush did win eighteen states and 37.7 percent of the popular vote to Clinton's 43.2 percent of the popular vote (Quirk and Dalager 1993). The media didn't help Bush's campaign, but Bush had a number of things working against him in 1992, foremost among them the very negative public perception of the economy and public doubts over whether Bush understood, or cared about, the plight of ordinary Americans trying to make ends meet in difficult times (Ceaser and Busch 1993; Quirk and Dalager 1993).

Is It Just Talk or a New Source of News?

The 1992 election will be remembered for the appearance of talk shows as an alternative to the mainstream media (Kurtz 1993; Owen 1996; Davis and Owen 1998). Independent presidential candidate Ross Perot launched his candidacy via appearances on *Larry King Live*, and throughout the 1992 election Perot and Clinton tried to use these venues for making their case to the country in a more direct way than by going through the campaign press corps.

The hosts of these shows—and the callers who contact them to ask questions of the candidates—are often seen by reporters as too easy for a useful exchange of issues and a useful challenging of the candidates. Michael Kinsley, then with the *New Republic*, said in 1992 that the mainstream media could learn something from the issue-oriented focus of citizen and talk show host questions. But Kinsley also said he nevertheless felt uneasy about the whole process of having candidates campaign in this way.

> First . . . untrained amateurs are no match for skilled professionals in exposing a candidate's flaws and weaknesses. And second, that semi-journalists like [Phil] Donahue and [Larry] King, not to mention non-journalists like Arsenio [Hall], unhealthily—or at least surrealistically—muddy the distinction between serious politics and trivial show biz. There is, no question, something eerie about the same show discussing men-who-would-be-president one day and women-who-hate-their husbands the next. (Kinsley 1992)

Conversely, Bill Clinton, a leading practitioner of talk show campaigning in 1992, portrayed the mainstream press as the source of triviality.

> I think the watchdog function is fine. But it's often carried to extremes in a search for headlines. For instance, the missing pages from my State Department file—here was a deal where *Newsweek* bit on a rumor. So you had these serious reporters who just wanted to grill me about that—when the economy is in the tubes, when 100,000 people a month are losing their health insurance. . . . And I'm supposed to take these people seriously as our sole intermediaries to the voters of this country? Sure, they should do their watchdog function, but anyone who lets himself be interpreted to the American people through these intermediaries alone is nuts. (quoted in Lichter and Noyes 1995:261)

So what does the evidence say? CMPA's content analysis of thirty-four national TV talk shows in 1992 found that this format did a far better job of focusing on the issues than did any of the journalist-centered media outlets. Based on the same criteria we used to evaluate the content of newscasts, we found that 74 percent of the segments on TV talk shows focused on substantive matters (primarily policy issues and candidate qualifications). In comparison, CNN's *PrimeNews* was only 53 percent substantive, PBS's *NewsHour* was 48 percent substantive, and the Big Three television networks ranged from 26 percent to 34 percent substantive. The somewhat higher rating for CNN may be the result of a $3.5 million grant from the Markle Foundation designed to improve the quality of campaign news coverage (Kerbel 1998:132). It appears that the news media *can* be more substantive in orientation, particularly if you pay them to be so!

The focus of discussion was also quite different on the talk shows in 1992. The top four topics of candidate discussion on the traditional news media (the three networks, CNN, the *Wall Street Journal*, the *New York Times,* and the *Washington Post*) were general candidate viability (22 percent), poll standings (14 percent), general candidate assessments (13 percent), and issue stances (13 percent). The top four topics on the television talk shows were candidate records (23 percent), campaign conduct (20 percent), issue stances (19 percent), and general candidate assessment (12 percent). Once again, the evidence shows that the less-mediated formats do a better job of focusing on issues. Even though some programs in this group are not news shows, policy issues received a more extensive hearing on the television talk show circuit than on the nightly newscasts that ostensibly are designed to provide citizens with the information they need to evaluate the candidates and to cast an informed ballot.

Is It Comedy or Is It News?

Daytime talk shows are not the only unlikely places where citizens dissatisfied with network television news coverage have turned in recent years for more information about presidential candidates. A January 2000 Pew Research Center survey found that 28 percent of Americans said they learned about the presidential campaign from late night comedy and talk shows like *The Tonight Show*, *The Late Show with David Letterman*, *Late Night with Conan O'Brien,* and *Politically Incorrect.* Among those under thirty years old, the figure rose to 47 percent (Media Monitor 2000). That fall, both nominees demonstrated the importance of this venue by appearing on the Jay Leno and David Letterman shows and engaging in some serious discussion of political issues as well as the usual banter. Researchers have started to consider these entertaining venues as important areas for at least some citizens to receive political cues away from the stuffier—and for many, less entertaining—news programs (Jones 2001; Media Monitor 2000).

Of course comedians are not subject to the same standards of objectivity and fairness that one would expect of the network newscasts, but for those who are interested, CMPA tabulations of Leno and Letterman monologues found that Bush was the target of 254 jokes during the general election campaign, while Gore was the subject of 165. The 1996 contest produced a split decision, with a more balanced result of 242 jokes by late night comedians skewering Clinton and 228 targeting Dole.

Ironically, at a time when candidates are relegated to eight-second sound bites on the traditional evening news shows, they can present themselves to viewers and voters in extensive give-and-take sessions in that fluffiest of entertainment formats, the variety show. For example, George W. Bush was on screen for 13 minutes during his October 19, 2000, appearance on Letterman's show, which exceeded his entire speaking time on all three network news evening shows during the month of October. Similarly, Al Gore received more time on his September 14, 2000, appearance on Letterman's show than on all three network newscasts during the entire month of September. Several other candidates, including Green Party candidate Ralph Nader and Democratic vice presidential nominee Joseph Lieberman, also made appearances on the late night talk show circuit. Nader was rarely covered by network news reporters during the campaign, even though his candidacy proved to be of historic significance, dealing a fatal wound to Gore's hopes for the White House in 2000.

Conclusion

After watching his ragtag New York Mets blow yet another game in their miserable first season as an expansion team, manager Casey Stengel famously lamented, "Can't anybody here play this game?" More and more viewers—and voters—seem to be asking, "Can't anybody here cover this election?" Something is very wrong with election coverage when the one-liners are on the evening news and the serious discussions are on Leno and Letterman.

Throughout this chapter, we have tried to determine whether anybody can cover campaigns better than the Big Three networks. From the volume to the substance to the tone of the coverage, we can find somebody who does it at least as well, if not better. Over four presidential elections, and through many different comparisons among information sources, we rarely found an instance in which the Big Three television networks did a better job of covering the presidential election than the other news sources we examined. This was the result when we compared the flagship network evening newscasts to the PBS *NewsHour*, to CNN *PrimeNews*, to the major newspapers, and to a composite local newspaper. Even more troubling, considering the role that the news media play in building links between the government and citizens, was that the networks did not even do a better job of allowing candidates to speak to voters than the entertainment-oriented talk shows, which enjoy far smaller audiences. Our content analysis found that the networks consistently focused heavily on the horse race, ignored matters of substance, and accentuated the most negative aspects of the campaign trail, and in so doing failed to provide an accurate and fair reflection of the presidential campaigns. This litany of failure nears the point of absurdity when it is possible to learn more from a candidate from one night with a late-night comedian than from a month of watching network nightly newscasts.

Despite the emergence of several new sources of political information in recent years, the flagship evening newscasts of the Big Three broadcast networks still command by far the largest audience for election news (Kurtz 2002b). Unfortunately, they also most clearly represent what has gone wrong with election news. The single most troubling finding of this analysis is the massive chasm between what the campaigns say in their various unmediated forms—including candidate free-airtime segments, paid campaign ads, candidate speeches, and candidate web pages—and what citizens learn about those campaigns from the networks' nightly news programs. That the chasm narrows somewhat when we compare the campaigns' unmediated discourse with other media outlets is hardly a cause for rejoicing, particularly when one considers the size of the gap that separates the campaign communication from the print outlets and from even CNN and PBS.

In recent years, as intensified partisan strife suggests the civility has gone out of politics and of public life, the news media have actually made campaign messages seem more negative and less substantive than they really are. Reporters often argue that they are far better interpreters of campaigns and elections than the candidates and their handlers, because people connected to the campaigns are anything but objective in the information they put out. Their goal, after all, is to win an election, not to tell the truth.

That is true enough in theory, but our findings show that even these self-interested politicians are more informative and useful sources about the campaigns than the news organizations that claim to improve upon them. Candidate speeches, advertisements, and web pages are far more issue-oriented in their substance and more positive in their tone than any of the television and print outlets we examined, even outdoing the generally high-scoring PBS. It is difficult to imagine a more damning indictment of network television than this fact: even the obviously biased campaigns do a better job of informing citizens about candidates and issues than do the armies of highly trained and supposedly dispassionate professionals who spend years following the candidates from Iowa to New Hampshire, through Super Tuesday, the nominating conventions, the general elections, and perhaps ultimately to the White House.

At its best, American politics represents a marketplace of ideas, an area where truth and the most appealing public policies can emerge from the muscular democratic competitions waged by candidates, their campaigns, and other political actors, including citizens. Even the Founders, who had anything but an elevated view of human nature, nevertheless ultimately trusted citizens' abilities to sort out the wheat from the chaff. Reporters don't have to be self-appointed, latter-day versions of Plato's guardians, protecting citizens from the candidates they think we should not elect. Nobody asked network correspondents to do this job. Their efforts to place an imprimatur on campaigns, or more precisely, to cut every candidate down to size, diminishes everyone concerned. Journalists have descended into a mode of reporting that is notable for its negativity, for its near-silencing of the candidates themselves, and for its obsessive pursuit of the trivial. As a result, reporters are less likely to be listened to and respected by citizens. Voters turn away from all the candidates in disgust, or if they do venture to the polls, they cast their votes while figuratively holding their noses. The candidates fear to be nominated "court jester" by the media framers, but even more than that they fear being ignored by the press pack, which is an even surer kiss of political death. America's elections, its central marketplace of ideas, is being filled by mainstream media with junk food that slowly rots our political discourse. Today's high-fat journalism doesn't make for a healthy democracy.

The *NewsHour* content analysis for Campaign 2000 that began this chapter, together with the comparative analysis involving PBS, CNN, newspapers, and even entertainment media outlets show there is more than one way to cover presidential elections. The trivialized and negativistic network news coverage is not simply a reflection of either reality or of the structural limitations of news programming generally or the broadcast evening news format in particular. Of course, even if this critique of election news coverage were to be embraced by broadcast journalism, it would not necessarily stimulate substantial changes in news practices and content. To paraphrase Marx: the scholars have interpreted the news; the point, however, is to change it. Nonetheless, there are two external factors whose interaction may yet substantially alter the broadcast news format. The first is the growing disaffection of the viewing audience. The second is the rise of new methods of obtaining information, which provide alternatives for those disaffected viewers. We now turn to the prospects for change.

Notes

1. The *NewsHour* candidate totals were 85 minutes for Gore, 77 minutes for Bush, 15 minutes for Ralph Nader, and 14 minutes apiece for Joe Lieberman and Dick Cheney. In addition to the overall totals for the major party tickets, this indicates the attention that PBS gave to the vice presidential and minor party candidates who received almost no airtime on the networks.

2. Kerbel et al. (2000) conducted a story-level "frame analysis" of a sample of 1996 election coverage comparing PBS with ABC. The authors concluded that the PBS version was no more substantive, thoughtful, or "empowering" to voters than was its commercial counterpart: "The evidence points with few exceptions to the similar fashion in which the two networks portray the electoral process" (16). However, this conclusion may reflect methodological limitations of their research method, which applied a less precise content analysis system to a much smaller sample of stories. Further data analysis of CMPA's election news demonstrated the robustness of our findings. First, the same pattern emerged whether the unit of analysis was the story or the message units that comprised it. Second, analysis of our PBS data from the expanded 1996 primary and general election data sets replicated the findings for 2000. Kerbel and his colleagues' conclusion derives primarily from a single variable (the "frame"), whose variates are not mutually exclusive and which was coded for a small sample (ninety PBS stories for the entire period from January 1 to Election Day, or about two stories per week), with the entire story serving as the unit of analysis. Thus, for example, a story might be coded as being framed in terms of the horse race and the political process but not in terms of issues or personal character. This coding system lacks the precision of a message unit analysis that encodes each statement within a story for its source, object, and valence. These codes can be used as the individual building blocks for story-level analysis, rather than relying on a single code to represent an entire story, which contains numerous discrete pieces of information. As they note, "These classifications [frames] are meant to provide no more than a broad framework for understanding the various ways that the election

story may be told" (Kerbel et al. 2001:14). Thus, as a further check, we reanalyzed our data by building horse race and substance variables out of individual message units. The results strongly reinforced the conclusions that were found on CMPA's story-level variables. In addition, the CMPA study coded the entire universe of general election news for all 218 stories on PBS and 462 stories on ABC, CBS, and NBC. And the same core instrument has been applied by the same researchers to four conservative presidential elections with evidence of independent replication. But the case for accepting CMPA's findings is not merely inferential. The expanded 1996 study included PBS data for both the primaries and the general election. We combined content categories related to policy issues and candidate qualifications into a story-level index of substantive news, in order to make our measure of substance more comparable to Kerbel et al.'s frames. By this measure, during the primaries the *NewsHour* offered 50 percent substantive coverage, compared to 42 percent for CBS, 37 percent for ABC, and 34 percent for NBC. During the general election a remarkable 68 percent of PBS coverage was substantive, compared to 49 percent on CBS, 39 percent on NBC, and only 27 percent on ABC. In light of this evidence, it would seem that the burden of proof for their counterintuitive interpretation of PBS election coverage rests with Kerbel and his colleagues.

CHAPTER 6

MAYBE NEXT YEAR?
The Future of Campaign Coverage

The consequences of the many media failings we have catalogued in previous chapters are not trivial for our polity. Democracy depends on a free exchange of ideas and a fruitful discussion of issues among citizens and public officials through communication vehicles such as a vibrant, independent mass media. Yet our findings show that the mass media, and especially the television networks, are far from being as helpful as they could be, with reporters and editors cutting the time devoted to politics and focusing in the reduced time that remains on horse race standings rather than the vital issues the nation's leaders will have to face.

The First Amendment guarantee of a free press is one of our most sacred Constitutional birthrights. Reporters have performed vital roles throughout our nation's history in exposing corruption and official misconduct, ranging from attacking the partisan political machines and the corporate trusts of a century ago to exposing the more recent deceits surrounding Watergate and Vietnam. Democracy depends on a fair and critical news media to investigate public wrongdoing and to evaluate objectively the claims of the self-interested partisans who populate the fields of politics and government. At the same time, however, the television networks have behaved irresponsibly in their reporting of recent presidential elections, particularly regarding the heavy emphasis on the horse race (even for one-sided campaigns like 1996 where there was at most a "horse trot" to cover) and their overly negative orientation. Campaigns that are conducted on a surprisingly positive basis are badly mischaracterized on the network evening news shows. By using these mostly positive campaigns as opportunities for expressing little more than cynicism, today's television journalists do not help, and sometimes may even hinder, democratic practices. Why should you as a citizen take the trouble to vote when, judging from what the networks report, it looks as if there are no important issues, and none of the candidates deserves your attention, much less your respect? With rights come responsibilities, and this is true not only for citizens but also for the Fourth Estate.

This chapter, then, is about possible ways to improve the communication links between citizens and presidential candidates, with an emphasis on television's vital role. We consider ways that television could improve its performance through such changes as hour-long newscasts; weekday editions of interview shows like *This Week*, *Face the Nation,* and *Meet the Press* (at least during presidential election years); and an expansion of the free-airtime-for-candidates initiative that has been tried sporadically in past elections.

But, as Publius observed in *Federalist* 51, "Experience has taught mankind the necessity of auxiliary precautions." Therefore we also consider a variety of reforms to enhance this link between presidential candidates and citizens in ways that do not directly involve the Big Three broadcast networks. Despite the near-universal conviction among scholars and even many reporters that the television news should do better, the performance of network television news continues to decline. So we also consider the prospects for reforming the nomination and electoral process, as well as the potential uses of other news outlets to supplement the woefully inadequate coverage offered by network television news. The Internet is a particularly appealing alternative venue for additional information, at least in theory, as more people spend more time online in the years ahead. Perhaps a newly competitive environment along the lines envisioned in this chapter will spur network television on to a higher quality performance. But we must admit the networks' response so far to the increasingly fluid news environment is not encouraging.

A Brief Review of the Content Analysis Evidence

The purpose of this research is to evaluate the degree to which the network evening news shows have succeeded in their often-stated desires to produce serious, substantive, and evenhanded coverage of presidential elections. Unfortunately, the results have been disappointing. CMPA's initial study of the 1988 campaign documented the predominance of the horse race over substantive issues, the negative treatment of both major party nominees, and a heavily mediated approach that lets journalists rather than candidates do most of the talking. After that campaign was widely criticized for its negativity and lack of substance, the networks introduced numerous reforms designed to produce coverage that was more serious, fair, and informative to voters. But CMPA's subsequent studies have shown little evidence of improvement and considerable evidence of decline over the past several presidential election campaigns. The airtime devoted to campaign news has dropped sharply, candidate sound bites have continued to shrink, and candidate airtime has remained static. The proportion of horse race news declined in 1996, but in 2000 it shot back up to well above 1988 levels. Because the total volume of election news has dropped, the amount of substantive information available to viewers has declined.

The tone of the 2000 coverage was as negative overall as in the 1988 race that led to numerous calls for changes in the coverage. Unfortunately, coverage in 1992 and 1996 seemed more biased in a quite different sense, with Clinton receiving more positive evaluations that either Bush or Dole. The tone was more balanced overall in 2000 than in the previous two elections, although that balance shifted during the course of the race. Gore led the race for positive press in September, while Bush was favored in October and November. Both candidates received a majority of negative on-air evaluations, although their combined ratings were slightly more positive than was the case in 1988. The inclusion of off-year election data reinforced the patterns of valence observed in presidential campaigns.

Thus, network election news coverage has been characterized in this analysis by declining volume, little substance, pervasive negativism, a sometimes partisan tilt, and heavy mediation. Despite the good intentions announced by journalists anxious to improve the coverage after the 1988 campaign (and after subsequent campaigns as well), we seem to be getting the same approach, only less of it. As we have demonstrated, this pattern cannot be attributed mainly to manipulation of the coverage by candidates and their "spin doctors." CMPA's 1996 study directly compared candidate discourse to media discourse and found the latter to be more negative and less substantive. Of course, most voters experience the campaign through media images rather than direct contact with the candidates. One likely reason they perceive the process as lacking in substance and civility is that campaign news accentuates the least attractive elements of electoral realities. One source of optimism is that polls indicate that citizens can see the differences among various source of campaign news and information. Surveys show that most voters direct most of their ire at reporters, not at the candidates, the political parties, or even the much-maligned political consultants.

The Declining Network News Audience

Not only is the declining quality of network television's coverage of presidential elections bad for candidates and citizens but it hurt the media companies themselves. The rapid movement of viewers in recent years from network television to cable news and to a lesser extent to the Internet, is well documented. It should provide a significant incentive for the network newscasts to adjust their approach toward less negative and more issue-oriented coverage than they have offered in recent elections (Farnsworth and Owen 2001; Norris 2001; Pew 2000a, 2000b). The sharp decline in citizen use of network television as a source of campaign news was illustrated in the first chapter of this work (table 1.1). These roving eyeballs demonstrate that the television networks have a sound financial reason for addressing some of the problems we have raised with respect to the trivial, negative, and skewed campaign material that dominates the nightly newscasts. Higher-quality outlets are increasing market share, or declining at a less rapid pace than network television.

Noted political scientist V. O. Key once quipped, "Voters are not fools." The same appears to be true for news media consumers. Citizen evaluations of news sources demonstrate once again that the news media's effects are modest, not all-powerful—nothing along the lines projected by the old hypodermic effects model. The declining market share for network news seen in table 1.1 is consistent with the negative ratings citizens give the television networks after every presidential contest. In 1992, 37 percent of the voters gave the news media a grade of "A" or "B" based on their performance during the campaign. This was seen as a vote of no confidence at the time, but in surveys conducted to assess coverage of the 1996 and 2000 presidential elections, the media's score fell to only 29 percent awarding those grades during both years (Pew 2000a). This demonstrates that the same public frustration with mainstream news sources seen through news source preferences is reflected in campaign information source evaluations.

Voters also seem to have identified the differences among information sources that we found through our systematic content analysis. For example, the proportion of those surveyed that gave Bill Clinton an "A" or "B" for his 1996 campaign (58 percent) was twice the percentage of good grades that the news media received. Bob Dole, who did not run a particularly effective campaign, also received a higher percentage of good grades (34 percent) than those awarded the news media. The same pattern of higher grades for the candidates was found in 2000, when Al Gore received 54 percent "A" and "B" grades and 53 percent of citizens gave George W. Bush these grades, again both markedly higher than the scores given reporters. The only presidential candidate to receive a lower grade than the press over the last four presidential elections was George H. W. Bush in 1992. Even the much-maligned political parties outscored the media, with 49 percent good grades for Democrats in 2000 and 48 percent for Republicans (Pew 2000a). Thomas Jefferson once said they he would prefer a vibrant press and no government to the reverse. Were he alive today he would find it quite difficult to make a similar observation regarding network television, as candidates offer far more relevant and informative campaign discourse than the supposedly consumer-sensitive network television news companies.

Voters also rate talk show hosts higher than the news media, with 49 percent of survey respondents giving the talk shows "A" or "B" grades of in 1992 and 41 percent in 2000 (Pew 2000a). Support for talk show hosts was considerably more negative in 1996, when the percentage of good grades fell to 28 percent, about the same as the 29 percent score for the press. The low score registered by talk show hosts in 1996 may be an exception caused by the political circumstances that year; partisan voters in 1996 were primed to focus on talk radio hosts like Rush Limbaugh, who regularly attacked Clinton and who was among those voices who supported the Republicans as they engaged in the unpopular shutdown of the federal government a year earlier (Davis and Owen 1998; Laufer 1995; Owen 1996, 1997). The 1992 and 2000 evaluations were far less likely to be colored by evaluations of talk radio celebrities like Limbaugh, who in the mid-1990s was something of a lightning rod for liberals (Franken 1999).

These findings regarding citizen choices and media evaluations demonstrate that the corporate owners of the three television networks—General Electric, Disney, and Viacom—have sound financial reasons for improving the quality of presidential election coverage. People are moving away from the network news in the direction of more effective and informative media sources.

So far, though, the networks have responded to negative evaluations and declining viewer interest mainly by trying to improve the quality of their media offerings through expanding alternative news outlets. NBC uses its cable partner MSNBC to provide more-extensive evening newscasts beyond its 30-minute (before commercials) *Nightly News* program, and it promotes the cable offshoot heavily on its flagship news program. All three network newscasts regularly refer viewers to their news web sites for more information than that provided on-air. But these media modifications do not seem sufficient, particularly when we consider that only a small, elite audience turns to the Internet for information about politics. In 2000, only one-third of citizens surveyed by the Pew Research Center for the People and the Press said they went online for news about the elections, and most of those who did so surfed the web quite infrequently. Only 10 percent of citizens in a Pew survey in 2000 said they went online for election information once a day or more (Farnsworth and Owen 2001; Pew 2000b).

Reforming Network News?

All this suggests that the most significant changes in the delivery of election news are originating less from conscious intentions than from rapid market changes and technological innovations. Even as journalists struggle to improve the news product from within, they find themselves adapting to outside forces that are reshaping audience expectations as well as newsroom norms and practices. The initial impact of these changes in recent years has not always inspired confidence, to put it mildly (Kovach and Rosenstiel 1999). Reporters have long been among the harshest critics of television news and are among the most insistent in their demands for reform. Writing about the television's shortcomings in its coverage of the 1984 presidential election, for example, Roger Mudd—formerly a top reporter and anchor for CBS—called for the networks to establish a 30-minute weekly segment to report on the campaign (Mudd 1987).

Now, as Mudd's thoughtful suggestion moves through its teenage years, it is long past time to reconsider this modest proposal. One possible explanation for why television news is so fragmented and trivialized is that a 30-minute newscast is simply too small an amount of time to report on anything all that well. The much longer segments on PBS's hour-long *NewsHour* and on the network-affiliated MSNBC's hour-long nightly newscast allow for more extensive treatment of issues than would be possible in the shorter format that has long been the network newscast standard. CBS's *60 Minutes* has been one of the most commercially successful and highly rated shows in the history of broadcast television, demonstrating that being informative and being profitable are not mutually exclusive. In other words, success in televised news delivery does not have to come in 30-minute packages.

One possible reform along these lines, as Roger Mudd suggested, would be for the networks to produce a weekly 30-minute program during presidential election years, perhaps airing right after the news on a Tuesday night, corresponding with the day of the week that Americans will go to the polls. This additional program could take a variety of shapes, perhaps a weeknight version of the networks' Sunday news programs. These interview shows, as the CMPA content analysis shows, offer far more information and less negativity than the nightly newscasts. Alternatively, the half-hour could be spent going through an important issue or two, perhaps even with a deliberative public assembly convened to debate the issue on television (Fishkin 1991, 1995; Georges 1993; Harwood Group 1991, 1993; Janowitz 1983). There could even be mini-debates among the leading candidates, perhaps with extended versions of the free-airtime remarks by the candidates that have been used in the past (Taylor 2002). In addition to improved candidate discourse, free-airtime policies would reduce the pressure on candidates to raise vast sums of money needed for campaign advertising from special interests, an important reason for citizen distrust of government (Farnsworth 1997, 2001). Experimentation and diversity could mark this half-hour block in its early going.

Only execution of these various proposals can determine what would be most appealing for citizens and most effective for expanding the audience for network newscasts and reinvigorating political discourse. What the above ideas have in common is that the news programming should be expanded, since a lack of time for covering issues is a major impediment to serious discussion and analysis of campaigns on network television. Ross Perot's high ratings for his televised lectures on the economy demonstrate that a substantial number of citizens are interested in watching serious presentations of issues on television, as does the decades of success enjoyed by *60 Minutes* and various imitators. Further evidence of such a public willingness for higher-quality news programming is found in the steady erosion of the influence of network news in election politics and the relative strength of those media outlets, including print and cable, that our content analysis demonstrates offer far more substantial coverage.

Along these same lines, the media's exercise of their vital linkage functions between candidates and citizens, and between government and citizens, would be enhanced by doubling the length of the nightly network newscasts to an hour. The superficial treatment that is television's hallmark could be replaced by more extended discussions of the important issues of the day and the differences of the candidates. Local television newscasts usually run for at least an hour, and some last considerably longer than that. Are not the networks' evening newscasts equally important? Since the evidence suggests that citizens are deserting network news for more substantial media outlets, the best ways for television to compete would be by offering more coverage and by offering better coverage. The only real cost to an hour-long newscast would be that local stations would lose some of the revenue from rerunning half an hour of one of yesterday's hit shows, like *M*A*S*H* or *Seinfeld*. The local affiliates could be compensated with more advertising slots during the newscasts or perhaps rebates to make the decision to move to an hour-long newscast revenue-neutral to local stations. Democracy would be better off with once-a-week news specials or hour-long network newscasts, and we believe the networks would be better off under such a change as well.

Our argument in favor of voluntary increases in the amount of evening news the networks provide rests on the free-market assumption that it is in the rational self-interest of a profit-making corporation to respond to consumer desires. To fail to take account of the evidence that suggests viewers want more and better news is simply not—from the perspective of the news operations—a rational decision on the part of these companies. The dramatically declining audience for network news translates into lower advertising revenues for the television networks and local stations, since advertisers pay rates based on the size of each show's viewing audience. Indeed, the disproportionately older audience that watches television news is not all that appealing to most advertisers. The advertisers most interested in buying spots during evening news programs sell insurance, arthritis pain medications, and other products of particular interest to older viewers. Younger viewers are likely to have greater disposable income, and so are particularly appealing to many advertisers. But apparel retailers, soft drink makers, and other businesses most interested in younger audiences hawk their wares elsewhere. The networks' failure to attract large numbers of younger viewers—and the advertisers who court them—to their evening news shows indicates that the audiences and revenues associated with these network news shows will be even smaller in the years ahead.

Perhaps historical trends in network television explain this disconnect. The broadcast industry has been heavily regulated in the past through such policies as the fairness doctrine and tight limitations on cross-ownership of media properties (McChesney 1999). The old regulatory structures, in other words, may not have prepared the news media to be all that responsive to current citizens' wishes. But if these network news dinosaurs do not evolve into news organizations capable of responding more effectively to the public's search for higher-quality media sources, the nightly newscasts are unlikely to thrive in the years ahead (Kurtz 2002b).

The networks' approach, an apparently consistent denial of market forces, may result from the fact that even well-watched network newscasts do not have the potential to generate profits of the magnitude possible with prime-time evening entertainment programs. Network news exists in a world of limited resources, and the media acquisitions of recent years have made many media outlets deeply indebted. Given such circumstances, it may be rational for a media company to focus its finite energies and resources on building a new *Survivor* or new shows to replace the holes caused by the end of long-running hits like *Seinfeld* and *Friends*. What seems irrational from a news-oriented perspective may be rational when considered in the light of the network's entertainment division priorities. Rational or not for the networks, decisions to close foreign bureaus, to keep the newscasts to 30 minutes, and to provide the news content that has been found wanting so often in this analysis clearly do not help build an informed citizenry. These trends don't help expand network news ratings, either.

A network news operation more responsive to public desires, our evidence suggests, would allow candidates to say more, offer more even-handed commentary, provide a greater volume of information on-air, and focus more on the country's key issues. One of the easiest ways to reduce the pressures that induce the networks to offer trivial, superficial, sound-bite coverage is for those news programs to be longer, at least once a week but perhaps every night. We believe it is in the news media's best interests, commercially speaking, to make these changes voluntarily.

There are other ways that today's media undermine their potential. To paraphrase Thoreau: the issue here is not so much that the news media are often negative, but rather the question is what are they so negative about? Bruce Sanford, one of the nation's leading press lawyers, has argued that today's large media companies actually have backed away from the aggressive reporting that tells people what they need to know. Rather than offer real investigative reporting, today's wary media companies prefer to offer trivial and largely litigation-proof distractions like the O. J. Simpson case and the Clinton/Lewinsky scandal, according to Sanford (1999). The rush to get the news first—rather than worrying first about getting the news right—undermines the media's credibility, as does negative treatment of figures like Donna Rice, the overnight houseguest of 1984 and 1988 Democratic presidential hopeful Gary Hart (in media sex-scandal terms, Rice might be described as the Monica Lewinsky of the 1980s). The media's credibility is not being compromised by the lack of effective investigative reporting that was once a more significant part of network news; network news credibility is undermined by the focus on the trivial (cf. Kurtz 1994).

The change in focus is immense. Newspapers that not so long ago defied the government and published the Pentagon Papers in the midst of the Vietnam War now write obsessively about the sexual scandal of the week, whether it is Bill Clinton's paramour, Jesse Jackson's illegitimate child, or Madonna's latest boyfriend or husband. "It is not death or torture or imprisonment that threaten us as American journalists," Ted Koppel of *Nightline* remarked in 1997 when he received a lifetime achievement award from the Committee to Protect Journalists. "It is the trivialization of our industry" (quoted in Sanford 1999). Koppel was incredibly prophetic in his comments; five years later his own show was in jeopardy as Disney tried to lure David Letterman by offering him Koppel's ABC time slot (Ahrens 2002; Rosenstiel and Kovach 2002). Although the late-night talk show host decided in March 2002 to remain at CBS, the long-term future of Koppel's award-winning show—a fixture at ABC for more than two decades—remained uncertain (Kurtz 2002a).

The constant sniping and negativity found in much media campaign coverage undermine the ability of journalists to do the sort of effective investigative reporting that brings important matters to life. Readers and viewers see the silliness of what often passes for effective criticism with these reporters, and the credibility of the news business itself is compromised. If today's reporters were fairer in their treatment of campaigns and politicians, their news organizations would be more respected and reporters would have greater support to expose wrongdoing by corporations and public officials. They wouldn't need to fear huge damage awards from judges and juries turned off by trivialized media coverage (Sanford 1999). Today's Woodwards and Bernsteins may be more likely to be struggling to write clever put-downs of candidates and looking for the girlfriends of congressmen than to be burrowing through government files to find the latest abuses of power, the latest cases of corruption, the latest threats to civil liberties.

If the news media remain unmoved by any sense of public purpose, and if they remain unmoved by the corporate self-interest argument presented here, some would argue that there is another—albeit highly unlikely—alternative to voluntary change. We, the people, own the nation's airwaves, and the broadcast television stations are permitted to use those airwaves without charge in exchange for providing public service programming, including news and educational shows (Graber 2002). When the federal government says that a particular station has a license to broadcast on Channel 3, for example, no one else can be Channel 3 in that viewing area. Despite recent declines in viewership discussed here, the broadcast television business remains enormously profitable. Recent changes in telecommunications laws allow greater ownership concentrations that have made the television business even more valuable (McChesney 1999). Even though the television networks are facing a steady drain of their audience to cable and satellite subscribers, in 1999 Viacom paid $37 billion to acquire and run CBS (Graber 2002; McChesney 1999). The Federal Communications Commission (FCC) has the authority to terminate broadcast licenses for poor performance, and it has done so in the past to punish stations that have engaged in discriminatory hiring practices (Graber 2002:54). Some media critics may observe that under existing law the FCC could more precisely define what is meant by "programming in the public interest," perhaps by saying that this phrase should be construed to require an hour-long nightly network newscast.

The thought that the government would establish an hour-long network newscast by demanding higher public interest standards seems to us a vain hope. This proposal ignores the fact that the broadcasters' lobby is one of the most powerful in Washington and one not likely to be pushed around by a regulatory agency (West and Loomis 1999). The broadcasting industry is also not likely to be pressured in any meaningful way by lawmakers who want to stay in the good graces of television station owners from whom they will buy advertising time and from whom they will desire favorable news coverage of their next campaign (West and Loomis 1999). An aggressive stand by government to force expansion of the media's response to the industry's public interest obligations would likely occur only in the wake of sustained citizen pressure for change, something that in a few instances has triggered FCC license nonrenewals in the past (Graber 2002). Americans, of course, are not known for their aggressive demands upon governmental authorities, though we often mutter our complaints about governmental performance. The powerful cynicism most voters have toward the national government most of the time—together with America's Constitutional traditions to keep the news media as far away from government control as possible—are highly effective barriers to government intervention even in the volume of news programming provided, regardless of how low the quality of those programs may sink. While others may call for greater government regulation in this area, we consider voluntary network news reform the best way—and the only politically viable one—for the news business to move in the direction of higher standards for network news coverage.

A Miscast Institution?

Nearly a decade ago, media scholar Thomas Patterson (1994) described the news media as a "miscast institution." Reporters have come to replace the political parties as the overseers of the presidential nomination and election process, leaving a country focusing on images such as Michael Dukakis peering out of a tank like a cartoon character and the dueling "he said, she said" stories of Bill Clinton versus Gennifer Flowers, Paula Jones, and later Monica Lewinsky. The weakening of political parties over the past several decades through various political reform efforts has created a power vacuum (Polsby 1983; Polsby and Wildavsky 2000). Reporters ended up being swept into the vacuum, as the role of citizens in selecting presidential nominees through primaries increased greatly in recent decades. Reporters did not particularly want to do this, Patterson argues. They are not very good at it either, but they just cannot stop.

In response to this observation of a miscast news media, Patterson proposed shortening the length of the primary season as a way of reducing media influence in the presidential nomination process. Reporters would have less time to pound their horse race messages into voters' brains and less time to dig up dirt from the candidates' distant pasts. The primary season has been compressed (though not shortened) over the past several elections—states want to hold their primaries while the partisan outcomes remain in doubt and therefore have crowded near the front of the nomination contest line—but the influence of the news media has hardly been reduced in the days since Muskie cried (or, by some accounts, had his face moistened with melting snow) outside the Manchester (N.H.) *Union Leader* in 1972 (Shogan 2001) or since Clinton declared himself "the comeback kid" after finishing second in the 1992 New Hampshire primary (Barilleaux and Adkins 1993). Miscast or not, presidential campaigns continue to be geared around the media, and network news content continues to be highly influential throughout the presidential nomination and election process, even in New Hampshire, the first and most important primary state (Farnsworth and Lichter 1999, 2001,

2002). In fact, the accelerated campaign schedule may have made campaigns even more media-dominated. Certainly the candidates in 2000 engaged in heavy media campaigning: Bush spent tens of millions of dollars on campaign advertising during the primaries alone, and McCain came close to becoming his own cable channel on his "Straight Talk Express" campaign bus (Corrado 2001; Sabato and Scott 2002; Stanley 2001).

Thus, the same law of unintended consequences that often applies to government policies may also apply to media influence in elections. Despite well-intentioned proposals to reduce this influence in politics, it remains and may even have *grown* in the wake of recent attempts to reform campaigns to make them *less* influenced by the news media.

Another possible reform to reduce the news media's influence—returning authority for the presidential nomination process back to the political party bosses—may be a cure worse than the disease. Primary voters have been decisive in the selection of presidential nominees for both major political parties starting with the 1972 nomination contests. Four years earlier, Democratic party bosses had nominated Vice President Hubert Humphrey rather than a candidate opposed to the Vietnam War, an act that triggered massive youth rioting in Chicago. The many political controversies of 1968, and Humphrey's subsequent loss to Richard M. Nixon, led to major reforms in the nomination process that gave rank-and-file partisan voters effective control over both the Democratic and Republican presidential nominations in 1972, and for every presidential campaign since then (Ceaser 1979; Maisel 2002; Polsby 1983; Polsby and Wildavsky 2000). Reducing media influence in presidential nominations by reducing the citizen influence in them would be a terrible idea from the standpoint of political participation, particularly when half the country's adults don't vote in presidential elections as it is.

Reducing the Mediation, at Least Some of the Time

Technological developments increase the opportunities for candidates to send campaign news, information, and messages directly to citizens. Today's candidates can far more easily communicate directly with more voters than was possible when reporters functioned as a presidential campaign's only real gatekeeper in the electoral process. Technological advancements likewise offer candidates the opportunity to reach voters through a wider range of media channels, includinng channels that allow candidates to communicate in a less mediated way with citizens.

One of the most notable improvements in the campaign environment in recent years is an increase in opportunities for the candidates to be heard in their own words and at greater length than the brief sound bite that is the norm in network news coverage. The rise of cable talk shows has dramatically expanded the opportunities for candidates to speak without mediation. Even on the networks, substantial opportunities for unmediated discourse sometimes can be found in the morning shows and the evening humor/talk shows. This is a particularly important change for campaign discourse. Our content analysis that has shown that the unmediated campaign—be it through speeches, web pages, talk show content, or even political advertising—is far more substantial, far more issue based, and far less negative in orientation than the campaign described in network news accounts. Viewership patterns demonstrate the popularity of these formats, and the opportunity for less-mediated communication by campaigns seems likely to grow given the public interest. This should be a naturally occurring development in future elections, and one that should be applauded. These unmediated and less-mediated avenues should not replace the network news, but the less-mediated communication channels seem likely to provide a healthy diet of issues and substance that can supplement and perhaps reduce the consumption of the high-fat, high-cholesterol offerings provided by today's network newscasts, the purveyors of fast-food journalism. The more visible these formats become, the more they can illustrate a news media credibility gap between what the candidates actually say and what network news reporters tell us the candidates are saying. Growing public awareness of this gap should help push the media in the direction of higher quality and more representative reporting.

Greater opportunities for unmediated discourse may improve the performance of network television in the future, but our current findings do not identify any such trends in the content of network newscasts. One glimmer of hope is CBS's decision to devote part of its *Evening News* program to the recorded unmediated messages of presidential candidates. Although these presentations represented a tiny fraction of the network's broadcast time during the two-month period before the general elections, they at least provide a model that might be built upon in the future.

Many of our suggestions earlier in this chapter are designed to improve network news, not replace it. Our proposals in this realm include hour-long newscasts every weeknight (or failing that, once a week); the use of the additional time for more substantive, issue-based reporting; extended interview sessions; free airtime and perhaps even several mini-debates focusing on different issues. With more time for network news, there would be less need for candidates to try to reach voters through eight-second sound bites, less pressure to squeeze in as much commentary as possible through heavily reporter-mediated stories, and less of a demand for the barrage of negative commentaries that are the hallmarks of today's evening news programs.

It is our belief that network newscasts should change in ways that make them simultaneously more useful to democracy, more appealing to viewers, and more profitable to the corporate giants that control ABC, CBS, and NBC. The evidence of poor performance and declining market share for the network newscasts is overwhelming. From within the media industry often come calls for change, but these changes do not often occur, and when they do, they usually turn out to be temporary. Despite promises to improve and sometime efforts in that direction, the networks often end up slipping back soon into the same tired, unproductive routines of the past. If the first step on the road to recovery is recognizing that you have a problem, the media industry is now ready for the second step. The path back to higher-quality reporting has already been blazed by PBS, cable, and the print press, and the less-mediated commentary of candidates and campaigns themselves also helps mark the way.

An Internet Revolution?

The 2000 presidential election was the "revolution that wasn't" for cyberspace (Farnsworth and Owen 2001). Relatively few citizens went online for news and information, and those who did tended to use the Internet for election news infrequently. When compared to other media genres, the Internet lagged far behind newspapers, cable news, network news, and even local TV news as a leading consumer media choice for information about the 2000 presidential election (see table 1.1 in chapter 1). Many media scholars and practitioners nevertheless have high hopes for a new form of democratic communication in the age of cyberjournalism (Drudge 2000; Hall 2001). Others are troubled by what they imagine to be the dystopias of unaccountable cybergossips and personalized "daily me" news diets that we consume alone (Seib 2001; Sunstein 2001). But the quantitative evidence so far suggests that neither the hopes nor the fears have yet come to pass (Davis 1999; Davis and Owen 1998; Farnsworth and Owen 2001; Margolis and Resnick 2000; Owen 2002).

For the moment, the most frequent users of the web are those same highly informed citizens who already are very interested and very active in politics. Likewise, the dominant sources used in cyberspace are the web pages of the mainstream media, whose offline successes contribute to the online attention they receive. The online offerings of the Big Three broadcasts networks seem to be having even more of a problem with market share than the networks' offline flagship newscasts. In a 2000 survey regarding citizen uses of cyberspace (Pew 2000b), citizens who went online for election news and information said they relied most often on CNN (24 percent), America Online (16 percent), Yahoo (8 percent), MSNBC (6 percent), Microsoft/MSN (4 percent), local news sites (3 percent), and the *New York Times* (3 percent). Among those who said they went online for election news, only 2 percent of those said they would turn to the Internet offerings of ABC News, 1 percent said NBC News, and less than one-half of 1 percent said CBS.

There is certainly an opportunity for important changes in media and politics as the Internet develops. In the same way that viewers have voted with their television remote controls for news sources that offer better election coverage than the networks, citizens can search out precisely the information they desire without having to wait for it to appear on a newscast or in print (Cornfield 2000; Glass 1996; Rash 1997). This individual-level control over what information a citizen attends to—and what is ignored—may offer the opportunity for a rejuvenated democracy of citizens who insist upon more responsive media sources and even more responsive candidates and elected officials (Grossman 1995; Hall 2001). Some day this may be the case, but that day was not the 2000 election.

Our content analysis of campaign web sites in the 1996 campaign suggests that these forums, like candidate interview programs, candidate speeches, and even candidate advertising, are excellent places for candidates to conduct campaigns that are more positive and issue-based than they are presented in the mainstream media, especially on the network evening newscasts. The networks can get into the act as well, through more issue-oriented web sites and news presentations on-air. As the volume of Internet users grows, and as the influence of less-mediated forms of campaign news and information expand in influence, the networks may be under even greater pressure to abandon the status quo coverage that focuses on horse race politics, largely ignores issues, casts politics in a negative light, and rarely gives candidates more than a few seconds to speak to the American people in a nightly newscast. While those who see the Internet as a revolutionary new development in American politics may find themselves disappointed, the web clearly can provide some relief for citizens seeking accurate representations of what candidates stand for. This medium can also help candidates find a more direct route to citizens than the network newscasts. In this way, competition from the expanded, less-mediated formats could indirectly nudge the quality of network newscasts upward.

The New Network News: The 2001 War on Terror

The September 11, 2001, terrorist attacks on the World Trade Center in New York City and on the Pentagon outside Washington, D.C., were seen almost immediately as a watershed event in the American public's sense of security. The simultaneous hijacking of four different planes by teams of suicidal terrorists led to the deaths of more than three thousand people, a larger death toll than at Pearl Harbor on December 7, 1941, the disaster that triggered American involvement in World War II. As Americans in fall 2001 surveyed the Pentagon wreckage and the devastation in lower Manhattan, mourned the horrific loss of life, agonized over the lapses in airport security, and eventually turned public attention to a retaliatory military campaign in Afghanistan, network television news was always there. The broadcast and cable networks alike seemed to spare no expense, covering the immediate aftermath of the attacks without commercial interruptions for hours on end. The sober and informative network news focus was on collecting the facts, a focus on substance over triviality.

The consequences to the financial bottom lines of these companies may end up being immense, but network news' nonstop coverage paid clear dividends in the court of public opinion, where network television has long been in disrepute.

A nationwide survey of public opinion regarding the news media fielded November 13–19, 2001, by the Pew Research Center found dramatically increased respect for reporters. In November 2001, 46 percent of those surveyed thought the news media usually get their facts straight, up from 35 percent in a mid-September poll. The November 2001 number was the highest level recorded on this question since 1992, shortly after the Gulf War (Pew 2001).

As network correspondents wear flag pins in their lapels and the network studios use American flag backdrops and logos, the public's sense of the news media as being too critical of America has fallen from 42 percent in February 1999 to 36 percent in mid-September 2001 and to 17 percent in November 2001. The percentage of those who believe that the news media "stand up for America" reached 69 percent in November 2001, up from 43 percent in mid-September and 41 percent in February 1999. The percentage of those who see the news media as protecting democracy rather than hurting it stood at a record high of 60 percent in November 2001. This is far higher than the 45 percent recorded in February 1999 and 46 percent in mid-September 2001 (Pew 2001). The previous high point on this measure was a 53 percent reading in 1987.

The networks' war reporting likewise received strikingly high marks from the public. In the November 2001 survey, 77 percent rated the media's coverage as excellent or good, slightly below the 89 percent recorded in mid-September. Numbers like these have not been recorded since the Gulf War in 1991 (Pew 2001).

The great investment that network news made in more extensive, issue-based reporting in the wake of the terrorist attacks and their aftermath may not have been enough to erase entirely the image of network news as a comparably weak news performer. Although the networks were named as a leading source of news by 30 percent of those surveyed in the days after the terrorist attacks, second only to the 45 percent listing cable news, the networks fell much further back in the November 2001 survey (Pew 2001). Two months after the September 11, 2001, attacks, cable news was named in the Pew (2001) survey as a leading information source by

53 percent of those surveyed, as compared to 34 percent who identified newspapers, 19 percent who relied on radio news, 18 percent who favored local TV news, 17 percent who listed the network newscasts, and 13 percent who relied on the Internet as one of their leading sources of news and information (because survey respondents were allowed up to two responses, the percentages listed exceed 100 percent).

The news media lag considerably behind the government on most such measures. Public approval of President Bush in the November 2001 poll stood at 84 percent, and support for the president was consistently at 80 percent or higher in the first three months following the attack. Prior to the September 11, 2001, attack, Bush's first-year approval ratings had ranged from 50 percent to 56 percent (Pew 2001).

Part of the reason for Bush's high approval ratings may be a "rally around the flag" effect, when citizens express great loyalty to a president in times of military crisis (Adams et al. 1994; Lowi 1985; Nincic 1997). Presidents during military interventions generally enjoy high public approval, particularly in the early stages of conflict. President George H. W. Bush saw an 18-percentage-point improvement in his public approval during the 1991 Gulf War and a 9-point increase following the U.S. military's removal of Panama's president in 1989 (Nincic 1997). In a study of eighteen military interventions since World War II, citizen evaluations of a president rose by an average of 3.4 percentage points in the wake of a military crisis, and only fell four times—a 1982 intervention in Lebanon by Ronald Reagan, a 1971 intervention in Laos by Richard Nixon, Lyndon Johnson's decision in August 1964 to resume bombing in North Vietnam in the wake of the Tonkin Gulf incident, and Harry Truman's decision to take the Korean War north of the 38th Parallel in October 1950 (Nincic 1997).

Another part of the reason may be the extraordinarily positive coverage President Bush received on network television in the first two months following the attack. A CMPA content analysis of network news from September 11 to November 19 found that sound bites for Bush were positive by a margin of nearly two to one, 64 percent positive to 36 percent negative (Media Monitor 2001). Bush's evaluations on network news were 77 percent positive from September 11 to September 30, 67 percent positive in October, and 59 percent positive during the period November 1 to November 19. The growing presence of foreign sources opposed to the war in Afghanistan account for most of the decline, as three out of every four domestic sources supported the president throughout the study period (Media Monitor 2001). Even the Bush administration's controversial plan to create military tribunals to try suspected terrorists garnered 58 percent positive support from on-air sources, even though this proposal and others to restrict civil liberties during the crisis have been condemned by a number of influential constitutional experts (cf. Califano 2001; Dellinger and Schroeder 2001).

Prior to the terrorist attack, coverage of Bush had been far more negative, by a roughly two-to-one margin. As one would expect, there has a been a dramatic shift in the focus of network news coverage of the president. Ninety percent of Bush's postattack evaluations focused on foreign policy matters, while 80 percent of presidential evaluations before the attack involved domestic policy concerns. (During the 2000 presidential campaign, 96 percent of the issue-related evaluations of Bush and Al Gore combined were directed toward domestic policy.)

Bush's 64 percent in positive evaluations was also higher than that of his two predecessors during the key military crises of their administrations, according to previous CMPA content analyses. President Clinton received 62 percent positive coverage during the early phase of military action in Kosovo (on newscasts from March 24 through May 25, 1999) and President George H. W. Bush received 56 percent positive coverage on network news during the Persian Gulf War (on newscasts from January 17 through February 27, 1991).

The high level of popularity enjoyed by media outlets in the months that followed the September 11, 2001, terrorist attack does not necessarily demonstrate that the media are doing their jobs well. Some of the best reporting in recent decades, after all, was the critical analysis of government misconduct and deceit relating to Vietnam and Watergate. While the survey responses may suggest that the news media are enjoying boosts in the public's evaluation of the Fourth Estate, support for the news media may fall quickly once the hostilities in Afghanistan are resolved. Indeed, it looks like the public's evaluations of the media began to fall within ten weeks of the attack. Other political institutions and political figures may face similar patterns. After all, the senior Bush received stratospheric approval ratings in the wake of the 1991 Gulf War, only to be soundly defeated by Clinton in the 1992 presidential contest.

Whatever the future trajectory of public assessments of the press, the media's coverage of the terrorist attack and its aftermath has demonstrated what network television news is capable of: sustained serious discourse regarding national problems. Although the content of the coverage may be subject to criticism, the fact that the investment of media time and resources has been immense offers some opportunity to see the media's potential for political coverage. The negative coverage seen throughout our analysis of the past four presidential elections had made us wonder whether network television was even capable of presenting extensive, substance-oriented reporting; the performance of the networks and anchors doing their jobs in the wake of September 11, 2001, shows they can if they choose to do so.

Final Thoughts

In the end, we find ourselves astonished, above all, that the evening network newscasts have been able to do so little with so much. On virtually every measure we have considered in this analysis of presidential campaign coverage—from volume, to horse race, to content, to tone, to issues, to sound bites—the Big Three network news programs have been weighed in the balance and found wanting. They have repeatedly been compared unfavorably to other news outlets and, most dramatically, even to the candidates' campaigns themselves. To make matters worse, on several measures the networks seem to be doing worse with each passing presidential election.

We hope the content analysis of this book offers ammunition to the many serious journalists in network television who have been trying, in some cases for decades now, to push their television companies in the direction of greater substance and of higher-quality content in general. Network television needs all the internal agitators for quality that it can get, and it is our hope that the results here can allow the activists to agitate with renewed vigor. Simply put, the content analysis and survey information presented here demonstrate that network newscasts need massive overhauls if they hope to remain influential sources of news and information for America's news consumers. Viewer surveys and technological advancements suggest that time may be running out for network television news.

The future is never certain, but the evidence here suggests that network news is not likely to thrive if it retains an approach to presidential election news marked by reduced news volume, coverage dominated by the horse race, and a corrosive negativity that can undermine efforts to keep a sense of civic society alive in this country. The news media, the CMPA content analysis and the viewer surveys indicate, have lost their way for the past several presidential elections and are on a course to irrelevance. When the networks will make landfall there we cannot say, but changing course seems long overdue.

Perhaps the networks will retain their renewed sense of mission found in fall 2001. Perhaps they will not. Who may replace the networks if they fail to adjust their coverage of presidential elections is subject to debate. Despite their growing pains and the questionable news practices associated with them, the new news media delivery systems do at least provide a laboratory of innovation and a natural experiment in the redefinition and presentation of election news. Print and cable have proven to be effective competitors and should be even more competitive as Internet use expands in the coming years.

The web may offer the greatest new opportunity to revitalize print journalism. The Internet gives newspapers the chance to take greater advantage of their most powerful assets: huge, well-trained newsrooms. It also removes what for decades has been their greatest disadvantage, the once-a-day news cycle. Perhaps the coming years will be marked by the resurgence of once-dominant newspaper companies in cyberspace. It would be ironic if network television, which came to prominence and dominance over print because of its technological advantages, falls victim to still newer technology wielded in cyberspace by the more informative and substantive print press. Newspapers, once practically left for dead beside technology's high-speed highway, may turn out to be the once and future king of the media world.

An even greater irony, suggested by citizen surveys and by the CMPA content analysis, is that future of campaign discourse may be far less mediated than the past heyday of network news. The most popular, most informative, and most effective campaign discourse is actually the less-mediated campaign discourse of debates and interview shows, as well as the unmediated campaign discourse of the campaign speeches and web pages. The candidate interviews shows on cable television are positive developments, as is the unmediated communication potential offered by cyberspace. As information sources, these less-mediated and unmediated information outlets seem likely to grow in influence as more people venture online and turn to cable to answer their own questions about issue-based politics.

It is impossible to predict what new amalgam will eventually emerge from these competing voices. To appropriate another Marxist metaphor, however, without substantive improvement from its performance in recent presidential elections, the broadcast network model that dominated election news in the latter half of the last century may simply wither away in the next one. If these thirty-minute newscasts continue their decline, they will do so for very capitalist reasons. Other news media outlets, and the unmediated campaign information sources themselves, are providing great competition for these horse race–dominated, issue-starved, negatively oriented programs. Network television evening news shows, as America has known them since the 1960s, must evolve or they will likely die like the dinosaurs before them.

APPENDIX

CAMPAIGN INFORMATION ITEMS USED IN THE CONTENT ANALYSIS

The four presidential election studies included 22,436 campaign information items. These items include all network evenings news segments on ABC, CBS, and NBC in all presidential election cycles: 1987–1988, 1991–1992, 1995–1996, and 1999–2000. Depending on the year, the content analysis draws from other news media, including PBS news programs; CNN programs; campaign news stories from daily newspapers, among them the *New York Times*, the *Washington Post;* the *Wall Street Journal;* and others newspapers and magazines. In 1996, candidate speeches, advertising, interviews, and web pages were also contained in this content analysis and compared to the news coverage during that years. Details from individual years follow.

1987–1988

The 1987–1988 presidential election campaign cycle content analysis examines a total of 8,550 news items. On the Big Three network evening news programs there were 379 preseason stories (February 1 through December 31, 1987), 597 primary season stories (January 1 through March 15, 1988), and 589 stories during the general election campaign (September 8 through November 8, 1988). Those 589 stories were part of a total of 7,575 campaign news stories and editorials examined during the general election campaign from PBS, CNN, the *New York Times,* the *Washington Post,* the *Christian Science Monitor,* the *Wall Street Journal,* the *Los Angeles Times, Newsweek, Time, U.S. News & World Report,* the *National Journal,* the *New York Daily News,* the *Chicago Tribune,* the *Houston Chronicle,* and the *Sacramento Bee.* The 1987–1988 content analysis was provided by Bruce Buchanan (1991, 1995), and his analysis parameters were used by the Center for Media and Public Affairs (CMPA) in subsequent years.

1991–1992

The 1991–1992 presidential campaign content analysis examines a total of 4,434 news items. There were 211 stories on the Big Three network evening news programs during the preseason (January 1 through December 31, 1991), 424 stories during the primary season (January 1 through March 17, 1992), and 772 stories during the fall campaign (between September 7 and November 3, 1992). Also analyzed during the fall campaign period are 124 speeches and a total of 2,903 stories from CNN's *Prime-News*, PBS's *NewsHour,* the *New York Times*, the *Washington Post*, and the *Wall Street Journal.*

1995–1996

The 1995–1996 presidential campaign content analysis examines a total of 7,928 items. There were 485 stories on the Big Three network evening news programs during the preseason (January 1 through December 31, 1995), 699 stories during the primary season (January 1 through March 10, 1996), and 483 stories during the fall campaign (between September 2 and November 5, 1996). The 699 network news stories during the primary period and the 483 news stories during the fall campaign were part of a total primary season and general election season campaign news analysis of 4,325 campaign news stories and editorials from the Big

Three, PBS's *MacNeil-Lehrer*, the *New York Times*, the *Wall Street Journal,* and a local newspaper sample compiled from fifteen local newspapers. An additional 1,103 news stories and editorials from three leading New Hampshire media outlets—the *Concord Monitor*, the Manchester *Union-Leader,* and WMUR-TV (6 P.M. broadcast)—were analyzed from the period of January 20 to February 20, 1996 (the month before the crucial New Hampshire primary).

The 1996 content analysis paid particular attention to candidate discourse. The 1996 primary and general election campaign content analysis was also applied to 1,171 files posted on the Bill Clinton, Bob Dole, and Ross Perot campaign web sites at the close of the campaign, 396 television commercials, 270 campaign stump speeches, 164 television interview segments, 54 free candidate airtime speeches during the fall, and 50 candidate exchanges during the presidential debates.

1999–2000

The 1999–2000 presidential campaign content analysis examines a total of 1,524 items. There were 294 stories on the Big Three network evening news programs during the preseason (January 1 through December 31, 1999), 550 stories during the primary season (January 1 through March 7, 2000), and 462 stories during the fall campaign (between September 4 and November 6, 2000). In addition, the content analysis includes 218 news items from the *NewsHour* on PBS during the general election campaign period.

REFERENCES

Abramson, Paul R., John H. Aldrich, and David W. Rhode. 2002. *Change and Continuity in the 2000 Elections*. Washington, D.C.: CQ Press.

Adams, William C. 1984. "Media Coverage of Campaign '84." *Public Opinion* 7(2):9–13.

———. 1987. "As New Hampshire Goes . . ." In *Media and Momentum: The New Hampshire Primary and Nomination Politics*. Edited by Gary R. Orren and Nelson W. Polsby. Chatham, N.J.: Chatham House.

Adams, William C., et al. 1994. "Before and After 'The Day After': The Unexpected Results of a Televised Drama." In *Media Power in Politics*. Edited by Doris Graber. 3d ed. Washington, D.C.: CQ Press.

Adatto, Kiku. 1990. "Sound Bite Democracy." Research paper, Kennedy School Press Politics Center, Harvard University.

Ahrens, Frank. 2002. "In TV's Numbers Game, Youth Trumps Ratings." *Washington Post,* March 13.

Aitken, Jonathan. 1993. *Nixon: A Life*. Washington, D.C.: Regnery.

Alliance for Better Campaigns. 1999. *Money Shouldn't Be All That Talks: Reinventing Political Campaigns on Television*. Washington, D.C.: Alliance for Better Campaigns.

———. 2001. *Gouging Democracy: How the Television Industry Profiteered on Campaign 2000.* Washington, D.C.: Alliance for Better Campaigns.

Alter, Jonathan. 1988. "How the Media Blew It." *Newsweek,* November 28.

———. 1992. "Go Ahead, Blame the Media." *Newsweek*, November 2.

Alterman, Eric. 2000. *Sound and Fury: The Making of the Punditocracy*. Ithaca, N.Y.: Cornell University Press.

Arterton, Christopher. 1984. *Media Politics*. Lexington, Mass.: Lexington Books.

AuCoin, Don. 2000. "Low Ratings Mark Slim Convention Coverage." *Boston Globe*, August 5.

Baker, Ross K. 1993. "Sorting Out and Suiting Up: The Presidential Nominations." In *The Election of 1992: Reports and Interpretations*. Edited by Gerald M. Pomper. Chatham, N.J.: Chatham House.

Baker, Russell. 1996. "'Liberal Media' Are a Fiction." *New York Times*, July 9.

Barilleaux, Ryan J., and Randall E. Adkins. 1993. "The Nominations: Process and Patterns." In *The Elections of 1992*. Edited by Michael Nelson. Washington, D.C.: CQ Press.

Barstow, David, and Don Van Natta, Jr. 2001. "How Bush Took Florida: Mining the Overseas Absentee Vote." *New York Times*, July 15.

Bartels, Larry M. 1985. "Expectations and Preferences in Presidential Nominating Campaigns." *American Political Science Review* 79:804–15.

———. 1988. *Presidential Primaries and the Dynamics of Public Choice*. Princeton: Princeton University.

———. 1993. "Messages Received: The Political Impact of Media Exposure." *American Political Science Review* 87:267–85.

Baxter, T. 1992. "The Year the Voters Tuned In." *Atlanta Journal-Constitution*, November 1.

Bennett, Dick. N.d. American Research Group, Inc., 2000 Polls. Manchester, N.H.

Bennett, W. Lance. 2001. *News: The Politics of Illusion*. 4th ed. New York: Addison Wesley Longman.

Bernstein, Carl, and Bob Woodward. 1974. *All the President's Men*. New York: Warner.

Bode, Ken. 1992. "Pull the Plug." *Quill* (March): 10–13.

Boot, William. 1989. "Campaign '88: TV Overdoses on the Inside Dope." *Columbia Journalism Review*, 27(5) (January–February): 23–29.

Bozell, L. Brent, and Brent H. Baker. 1990. *And That's the Way It Wasn't*. Alexandria, Va.: Media Research Center.

Braestrup, Peter. 1983. *Big Story*. New Haven, Conn.: Yale University Press.

Broder, David. 1990. "Five Ways to Put Some Sanity Back in Elections." *Washington Post*, January 14.

———. 2001. "Election '04 Early Birds." *Washington Post*, November 28.

Broh, C. Anthony. 1980. "Horse Race Journalism." *Public Opinion Quarterly* 44:514–29.

Buchanan, Bruce. 1991. *Electing a President: The Markle Commission Research on Campaign '88*. Austin: University of Texas Press.

———. 1995. "A Tale of Two Campaigns or Why '92's Voters Forced a Presidential Campaign Better Than '88's and How It Could Happen Again." *Political Psychology* 16(2):297–318.

Buckley, C. 2000. "Talk the Vote." *TV Guide,* November 25.

Bugliosi, Vincent. 2001. *The Betrayal of America: How the Supreme Court Undermined the Constitution and Chose Our President.* New York: Avalon/Nation Books.

Buhr, Tami. 2001. "What Voters Know about Candidates and How They Learn It: The 1996 New Hampshire Republican Primary as a Case Study." In *In Pursuit of the White House 2000: How We Choose Our Presidential Nominees.* Edited by William G. Mayer. New York: Chatham House/Seven Bridges.

Burger, Timothy J. 2002. "In the Driver's Seat: The Bush DUI." In *Overtime: The Election 2000 Thriller.* Edited by Larry Sabato. New York: Longman.

Burns, James MacGregor, and Susan Dunn. 2001. *The Three Roosevelts: Patrician Leaders Who Transformed America.* New York: Atlantic Monthly Press.

Butterfield, Fox. 1990. "Dukakis Says Race Was Harmed by TV." *New York Times,* April 22.

Califano, Joseph A. 2001. "Too Many Federal Cops." *Washington Post,* December 6.

Campbell, James E. 1992. "Forecasting the Presidential Vote in the States." *American Journal of Political Science* 36(2):386–407.

———. 2001. "The Referendum That Didn't Happen: The Forecasts of the 2000 Presidential Election." *Political Science and Politics* 34(1):33–8.

Cantril, Hadley, Hazel Gaudet, and Herta Herzog. 1940. *The Invasion from Mars.* Princeton, N.J.: Princeton University Press.

Cappella, Joseph N., and Kathleen Hall Jamieson. 1997. *Spiral of Cynicism: The Press and the Public Good.* New York: Oxford University Press.

Ceaser, James W. 1979. *Presidential Selection: Theory and Development.* Princeton, N.J.: Princeton University Press.

Ceaser, James, and Andrew Busch. 1993. *Upside Down and Inside Out: The 1992 Elections and American Politics.* Lanham, Md.: Rowman & Littlefield.

———. 1997. *Losing to Win: The 1996 Elections and American Politics.* Lanham, Md.: Rowman & Littlefield.

———. 2001. *The Perfect Tie: The True Story of the 2000 Presidential Election.* Lanham, Md.: Rowman & Littlefield.

Clancey, Maura, and Michael J. Robinson. 1985. "General Election Coverage." In *The Mass Media in Campaign '84.* Edited by Michael J. Robinson and Austin Ranney. Washington, D.C.: American Enterprise Institute Press.

Committee of Concerned Journalists. 2000. *The Last Lap: How the Press Covered the Final Stages of the Presidential Campaign.* Washington, D.C.: Project for Excellence in Journalism.

Cook, C. 2000. "It's More, Much More Than Just a Kiss." *National Journal* 39: 2992–93.

Cook, Timothy E. 1998. *Governing with the News: The News Media as a Political Institution*. Chicago: University of Chicago Press.

Cornfield, Mike. 2000. "The Internet and Democratic Participation." *National Civic Review* 89(3):235–41.

Corrado, Anthony. 2001. "Financing the 2000 Elections." In *The Election of 2000*. Edited by Gerald M. Pomper. New York: Chatham House/Seven Bridges.

Craig, Stephen C. 1993. *The Malevolent Leaders*. Boulder, Colo.: Westview.

———. 1996. "The Angry Voter: Politics and Popular Discontent in the 1990s." In *Broken Contract? Changing Relationships between Americans and Their Government*. Edited by Stephen C. Craig. Boulder, Colo.: Westview.

Cronin, Thomas E., and Michael A. Genovese. 1998. *The Paradoxes of the American Presidency*. New York: Oxford University Press.

Dautrich, Kenneth, and Thomas H. Hartley. 1999. *How the News Media Fail American Voters: Causes, Consequences and Remedies*. New York: Columbia University Press.

Davis, Richard. 1999. *The Web of Politics: The Internet's Impact on the American Political System*. New York: Oxford University Press.

Davis, Richard, and Diana Owen. 1998. *New Media and American Politics*. New York: Oxford University Press.

De Moraes, Lisa. 2002. "Rukeyser May Have New Show up His Sleeve." *Washington Post,* April 2.

Deakin, James. 1983. *Straight Stuff: The Reporters, the White House, and the Truth*. New York: William Morrow.

Dellinger, Walter, and Christopher H. Schroeder. 2001. "The Case for Judicial Review." *Washington Post,* December 6.

Dionne, E. J. 1992. "GOP Accuses Media of Bias against Bush." *Washington Post,* August 13.

Downie, Leonard, Jr., and Robert G. Kaiser. 2002. *The News about the News: American Journalism in Peril*. New York: Knopf.

Drew, Dan, and David Weaver. 1991. "Voter Learning in the 1988 Presidential Election: Did the Debates and the Media Matter?" *Journalism Quarterly* 68 (Spring–Summer): 27–37.

Drudge, Matt. 2000. *Drudge Manifesto*. New York: New American Library.

Duncan, Dayton. 1991. *Grass Roots: One Year in the Life of the New Hampshire Presidential Primary*. New York: Viking.

Dye, T., H. Zeigler, and S. R. Lichter. 1992. *American Politics in the Media Age*. Pacific Grove, Calif.: Brooks/Cole.

Easton, David, and Jack Dennis. 1969. *Children in the Political System: Origins of Political Legitimacy*. New York: McGraw-Hill.

Edelman, Murray. 1985. *The Symbolic Uses of Politics.* Urbana: University of Illinois Press.

Epstein, Edward J. 1975. *News from Nowhere.* Chicago: University of Chicago Press.

Fair, Ray. 1978. "The Effects of Economic Events on Votes for President." *Review of Economics and Statistics* 40:159–73.

Farnsworth, Stephen J. 1997. "Political Support in a Frustrated America." Ph.D. diss., Georgetown University.

———. 1999a. "Federal Frustration, State Satisfaction? Voters and Decentralized Governmental Power." *Publius* 29(3):75–88.

———. 1999b. "Loving and Loathing Virginia: Feelings about Federalism in the Old Dominion." *Virginia Social Science Journal* 34:15–38.

———. 2000. "Political Support and Citizen Frustration: Testing Three Linkage Theories." *Virginia Social Science Journal* 35:69–84.

———. 2001. "Patterns of Political Support: Examining Congress and the Presidency." *Congress and the Presidency* 28(1):45–61.

Farnsworth, Stephen J., and S. Robert Lichter. 1999. "No Small Town Poll: Public Attention to Network Coverage of the 1992 New Hampshire Primary." *Harvard International Journal of Press/Politics* 4(3):51–61.

———. 2001. "The 2000 New Hampshire Democratic Primary and Network News." Paper presented at the annual meeting of the American Political Science Association, San Francisco, Calif.

———. 2002. "The 1996 New Hampshire Republican Primary and Network News." *Politics and Policy* 30(1):70–88.

Farnsworth, Stephen J., and Diana Owen. 2001. "The Revolution That Wasn't: The Internet and the 2000 Elections." Paper presented at the annual meeting of the Southern Political Science Association, Atlanta.

Fiedler, Tom. 2002. "Introduction: The Return of Key Largo." In *Overtime: The Election 2000 Thriller.* Edited by Larry Sabato. New York: Longman.

Fishkin, James S. 1991. *Democracy and Deliberation: New Directions for Democratic Reform.* New Haven, Conn.: Yale University Press.

———. 1995. *The Voice of the People: Public Opinion and Democracy.* New Haven, Conn.: Yale University Press.

Fitzwater, Marlin. 1995. *Call The Briefing! Bush and Reagan, Sam and Helen: A Decade with Presidents and the Press.* New York: Times Books/Random House.

Franken, Al. 1999. *Rush Limbaugh Is a Big Fat Idiot: And Other Observations.* New York: Delacourte.

Frankovic, Kathleen A., and Monika L. McDermott. 2001. "Public Opinion in the 2000 Election: The Ambivalent Electorate." In *The Election of 2000.* Edited by Gerald M. Pomper. New York: Chatham House.

Gallup News Service. 2000. "The First Time This Year, Gore's Image More Positive Than Bush's." *USA Today,* September 19.

Gans, Herbert J. 1979. *Deciding What's News.* New York: Pantheon.

Gellman, Irwin F. 1999. *The Contender: Richard Nixon, the Congress Years.* New York: Free Press.

Georges, Christopher. 1993. "Perot and Con: Ross's Teledemocracy Is Supposed to Bypass Special Interests and Take the Money out of Politics; It Won't." *Washington Monthly* 25 (June): 38–43.

Gergen, David. 2000. *Eyewitness to Power: The Essence of Leadership.* New York: Simon & Schuster.

Germond, Jack W., and Jules Witcover. 1989. *Whose Broad Stripes and Bright Stars? The Trivial Pursuit of the Presidency, 1988.* New York: Warner.

———. 1993. *Mad as Hell: Revolt at the Ballot Box, 1992.* New York: Warner.

Gillon, Steven M. 2002. "Election of 1992." In *History of American Presidential Elections, 1789–2001.* Vol. 11. Edited by Arthur M. Schlesinger, Jr., and Fred L. Israel. Philadelphia: Chelsea House.

Ginsberg, Benjamin. 1986. *The Captive Public: How Mass Opinion Promotes State Power.* New York: Basic.

Gitlin, Todd. 1980. *The Whole World Is Watching: Mass Media and the Making and Unmaking of the New Left.* Berkeley: University of California Press.

Glass, Andrew. 1996. "On-line Elections: The Internet's Impact on the Political Process." *Harvard International Journal of Press/Politics* 1(4):140–46.

Gold, Victor. 1994. "George Bush Speaks Out." *Washingtonian*, February.

Goldberg, Bernard. 2002. *Bias: A CBS Insider Exposes How the Media Distort the News.* Washington, D.C.: Regnery.

Goldberg, Robert, and Gerald J. Goldberg. 1995. *Citizen Turner.* New York: Harcourt Brace.

Goodwin, Doris Kearns. 1994. *No Ordinary Time.* New York: Simon & Schuster.

Graber, Doris. 1987. "Kind Words and Harsh Pictures." In *Elections in America.* Edited by K. Lehmann-Schlozman. Boston: Allen and Unwin.

———. 1988. *Processing the News.* 2d ed. New York: Longman.

———. 2002. *Mass Media and American Politics.* 6th ed. Washington, D.C.: CQ Press.

Greenfield, Jeff. 2001. *Oh Waiter! One Order of Crow! Inside the Strangest Presidential Election Finish in American History.* New York: Putnam.

Grossman, Lawrence K. 1995. *The Electronic Republic: Reshaping Democracy in the Information Age.* New York: Penguin.

Halberstam, David. 1979. *The Powers That Be.* New York: Knopf.

Haldeman, H. R. 1994. *The Haldeman Diaries: Inside the Nixon White House.* New York: Putnam.

Hall, Jim. 2001. *Online Journalism: A Critical Primer.* London: Pluto.

Hallin, Daniel C. 1984. "The Media, the War in Vietnam, and Political Support: A Critique of the Thesis of an Oppositional Media." *Journal of Politics* 46(1):2–24.

Hart, Roderick P. 1994. *Seducing America: How Television Charms the Modern Voter*. New York: Oxford University Press.

Harwood Group. 1991. *Citizens and Politics: A View from Main Street America*. Dayton, Ohio: Kettering Foundation.

———. 1993. *College Students Talk Politics*. Dayton, Ohio: Kettering Foundation.

Herman, Edward S., and Noam Chomsky. 1988. *Manufacturing Consent: The Political Economy of the Mass Media*. New York: Pantheon.

Hershey, Marjorie Randon. 1989. "The Campaign and the Media." In *The Election of 1988: Reports and Interpretations*. Edited by Gerald M. Pomper. Chatham, N.J.: Chatham House.

———. 2001. "The Campaign and the Media." In *The Election of 2000*. Edited by Gerald M. Pomper. New York: Chatham House.

Hertsgaard, Mark. 1989. *On Bended Knee: The Press and the Reagan Presidency*. New York: Schocken.

Hess, Stephen. 2000a. "Critical Information Not Covered by the Media." *USA Today,* September 25.

———. 2000b. "Viewers Seek Fairness in TV Political News." *USA Today,* October 23.

Hetherington, Marc. 2001. "Declining Trust and a Shrinking Policy Agenda: Why Media Scholars Should Care." In *Communication in U.S. Elections: New Agendas*. Edited by Roderick P. Hart and Daron R. Shaw. Lanham, Md.: Rowman & Littlefield.

Hibbing, John R., and Elizabeth Theiss-Morse. 1995. *Congress as Public Enemy: Public Attitudes towards American Political Institutions*. Cambridge: Cambridge University Press.

Hofstetter, C. Richard. 1976. *Bias in the News.* Columbus: Ohio State University Press.

Hollihan, Thomas A. 2001. *Uncivil Wars: Political Campaigns in a Media Age*. Boston: Bedford/St. Martin's.

Hunt, A. 1985. "Media Bias Is in the Eye of the Beholder." *Wall Street Journal,* July 23.

Iyengar, Shanto. 1991. *Is Anyone Responsible? How Television Frames Political Issues*. Chicago: University of Chicago Press.

Iyengar, Shanto, and Donald R. Kinder. 1987. *News That Matters*. Chicago: University of Chicago Press.

Jacobson, Gary C. 2001a. *The Politics of Congressional Elections*. 5th ed. New York: Addison Wesley Longman.

———. 2001b. "Congress: Elections and Stalemate." In *The Elections of 2000*. Edited by Michael Nelson. Washington, D.C.: CQ Press.

Jamieson, Kathleen Hall. 1996. *Packaging the Presidency*. 3d ed. New York: Oxford University Press.

———. 2000. *Everything You Think You Know about Politics and Why You're Wrong*. New York: Basic.

Jamieson, Kathleen Hall, and Paul Waldman. 2002. "The Morning After: The Effect of the Network Call for Bush." *Political Communication* 19(1): 113–18.

Janowitz, Morris. 1983. *The Reconstruction of Patriotism: Education for Civic Consciousness*. Chicago: University of Chicago Press.

Jones, Jeffrey P. 2001. "Forums for Citizenship in Popular Culture." In *Politics, Discourse, and American Society: New Agendas*. Edited by Roderick P. Hart and Bartholomew H. Sparrow. Lanham, Md.: Rowman & Littlefield.

Just, Marion R., et al. 1996. *Crosstalk*. Chicago: University of Chicago Press.

Karabell, Zachary. 2000. *The Last Campaign: How Harry Truman Won the 1948 Election*. New York: Knopf.

Kerbel, Matthew Robert. 1995. *Remote and Controlled: Media Politics in a Cynical Age*. Boulder, Colo.: Westview.

———. 1998. *Edited for Television: CNN, ABC, and American Presidential Elections*. 2d ed. Boulder, Colo.: Westview.

———. 2001. "The Media: Old Frames in a Time of Transition." In *The Elections of 2000*. Edited by Michael Nelson. Washington, D.C.: CQ Press.

Kerbel, Matthew R., Sumaiya Apee, and Marc Howard Ross. 2000. "PBS Ain't So Different: Public Broadcasting, Election Frames, and Democratic Empowerment." *Harvard International Journal of Press/Politics* 5(4):8–29.

Kinsley, Michael. 1992. "Ask a Silly Question." *New Republic*, July 6.

Klain, Ronald A., and Jeremy B. Bash. 2002. "The Labor of Sisyphus: The Gore Recount Perspective." In *Overtime: The Election 2000 Thriller*. Edited by Larry Sabato. New York: Longman.

Klapper, Joseph. 1960. *The Effects of Mass Media*. Glencoe, Ill.: Free Press.

Klein, Joe. 2002. *The Natural: The Misunderstood Presidency of Bill Clinton*. New York: Doubleday.

Kloer, P. 2000. "Networks Suffer Convention Deficit Disorder." *Atlanta Journal-Constitution*, August 3.

Kovach, Bill, and Tom Rosenstiel. 1999. *Warp Speed: America in the Age of Mixed Media*. New York: Century Foundation Press.

Kurtz, Howard. 1992a. "The Pundits, Eating Crow after Clinton Comeback." *Washington Post*, March 18.

———. 1992b. "Networks Adapt to Changed Campaign Role." *Washington Post*, June 21.

———. 1992c. "When the Media Are on a Roll, the Candidate Rides a Wave." *Washington Post*, July 25.

———. 1992d. "The Talk Show Campaign: TV Interviews Emerge as Preferred Forum." *Washington Post,* October 28.

———. 1994. *Media Circus: The Trouble with America's Newspapers.* New York: Times Books/Random House.

———. 1996a. "Bob Dole's Pollbearers." *Washington Post,* September 10.

———. 1996b. "A Big Story, but Only Behind the Scenes." *Washington Post,* November 13.

———. 1998. *Spin Cycle: Inside the Clinton Propaganda Machine.* New York: Free Press.

———. 2000a. "Will the 'Slow' Candidate Win the Big Race?" *Washington Post,* October 26.

———. 2000b. "Is the Press Helping Bush?" *Washington Post,* November 6.

———. 2001a. "Election Coverage Burned to a Crisp." *Washington Post,* February 15.

———. 2001b. "Press Takes a Step Up in the Public's Opinion." *Washington Post,* November 29.

———. 2002a. "At ABC, a Shaken News Dynasty." *Washington Post,* March 6.

———. 2002b. "Troubled Times for Network Evening News." *Washington Post,* March 10.

Ladd, Everett C. 1980. "Polling and the Press: The Clash of Institutional Imperatives." *Public Opinion Quarterly* 44:474–84.

Larson, Stephanie G. 2001. "Poll Coverage of the 2000 Presidential Campaign on the Network News." Paper delivered at the annual meeting of the American Political Science Association, San Francisco.

Laufer, Peter. 1995. *Inside Talk Radio: America's Voice or Just Hot Air?* Secaucus, N.J.: Carol.

Lawrence, Regina G. 2001. "Defining Events: Problem Definition in the Media Arena." In *Politics, Discourse, and American Society: New Agendas.* Edited by Roderick P. Hart and Bartholomew H. Sparrow. Lanham, Md.: Rowman & Littlefield.

Lazarsfeld, Paul F., Bernard Berelson, and Hazel Gaudet. 1948. *The People's Choice.* New York: Columbia University Press.

Lengle, James I. 1981. *Representation and Presidential Primaries: The Democratic Party in the Post-Reform Era.* Westport, Conn.: Greenwood.

———. 1987. "Democratic Party Reforms: The Past as Prologue to the 1988 Campaign." *Journal of Law and Politics* 4:223–73.

Lengle, James I., Diana Owen, and Molly W. Sonner. 1995. "Divisive Primaries and Democratic Electoral Prospects." *Journal of Politics* 57:370–83.

Lesher, Stephan. 1982. *Media Unbound: The Impact of Television Journalism upon the Public.* Boston: Houghton-Mifflin.

Lewis-Beck, Michael S., and Tom W. Rice. 1992. *Forecasting Elections.* Washington, D.C.: CQ Press.

Lewis-Beck, Michael S., and Charles Tien. 2001. "Modeling the Future: Lessons from the Gore Forecast." *Political Science and Politics* 34(1):21–3.

Lichter, S. Robert. 1988. "Misreading Momentum." *Public Opinion* 11(1):23–29.

———. 1996. "Consistently Liberal: But Does It Matter?" *Forbes Media Critic,* Fall, 26–39.

———. 2001. "A Plague on Both Parties: Substance and Fairness in TV Election News." *Harvard International Journal of Press/Politics* 6(3):8–30.

Lichter, S. Robert, Daniel Amundson, and Richard Noyes. 1988. *The Video Campaign.* Washington, D.C.: American Enterprise Institute.

———. 1989. "Election '88: Media Coverage." *Public Opinion* 11(5):18–19.

Lichter, S. Robert, and Richard E. Noyes. 1995. *Good Intentions Make Bad News: Why Americans Hate Campaign Journalism.* 2d ed. Lanham, Md.: Rowman & Littlefield.

———. 1998. *Why Elections Are Bad News.* New York: Markle Foundation.

Lichter, S. Robert, Stanley Rothman, and Linda S. Lichter. 1990. *The Media Elite.* New York: Hastings House.

Lopez, Steve. 2001. "You Gotta Admire TV's Commitment to Meaninglessness." *Los Angeles Times,* November 26.

Lowi, Theodore J. 1985. *The Personal President: Power Invested, Promise Unfulfilled.* Ithaca, N.Y.: Cornell University Press.

Lowi, Theodore J., Benjamin Ginsberg, and Kenneth Shepsle. 2002. *American Government: Power and Purpose.* 7th ed. New York: Norton.

Maisel, L. Sandy. 2002. *Parties and Elections in America: The Electoral Process.* 3d ed. Lanham, Md.: Rowman & Littlefield.

Margolis, Michael, and David Resnick. 2000. *Politics as Usual: The Cyberspace "Revolution."* Thousand Oaks, Calif.: Sage.

Mast, Gerald. 1971. *A Short History of the Movies.* Indianapolis, Ind.: Pegasus.

Mayer, William G. 1987. "The New Hampshire Primary: A Historical Overview." In *Media and Momentum: The New Hampshire Primary and Nomination Politics.* Edited by Gary R. Orren and Nelson W. Polsby. Chatham, N.J.: Chatham House.

———. 1996. "Forecasting Presidential Nominations." In *In Pursuit of the White House: How We Choose Our Presidential Nominees.* Edited by William G. Mayer. Chatham, N.J.: Chatham House.

———. 1997. "The Presidential Nominations." In *The Elections of 1996: Reports and Interpretations.* Chatham, N.J.: Chatham House.

———. 2001. "The Presidential Nominations." In *The Elections of 2000: Reports and Interpretations.* Chatham, N.J.: Chatham House.

McChesney, Robert W. 1999. *Rich Media, Poor Democracy: Communication Politics in Dubious Times.* New York: New Press.

McCombs, Maxwell E., and Donald L. Shaw. 1977. *The Emergence of American Political Issues: The Agenda-Setting Function of the Press*. St. Paul, Minn.: West.

———. 1993. "The Evolution of Agenda-Setting Research: Twenty-Five Years in the Marketplace of Ideas." *Journal of Communication* 43(2):58.

McGinniss, Joe. 1969. *The Selling of the President, 1968*. New York: Trident.

McLeod, Jack M., Gerald M. Kosicki, and Douglas M. McLeod. 1994. "The Expanding Boundaries of Political Communication Effects." In *Media Effects: Advances in Theory and Research*. Edited by Jennings Bryant and Dolf Zillmann. Hillsdale, N.J.: Lawrence Erlbaum.

McQuail, Denis. 2000. "The Influence and Effects of Mass Media." In *Media Power in Politics*. Edited by D. Graber. 4th ed. Washington, D.C.: CQ Press.

McWilliams, Wilson C. 1993. "The Meaning of the Election." In *The Election of 1992: Reports and Interpretations*. Edited by Gerald M. Pomper. Chatham, N.J.: Chatham House.

Media Monitor. 1997. *Network News in the Nineties*. Washington, D.C.: Center for Media and Public Affairs.

———. 2000. *Campaign 2000 Final*. Washington, D.C.: Center for Media and Public Affairs.

———. 2001. *News in a Time of Terror*. Washington, D.C.: Center for Media and Public Affairs.

Meyer, Philip. 1993. "The Media Reformation: Giving the Agenda Back to the People." In *The Elections of 1992*. Edited by Michael Nelson. Washington, D.C.: CQ Press.

Meyrowitz, Joshua. 1985. *No Sense of Place: The Impact of Electronic Media on Social Behavior*. New York: Oxford University Press.

Mnookin, Seth. 2001. "It Happened One Night." *Brill's Content*, February, 94–98, 150–53.

Morris, Dick. 1997. *Behind the Oval Office: Winning the Presidency in the Nineties*. New York: Random House.

Mudd, Roger. 1987. "Television Network News in Campaigns." In *Political Persuasion in Presidential Campaigns*. Edited by L. P. Devlin. New Brunswick, N.J.: Transaction.

Mueller, John E. 1973. *War, Presidents, and Public Opinion*. New York: John Wiley & Sons.

Mutz, Diana. 1992. "Mass Media and the Depoliticization of Personal Experience." *American Journal of Political Science* 36(2):483–508.

Nader, Ralph. 2002. *Crashing the Party: Taking on the Corporate Government in an Age of Surrender*. New York: St. Martin's.

Nelson, Michael. 2001. "The Post-Election Election: Politics by Other Means." In *The Elections of 2000*. Edited by Michael Nelson. Washington, D.C.: CQ Press.

Neuman, W. Russell. 1986. *The Paradox of Mass Politics: Knowledge and Opinion in the American Electorate*. Cambridge, Mass.: Harvard University Press.

Neustadt, Richard E. 1990. *Presidential Power and the Modern Presidents: The Politics of Leadership from Roosevelt to Reagan*. New York: Free Press.

Nie, Norman H., Sidney Verba, and John R. Petrocik. 1979. *The Changing American Voter*. Cambridge, Mass.: Harvard University Press.

Nincic, Miroslav. 1997. "Loss Aversion and the Domestic Context of Military Intervention." *Political Research Quarterly* 50(1):97–120.

Norris, Pippa. 1996. "Does Television Erode Social Capital? A Reply to Putnam." *Political Science and Politics* 29(3):474–80.

———. 2001. "A Failing Grade? The News Media and Campaign 2000." *Harvard International Journal of Press/Politics* 6(2):3–9.

Noyes, Richard, S. Robert Lichter, and Daniel Amundson. 1993. "Was TV Election News Better This Time?" *Journal of Political Science* 21(1):3–25.

Orren, Gary R., and Nelson W. Polsby, eds. 1987. *Media and Momentum.* Chatham, N.J.: Chatham House.

Owen, Diana. 1991. *Media Messages in American Presidential Elections*. Westport, Conn.: Greenwood.

———. 1995. "The Debate Challenge: Candidate Strategies in the New Media Age." In *Presidential Campaign Discourse: Strategic Communication Problems*. Edited by Kathleen E. Kendall. Albany: State University of New York Press.

———. 1996. "Who's Talking? Who's Listening? The New Politics of Talk Radio Shows." In *Broken Contract? Changing Relationships between Americans and Their Government*. Edited by Stephen Craig. Boulder, Colo.: Westview.

———. 1997. "The Press' Performance." In *Toward the Millennium: The Elections of 1996*. Edited by Larry Sabato. Boston: Allyn & Bacon.

———. 2000. "Popular Politics and the Clinton/Lewinsky Affair: The Implications for Leadership." *Political Psychology* 21(1):161–77.

———. 2002. "Media Mayhem: Performance of the Press in Election 2000." In *Overtime: The Election 2000 Thriller*. Edited by Larry Sabato. New York: Longman.

Page, Benjamin I., Robert Y. Shapiro, and Glenn R. Dempsey. 1987. "What Moves Public Opinion." *American Political Science Review* 81(1):23–43.

Paletz, David L. 2002. *The Media in American Politics: Contents and Consequences*. 2d ed. New York: Addison Wesley Longman.

Paletz, David L., and Robert M. Entman. 1981. *Media Power Politics*. New York: Free Press.

Palmer, Niall A. 1997. *The New Hampshire Primary and the American Electoral Process*. Westport, Conn.: Praeger.

Papai, L., and L. Robinson. 2000. "Campaign Reform." *American Journalism Review*, September.

Parmat, Herbert S. 2002. "Election of 1988." In *History of American Presidential Elections, 1789–2001*. Vol. 11. Edited by Arthur M. Schlesinger Jr. and Fred L. Israel. Philadelphia: Chelsea House.

Patterson, Thomas E. 1980. *The Mass Media Election: How Americans Choose Their President*. New York: Praeger.

———. 1994. *Out of Order*. New York: Vintage.

———. 2000. "Doing Well and Doing Good." Research paper, Kennedy School Press Politics Center, Harvard University.

Patterson, Thomas E., and Robert McClure. 1976. *The Unseeing Eye*. New York: Putnam.

Perlstein, Rick. 2001. *Before the Storm: Barry Goldwater and the Unmaking of the American Consensus*. New York: Hill & Wang.

Perret, Geoffrey. 2001. *Jack: A Life Like No Other*. New York: Random House.

Pew Research Center for the People and the Press (cited in text as Pew). 1996. Survey. September 25–29.

———. 2000a. "Voters Unmoved by Media Characterizations of Bush and Gore." July 27.

———. 2000b. "Media Seen as Fair, but Tilting to Gore." October 15.

———. 2000c. "Campaign 2000 Highly Rated." November 16.

———. 2000d. "Internet Election News Audience Seeks Convenience, Familiar Names." December 3.

———. 2000e. "Some Final Observations on Voter Opinions." December 21.

———. 2001. "Terror Coverage Boosts News Media's Image." November 28.

Polsby, Nelson. 1983. *Consequences of Party Reform*. Oxford: Oxford University Press.

Polsby, Nelson, and Aaron Wildavsky. 2000. *Presidential Elections: Strategies and Structures of American Politics*. 10th ed. New York: Chatham House/Seven Bridges.

Pomper, Gerald M. 1985. "The Presidential Election." In *The Election of 1984*. Edited by Gerald M. Pomper. Chatham, N.J.: Chatham House.

———. 1989. "The Presidential Election." In *The Election of 1988*. Edited by Gerald M. Pomper. Chatham, N.J.: Chatham House.

———. 2001. "The Presidential Election." In *The Election of 2000*. Edited by Gerald M. Pomper. New York: Chatham House/Seven Bridges.

Postman, Neil. 1985. *Amusing Ourselves to Death*. New York: Penguin.

Putnam, Robert D. 1995a. "Bowling Alone: America's Declining Social Capital." *Journal of Democracy* 6 (January): 65–78.

———. 1995b. "Tuning In, Tuning Out: The Strange Disappearance of Social Capital in America." *Political Science and Politics* 28(4):664–83.

———. 2000. *Bowling Alone*. New York: Simon & Schuster.

Quirk, Paul J., and Jon K. Dalager. 1993. "The Election: A New Democrat and a New Kind of Presidential Campaign." In *The Elections of 1992*. Edited by Michael Nelson. Washington, D.C.: CQ Press.

Ranney, Austin. 1983. *Channels of Power*. New York: Basic.

Rash, Wayne, Jr. 1997. *Politics on the Nets*. New York: Freeman.

Reich, Robert. 1998. *Locked in the Cabinet*. New York: Vintage.

Robinson, Michael J. 1976. "Public Affairs Television and the Growth of Political Malaise: The Case of 'The Selling the Pentagon.'" *American Political Science Review* 70:409–32.

———. 1985. "Where's the Beef? Media and Media Elites in 1984." In *The American Elections of 1984*. Edited by A. Ranney. Durham, N.C.: Duke University Press.

Robinson, Michael J., and Margaret A. Sheehan. 1983. *Over the Wire and on TV*. New York: Russell Sage Foundation.

Rosen, Jay. 1992. "Campaign Issues: Discourse." *Columbia Journalism Review*, November–December: 34–35.

Rosenstiel, Tom. 1994. *Strange Bedfellows: How Television and the Presidential Candidates Changed American Politics, 1992*. New York: Hyperion.

Rosenstiel, Tom, and Bill Kovach. 2002. "Why We Need 'Nightline.'" *Washington Post*, March 6.

Rueter, Theodore. 1988. "Reflections on the New Hampshire Primary." *Political Science and Politics* 21(Spring): 273–77.

Rusher, William A. 1988. *The Coming Battle for the Media*. New York: William Morrow.

Russert, Timothy J. 1990. "For '92, the Networks Have to Do Better." *New York Times*, March 4.

Ryan, Michael, and Douglas Kellner. 1988. *Camera Politica: The Politics and Ideology of Contemporary Hollywood Film*. Bloomington: University of Indiana Press.

Sabato, Larry J. 2000. *Feeding Frenzy: Attack Journalism and American Politics*. Baltimore, Md.: Lanahan.

———. 2002. "The Perfect Storm: The Election of the Century." In *Overtime: The Election 2000 Thriller*. Edited by Larry Sabato. New York: Longman.

Sabato, Larry J., and Joshua J. Scott. 2002. "The Long Road to a Cliffhanger: Primaries and Conventions." In *Overtime: The Election 2000 Thriller*. Edited by Larry Sabato. New York: Longman.

Sabato, Larry J., Mark Stencel, and S. Robert Lichter. 2000. *Peepshow: Media and Politics in an Age of Scandal*. Lanham, Md.: Rowman & Littlefield.

Sanford, Bruce. 1999. *Don't Shoot the Messenger: How Our Growing Hatred of the Media Threatens Free Speech for All of Us*. New York: Free Press.

Schneider, William, and I. A. Lewis. 1985. "Views on the News." *Public Opinion* 8(4):6–11.

Schudson, Michael. 1978. *Discovering the News*. New York: Basic.

Seib, Philip. 2001. *Going Live: Getting the News Right in a Real-Time, Online World*. Lanham, Md.: Rowman & Littlefield.

Shogan, Robert. 2001. *Bad News: Where the Press Goes Wrong in the Making of the President*. Chicago: I. R. Dee.

Sigelman, Lee, and David Bullock. 1991. "Candidates, Issues, Horse Races, and Hoopla: Presidential Campaign Coverage, 1888–1988." *American Politics Quarterly* 19(1):5–32.

Simon, Adam. 2001. "A Unified Method for Analyzing Media Framing." In *Communication in U.S. Elections: New Agendas*. Edited by Roderick P. Hart and Daron R. Shaw. Lanham, Md.: Rowman & Littlefield.

Simon, Roger. 2001. *Divided We Stand: How Al Gore Beat George Bush and Lost the Presidency*. New York: Crown.

Skocpol, Theda. 1997. *Boomerang: Health Care Reform and the Turn against Government*. New York: Norton.

Smith, Culver H. 1977. *The Press, Politics, and Patronage*. Athens: University of Georgia Press.

Smith, Ted. J., III, S. Robert Lichter, and Louis Harris and Associates. 1997. *What the People Want from the Press*. Washington, D.C.: Center for Media and Public Affairs.

Sparrow, Bartholomew. 1999. *Uncertain Guardians: The News Media as a Political Institution*. Baltimore: Johns Hopkins University Press.

Sprague, Stuart. 1984. "The New Hampshire Primary." *Presidential Studies Quarterly* 14 (Winter): 127–31.

Stanley, Harold W. 1997. "The Nominations: Republican Doldrums, Democratic Revival." In *The Elections of 1996*. Edited by Michael Nelson. Washington, D.C.: CQ Press.

———. 2001. "The Nominations: Return of the Party Leaders." In *The Elections of 2000*. Edited by Michael Nelson. Washington, D.C.: CQ Press.

Stephanopoulos, George. 1999. *All Too Human: A Political Education*. Boston: Little, Brown.

Sunstein, Cass R. 2001. *Republic.com*. Princeton, N.J.: Princeton University Press.

Sunstein, Cass R., and Richard A. Epstein. 2001. *The Vote: Bush, Gore, and the Supreme Court*. Chicago: University of Chicago Press.

Tapper, Jake. 2001. *Down and Dirty: The Plot to Steal the Presidency*. Boston: Little, Brown.

———. 2002. "Down and Dirty, Revisited: A Postscript on Florida and the News Media." In *Overtime: The Election 2000 Thriller*. Edited by Larry Sabato. New York: Longman.

Taylor, P. 2000. "The New Political Theater." *Mother Jones* (November–December): 30–33.

———. 2002. *The Case for Free Air Time*. Washington, D.C.: Alliance for Better Campaigns.

Terwilliger, George J., III. 2002. "A Campout for Lawyers: The Bush Recount Perspective." In *Overtime: The Election 2000 Thriller*. Edited by Larry Sabato. New York: Longman.

Vavreck, Lynn. 2001. "Voter Uncertainty and Candidate Contact: New Influences on Voter Behavior." In *Communication in U.S. Elections: New Agendas*. Edited by Roderick P. Hart and Daron R. Shaw. Lanham, Md.: Rowman & Littlefield.

Veblen, Eric. 1975. *The Manchester* Union-Leader *in New Hampshire Elections*. Hanover, N.H.: University Press of New England.

Wade, Steven M. 2002. "Election of 1972." In *History of American Presidential Elections, 1789–2001*. Vol. 10. Edited by Arthur M. Schlesinger, Jr., Fred L. Israel, and William P. Hanson. Philadelphia: Chelsea House.

Washington Post. 2001. *Deadlock: The Inside Story of America's Closest Election*. New York: PublicAffairs.

Wayne, Stephen J. 2001. *The Road to the White House, 2000: The Politics of Presidential Elections*. Boston: Bedford/St. Martin's.

———. 2003. *Is This Any Way to Run a Democratic Election?* 2d ed. Boston: Houghton Mifflin.

West, Darrell M., and Burdett A. Loomis. 1999. *The Sound of Money: How Political Interests Get What They Want*. New York: Norton.

White, Theodore H. 1961. *The Making of the President, 1960*. New York: Atheneum House.

———. 1978. *In Search of History*. New York: Warner.

Wlezien, Christopher. 2001. "On Forecasting the Presidential Vote." *Political Science and Politics* 34(1):25–31.

Woodward, Bob. 1994. *The Agenda: Inside the Clinton White House*. New York: Pocket Books.

———. 1999. *Shadow: Five Presidents and the Legacy of Watergate*. New York: Simon & Schuster.

Woodward, Bob, and Carl Bernstein. 1976. *The Final Days*. New York: Simon & Schuster.

INDEX

ABOUT THE AUTHORS

Stephen J. Farnsworth is associate professor of political science and international affairs at Mary Washington College in Fredericksburg, Virginia, and a former newspaper journalist.

S. Robert Lichter is president of the Center for Media and Public Affairs in Washington, D.C.